flour

flour

Spectacular Recipes *from* **Boston's Flour Bakery + Cafe**

by Joanne Chang

with Christie Matheson

Photographs by Keller + Keller

CHRONICLE BOOKS

SAN FRANCISCO

To Christopher, for making my life sweeter every day.

Text copyright © 2010 by **Joanne Chang**.
Photographs/Illustrations copyright © 2010 by **Keller + Keller**.

Library of Congress Cataloging-in-Publication Data available.
ISBN 978-0-8118-6944-7

Manufactured in China

Designed by **Anne Donnard**
Typesetting by **DC Typography, Inc.**

Chips Ahoy! and Oreos are registered trademarks of Nabisco Inc.; Duncan Hines is a
registered trademark of Hines-Park Foods, Inc.; Dunkin' Donuts is a registered trademark
of Dunkin' Brands; Fig Newtons and Jell-O are registered trademarks of Kraft Foods Global
Brands LLC; McDonald's is a registered trademark of McDonalds Corporation; Milky Way is a
registered trademark of Mars, Inc.; Nutella is a registered trademark of Ferrero S.P.A.;
Play-Doh is a registered trademark of Hasbro; Pop-Tarts is a registered trademark of
Kellogg, Inc.; Reddi-wip is a registered trademark of ConAgra Foods, Inc.; Twinkies and
Ding-Dongs are registered trademarks of Interstate Bakeries Corp.

10 9 8

Chronicle Books LLC
680 Second Street
San Francisco, California 94107
www.chroniclebooks.com

contents

introduction

Flour. On its own, it's an ordinary ingredient. Likewise, there's nothing special about a cup of sugar, a few eggs, or a stick of butter. But together, these seemingly pedestrian ingredients form the foundation of the magical world of baking.

Being able to create mouthwatering treats from a roster of such basic elements never fails to delight me. Every day I watch as the mixers and ovens and bakers work their magic to create the beautiful pastries that fill the counter at Flour, my bakery. The transformation of humble ingredients into delightful desserts inspires people to exclaim with joy following a single bite. It's a wonderful world to live and work in.

In some ways, baking reminds me of a theoretical math class I took in college. (Bear with me for a moment.) On the first day, we erased from our minds the number system as we knew it. Beginning only with the assumption of the existence of the idea of zero, we spent the next two weeks re-creating the modern-day number system. It seemed like a crazy exercise at the time (and I just barely passed that class), but it taught me that even very complex things start with the most basic building blocks. Baking isn't nearly as complicated as that class was, of course, but everything I bake—at Flour, or at home—starts with the fundamentals. That's why I named my bakery Flour. It's a reminder that in baking, as in life, simple things are best.

At Flour, we strive for perfection with every recipe we prepare and every item we serve. But that doesn't mean our offerings are complicated or fussy. In fact, the opposite is true. We bake the very best versions of wonderfully familiar and often nostalgic treats, from chocolate chip cookies and banana bread to such commercial classics as Oreos and Pop-Tarts. We wouldn't have it any other way.

In this cookbook, I am thrilled to share dozens of Flour's most popular recipes, carefully reformulated to work successfully at home, along with my best recipes for other delicious baked goods I've developed in more than fifteen years as a professional baker.

I've adored sweets since I was a little girl, but because I was brought up in a traditional Chinese household, I rarely had the chance to indulge my sweet tooth. Most Chinese meals end with nothing sweet at all. At our house, the occasional dinner with friends would inspire a plate of orange slices and some tea; on special occasions, we would pull out all the stops and serve moon cakes filled with red beans or crunchy almond cookies.

I wasn't introduced to the idea of dessert until I started spending time at my friends' houses. Everything I tasted was a novelty to me: Chips Ahoy! cookies, Oreos, Twinkies, Ding Dongs, Jell-O, instant pudding, chocolate cake from Duncan Hines. My sweet tooth knew no bounds. Whenever I could, I would sneak a new dessert.

What started out as a curiosity stemming from my love for sweets eventually developed into a full-blown obsession with desserts and pastries. I pored over baking books and food magazines; I read and reread dessert descriptions wherever I found them; I lingered at pastry cases at the supermarket. Most of the time I never tried the desserts I was dreaming about. Instead, I could only imagine how they must taste: Turkish delight (I read about it in *The Lion, the Witch, and the Wardrobe*), snickerdoodles *(Good Housekeeping)*, sticky toffee pudding *(The Joy of Cooking)*, double-crust apple pie *(Little House on the Prairie)*, New York cheesecake (first spotted at a Safeway in Houston!). Each one tasted better in my mind than the last.

Although I loved thinking about pastries, I never considered culinary school. I come from a fairly strict Asian family, and my parents expected me to go to college and pursue a practical career. So I went to Harvard and majored in applied mathematics and economics.

At Harvard, I had my first "professional" baking gig: I baked cookies and sold them at the Leverett House Grill. People loved them, and I became known as the Chocolate Chip Cookie Girl. Even though it was a lot of fun—and a great distraction from my endless problem sets—baking didn't cross my mind when it was time to look for a job. After all, I'd just spent four years and a lot of money (thanks Mom and Dad!) in pursuit of a "practical" degree, and I was determined to put it to good use.

After graduation, I went to work as a consultant at the Monitor Group, a large international management consulting firm based in Cambridge. It was a good job for someone like me who didn't know what to do for a career. It exposed me to a number of different industries and possible career paths. But none of them was where I wanted to be.

During my second year at Monitor, one of my responsibilities was running the undergraduate recruiting effort. I interviewed hundreds of students for our entry-level consultant position and my opening question, created to break the ice

and put anxious students at ease, was "What would you do with your life if you won the lottery?" Inevitably, I started thinking about my own response to that question. And the answer was easy: I would spend my days cooking and baking. I was always dreaming about food, especially pastries, and how I could make them taste more delicious.

I was tossing that pretty-much-out-of-the-question idea around in my head when I happened to pick up an adult education catalog at the grocery store. A seminar entitled "Open Your Own Restaurant" caught my eye. The teacher was Judy Rosenberg, founder of the successful chain Rosie's Bakery and author of a baking book I had read cover to cover and baked from pretty much every week. I signed up right away.

Rosenberg's advice for people who wanted to bake for a living was simple: go cook or bake! This inspired me to return to baking and selling cookies to those around me. Under the brand name Joanne's Kitchen, I baked cookies in my free time for friends and coworkers who were hosting parties or needed housewarming gifts. Finally, in 1993, after finishing two years at Monitor—when it was time to commit to more years as a consultant, go to business school, or change my path completely—I decided to go for it.

I sent letters to the top chefs in Boston at the time—Lydia Shire, Jody Adams, Todd English, Gordon Hamersley—explaining that I loved to cook and bake, had absolutely no experience or formal training, and was willing to start in any position to work in one of their restaurants. Lydia, who now owns Scampo and Locke-Ober in Boston and then was the groundbreaking chef and owner of the now-defunct Biba restaurant, responded right away. She interviewed me one day and called to hire me the next. Two weeks later, I traded my suit and pumps for a chef's coat and clogs and started as a bar food cook (basically one rung up from dishwasher). My first day, the sous chef asked me to julienne something for her, and I stammered, "Wh-what's julienne?"

I was pretty clueless, but I learned fast and was soon promoted to the garde-manger (appetizer) position, which just happened to be right next to the dessert-plating area. And while my hands were busy plating up knobby foie gras terrines and mustardy steak tartares, my mind and eyes were mesmerized by the sourdough chocolate cakes, caramelized banana *tartes Tatin*, and quince-thyme charlottes being plated next to me. I found myself rushing through my work just so I could lend a hand at the pastry station.

After a year of truffle oil, emulsions, and herbs, I asked Lydia if I could transfer to the pastry station. She didn't have an opening but she pointed me in the direction of Rick Katz, Biba's original pastry chef, who had left years prior to open his own bakery called Bentonwood. Once again my path to a new job was somewhat of a whirlwind. I took the train from Boston out to the suburb of Newton to meet Rick, he interviewed me and offered me a job, and two weeks later I made another trade, this time exchanging my chef's knife and tongs for an offset spatula and pastry bags.

Working for Rick was like enrolling in a rigorous baking school. He was fanatical about pastry and relentless in his pursuit of making the most delicious desserts I'd ever tasted. He used only the best ingredients. He preferred, for example, to make his own vanilla extract and shred his own fresh coconut. He was also a stickler for perfect technique, and after my shifts, the waste bins often overflowed with cakes he had deemed not tender enough or too heavy. I spent my days learning all I could about the proper way to whip meringue, cream butter, roll out puff pastry, and pipe frosting. I had been somewhat on the fence about my career change when I was surrounded by braised meats and stocks, but now that I was in the land of sugar and cream, I couldn't imagine ever going back to the corporate world. I was completely hooked on baking.

I would have stayed with Rick forever, but he closed Bentonwood, so I had to decide where to go next. I had heard that Rialto, an award-winning restaurant in Cambridge, was looking for pastry help. Jody Adams, the chef and co-owner, was one of the original chefs I had written to in search of a cooking job, and I was thrilled about the possibility of working with her. The position turned out to be head pastry chef. I didn't think I was nearly experienced enough to pull it off, but I loved the rapport I had developed with Jody during my interviews, and I knew I could learn a lot from her about balancing tastes and textures, writing a menu, and managing a staff.

Taking the pastry chef position at Rialto was like playing for the NBA right out of high school. I jumped into the frenetic, demanding world of restaurant desserts, where I was immediately responsible for creating a rotating menu of seasonal offerings, managing a small staff, and working directly with waiters, managers, and customers. I was learning every single moment: Jody taught me the importance of balancing a dessert with enough acid and salt to keep it from being one-dimensional, creating layers of texture and flavor in desserts to keep them from being flat, and being whimsical in my presentation so that every dessert was a treat for the eye as well as the palate. She encouraged me to test new ideas, and I constantly tried out pastries I'd only read about. I immersed myself in cookbooks, magazines, and my trusty *Dictionary of Pastries and Desserts*, eventually working my way from apricot to zabaglione.

After two intense, wonderful years at Rialto, I knew it was time for me to work on honing my pastry skills again. I needed to take a step back from overseeing other young pastry cooks and have someone teach me. I learned that acclaimed French pastry chef François Payard, who had won the James Beard Pastry Chef of the Year award in 1995 for his work at New York's Restaurant Daniel, was opening his own patisserie, so I took the train to the Big Apple to meet him. Following what had become the pattern in my cooking career, after only a brief interview, I found myself with a new job and a new life. I threw all of my stuff into the back of a rental car and moved to New York to become a pastry cook at Payard Patisserie. Located on

Manhattan's Upper East Side, it was a beautiful space known for exquisite French pastries, decadent cakes, and traditional French service—an elegant slice of Paris in New York City.

Before starting at Payard, I'd never had any formal training—and I'd never worked for anyone French. At Payard, I learned exacting techniques and studied methods for making the classics. It blew my mind that so many of the pastries I'd been making over the previous few years were historic French recipes that had been passed along from generation to generation through the centuries. I had baked cream puffs countless times at Rialto; at Payard I learned the exact same recipe from François, who had learned it from his father, who had learned it from his father, and so on. At the same time I was revisiting classics like puff pastry (*pâte feuilletée*), pastry cream (*crème pâtissière*), and almond cream (*frangipane*), I was also learning an entirely new vocabulary for pastry items, since my well-worn pastry dictionary focused primarily on American desserts.

We fashioned showstopping St. Honoré cakes and *croquembouches* out of cream puff dough. I labored over delicate sheet cakes imprinted with stunning chocolate designs and layered them with *crème bavarois* and fruit *gelées*. I pulled sugar into balloons and flowers and manipulated chocolate into bows and ribbons. The Payard way of looking at pastry was markedly different from the approach I'd learned at Bentonwood and then at Rialto, and that's when I discovered that pastry can be as much of an art form as it is a source of gustatory pleasure. I threw myself into my new world and soaked up as much as I could.

Working at Payard after my stint as a restaurant pastry chef reminded me of how much I love bakeries, and I began dreaming of opening my own. I relished the creativity-verging-on-obsession of making even the simplest sugar cookie delectable. I reveled in huge batches of scone dough and got caught up in the steady rhythm of producing dozens and dozens of tart shells. It thrilled me that the item I was baking that morning was going to be devoured by someone a few hours later, and that the cake I was decorating that afternoon would ring in a birthday celebration with family and friends that evening. I reminisced about my time with Rick making fruit-laden muffins, saucer-sized cookies, and seemingly countless loaves of bread. The tradition of French pastry with the precise recipes and fanatical attention to artful appearance was a terrific learning experience, but I knew I wanted my bakery to be resolutely American. I dreamed about bringing all of the pastries I'd fantasized about while I was growing up to life and serving them in a warm, bustling, friendly neighborhood bakery.

So after a year at Payard, I moved back to Boston to begin planning my own bakery. My now-husband, Christopher, suggested I call it Flour after I described to him what I was envisioning. He knew I wanted a simple, iconic name that would speak to the straightforward focus I was planning.

While I was searching for the perfect space for Flour, I needed a job, so I became pastry chef of the wildly popular Boston restaurant Mistral. By now, I had much more confidence in my abilities and used the time to polish my craft and focus on baking what customers really wanted. I was extremely lucky to work for chef Jamie Mammano, who has figured out how to give his customers what they want while still doing what he wants: use excellent ingredients in upscale classic dishes, jazzed up with modern twists.

We took tiramisu and made it special by serving it parfait style. Customers clamored for our apple tart with puff pastry and Tahitian vanilla anglaise—basically an apple pie in a fancy suit. I couldn't make enough of our molten chocolate cake, and I added my own touch by serving it with homemade hazelnut ice milk. I spent almost two years at Mistral satisfying the sweet tooths of countless customers until I left to open Flour.

"Make life sweeter . . . eat dessert first!" Flour's motto came to me quickly. I'd spent too much of my childhood oblivious to the world of desserts; once the door was opened to me, I made up for lost time by choosing to indulge in desserts above all else whenever possible.

I found a diamond-in-the-rough location on the outer edge of Boston's South End, then an up-and-coming neighborhood, and built the bakery of my dreams there. It has an open kitchen so the customers can see us and we can see them; lots of windows and natural light; wooden counters with ample room to present baskets of freshly baked scones, cookies, breads, and brioche; a pretty pastry case for fancier tarts and cakes and custards; and—my favorite part—a diverse stream of passionate, loyal customers who were thrilled a bakery had opened in their midst. I was just as excited to be part of the neighborhood as they were to have us. We opened to much local fanfare in September 2000. I took all the lessons I learned from my prior jobs and mentors and honed them to form the guiding principles of Flour: Make outstanding food, offer it with genuinely warm service, and have fun doing it.

A key goal for me in opening and running Flour has always been to make not only our customers' lives better, but also, and just as important, all of our staff members' lives better. And it has paid off. The staff at Flour is tremendous. Each person gives his or her all to the bakery, baking cakes, making coffee, cleaning the front, cooking pizzas, boxing up orders, and greeting customers.

After seven years of growing and learning and teaching, I realized I had a rare challenge: I had too many great employees, too many people ready to move up, and more customers than I ever dreamed possible. Flour was such a labor of love and personal sacrifice in the beginning that I never thought of opening a second bakery. It just didn't seem possible. And it would not have been if I didn't have some incredible people who wanted to help me grow Flour and to grow along with it. With their encouragement and commitment, I was ready to tackle a second location.

I opened the second edition of Flour in Boston's Fort Point Channel, an old warehouse district. Popular with artists who live and work in lofts and studios, Fort Point is being reinvigorated with residential and retail development. We opened in

January 2007, to the same warm welcome that South End Flour had received when it debuted. F2 (as we affectionately call our second store) was almost immediately as busy and popular as the original location. We offer the same neighborhood feel, personal service, and dedication to making each customer feel welcome that we do at the South End location. We combine that with the same menu of popular, scrumptious pastries and foods.

We did make a few improvements, however: The kitchen at F2 is much larger, and it allows extra room for production and testing—so we can add more delicious items to our repertoire. F2 also has more seats and an additional ordering area, both of which allow us to accommodate all our customers more quickly. But we have maintained the inviting, friendly atmosphere with an open kitchen where customers can watch our bakers churning out cookies and cakes. The F2 space also has lots of natural light and a great airy, lofty feel. Our customers still make our days—every day—with their compliments and repeat business.

Today, both bakeries are flourishing, and both kitchens hum with activity for about nineteen out of twenty-four hours, seven days a week. I remain amazed by the crowds that show up day after day. I think and hope they continue to come because everything they try is delicious. I teach the Flour bakers to apply what I call the "Mom Test" to each item we make: would you give this to your mom? If the answer is no, we start over. It's simple, and it works. We end each day feeling proud of the food and service we have offered our customers.

I know I am fortunate that I get to spend my days doing what I enjoy most—making the best pastries possible—and that by doing exactly that I can bring happiness to folks who visit my bakeries. I hope this book inspires you to bake for the people you care about and bring them joy each time you do.

techniques

Baking isn't difficult, especially once you are comfortable with certain techniques. Here are a dozen that every home baker should know.

APPLYING A CRUMB COAT

When assembling a layer cake, before you can finish with a luscious drape of frosting, you must first apply a crumb coat. This coat seals in any and all loose crumbs, so that your final coat is spotless and crumb free. Using an offset spatula and a small bit of frosting, spread as thin a layer of frosting as possible on the top of the cake. Then take a bit more frosting and spread it on the sides, again keeping the layer very thin. Don't worry too much about how the crumb coat looks, as it will eventually be entirely covered with more frosting. The important thing is to make sure the whole cake gets covered with a thin layer of frosting. If time permits, place the cake in the refrigerator or freezer for 20 to 30 minutes to set the crumb coat, which will make putting on the final coat of frosting a breeze.

BLIND BAKING

Tart shells and pie shells often need to be baked before they are filled, a technique known as *blind baking*. If you don't bake the shell first, it won't fully bake in the oven once it's filled and the result will be an underbaked, gummy, icky-tasting crust. Line your unbaked shell with parchment paper or a large coffee filter, and then fill the shell with pie weights, uncooked beans or rice, or even well-washed small pebbles. Press down lightly on the weights to make sure the shell is entirely and evenly filled, and place the whole thing in the oven. The pie weights will keep the shell from bubbling and puffing up. Check the shell for doneness by lifting the parchment and peeking at the color of the pastry. It should be lightly golden and look matte. If it is shiny, it needs to bake longer. Be careful when peeking that the weights (especially if you are using rice) don't slip under the parchment and bake into the dough. When the shell is done baking, remove it from the oven and let cool until you can remove the weights and parchment. Blind baking can refer to either partially baking a shell or fully baking a shell before filling it. If the recipe calls for baking the filled tart or pie shell for a long time after it is filled (more than 45 minutes), blind bake your shell until it is partially baked. If the recipe calls for baking the filled shell for only a short time or not at all after it is filled, blind bake it until it is completely baked through (see tip #10 on page 36).

COOKING SUGAR

Cooking sugar to make caramel or buttercream can be intimidating. Don't do it long enough and you won't get the right flavor. Do it too long and the sugar will burn. Don't do it quite right and the whole pot may crystallize. Eek!

Let's start at the beginning. When cooking sugar, be sure it is completely moistened with water before putting it on the stove.

Make sure no undissolved sugar crystals are clinging to the sides of the pot. (Sometimes when you moisten the sugar, a bit of it splashes onto the side of the pan.) Lingering sugar crystals can mess with your sugar when it is cooking, and start a chain reaction within your syrup that will crystallize the whole pot. It is easy to prevent: simply brush down the sides of the pot with a pastry brush dipped in water. Once the sugar is on the stove, bring it to a boil over high heat. I have found that if you cook sugar syrup on medium or low heat, it has a greater chance of crystallizing, so I always cook it on the highest heat possible. Once the syrup is boiling, don't jostle the pot and definitely don't stir it. Either action could trigger crystallization.

When the sugar syrup is boiling, you can check the temperature in one of two ways. The safest and easiest way is to use a candy thermometer. Clip it onto the side of the pan so the bulb is immersed in the syrup but not touching the pan bottom, or hold the thermometer in the syrup, then watch the temperature gauge. When it reaches the required temperature, the syrup is ready.

If you don't have a thermometer, you can test the syrup by dropping a tiny spoonful of it into a small cup of ice water and using your fingers to feel how the syrup responds in the water. Many recipes call for cooking syrup to the soft-ball stage (238 degrees F), or until the syrup you gather between your fingertips in the water is pinchable into a soft ball that holds its shape and then slowly flattens when you take it out of the ice water. If the recipe asks for the firm-ball stage (245 to 248 degrees F), the syrup will form a firm ball that doesn't flatten when you remove it from the water but will flatten when you squeeze it. If the recipe calls for the hardball stage (250 to 265 degrees F), the syrup will form a ball that holds its shape and does not give when you squish it. Once the syrup reaches the correct temperature, work with it quickly, as the temperature will continue to rise even when the pot is off the stove.

If you are making caramel, you don't need a thermometer or ice water. Your eyes will tell you when the sugar reaches the right point. As the syrup boils, the water will evaporate, slowly turning the syrup thicker and more viscous. Eventually, usually after 5 to 6 minutes, the sugar will start to color and become pale golden brown. If the heat on your stove isn't even, one side of the pot will typically color first. At this point, it is safe to move the pan, so you should swirl it gently so the sugar caramelizes evenly. Don't walk away from the pan now, because once the sugar colors, it doesn't take long for it to caramelize completely.

Here's the trick: Many cooks think that once the sugar is brown, the caramel is good to go, but usually it needs to cook a tiny bit longer to get that bittersweet caramel taste that is much more interesting than just sweet sugar. How to test? Tilt your pot to look at the thin layer of caramel that clings to the bottom. The color of this layer is the true color of your caramel, and this is the layer you want to be amber brown. Caramel in a small pot will look much darker than it really is simply because the layer is deep. By tilting the pot and peeking at a shallow layer of caramel on the bottom, you see the actual color. Once that color is a lovely amber brown, use the caramel immediately, as it will continue to darken even after you take it off the stove. Don't be afraid if it smokes just a bit. Add your cream or butter or pour it right away wherever you need it.

Remember, with caramel you need to watch the sugar mixture very carefully as it cooks, and you must not leave its side once it has started to turn the lightest shade of brown. As soon as the sugar begins to take on color, gently swirl the pan until the sugar mixture is evenly golden brown, and then quickly move on to the next step. A fine line exists between a beautifully cooked sugar and a smoky mess, but as long as you don't turn your back on the sugar, you can avoid the latter.

After the caramel is made, the residual sugar that remains in the pot looks like an impenetrable mess. To clean the pot, fill it with water and boil the water until the caramel dissolves. Or, if you don't need the pot again right away, simply fill it with water and leave it to soak until the caramel eventually breaks down.

CREAMING

Sugar crystals are magic. Think of them as thousands of little workers with shovels, burrowing into butter and creating zillions of small air pockets. When you cream butter and sugar together, if the butter is at the right temperature, the sugar digs into it, making lots and lots of air pockets that ensure your final product will be light and fluffy. What is the right temperature? The butter should be around 68 degrees—slightly cool room temperature. It should be soft enough for you to bend a stick of it, but not so soft that you can poke your finger through it. If it is too cold, the sugar won't be strong enough to dig those pockets; too warm and the sugar will slosh straight through the butter without creating any pockets.

Creaming is most important in cake and cookie recipes, which contain a hefty amount of both butter and sugar. It's best to beat together the butter and sugar for longer than you might think: as long as 6 to 8 minutes on medium speed with a stand mixer in some cases. Watch for the transformation from a yellow, sandy mixture to an ivory, fluffy mixture—the sign that you have properly creamed them together. When you're creaming butter with brown sugar, you'll see the mixture go from muddy looking to pale brown, and creamy.

FILLING A PASTRY BAG

To fill a pastry bag, first place your pastry tip inside the bag and poke it out the small hole in the bottom corner, wedging it tightly in place. Give the corner of the bag a twist, and push the twisted part of the bag into the tip. This will keep whatever you put into the bag from being forced out the tip as you fill the bag. Holding the bag with one hand, use the other hand to fold down the top of the bag to create a wide cuff. It should be about one-half the length of the bag. Don't cheat on the depth of the cuff or you'll have a mess on your hands later on—literally! Use your free hand to open up the bag to create a nice, big opening for your filling. Using a rubber spatula or a rounded plastic bowl scraper, carefully fill the bag half full. Don't overfill it, or you will spend your time cleaning up after yourself and messing up your cake or tart. Once the bag is half

 combining sugar and eggs

WHEN YOU ARE MIXING SUGAR AND EGGS TOGETHER, DO NOT CRACK THE EGGS DIRECTLY ONTO THE SUGAR AND LET THEM SIT. The sugar "cooks" the eggs (through a chemical reaction in which the sugar reacts with the yolks), producing little, hard lumps. Instead, crack eggs into a bowl, whisk them to break them up, and then slowly whisk in the sugar. Once the sugar is thoroughly mixed into the eggs, the two ingredients are fine sitting together.

full, uncuff it and push the filling to the bottom of the bag. Untwist the twisted part you jammed into the tip, and push the filling into the tip, forcing out any air bubbles at the same time. Twist the top of the bag several times at the point at which the filling ends.

Handling and piping properly with a filled pastry bag takes practice. If you are right-handed, hold the top of the bag where you made the twists with your right hand (I wrap the twisted plastic or cloth from the bag firmly around my index finger to keep it from untwisting) and use your left hand to guide the tip as you pipe. With your right hand, apply pressure to the bag to force the contents down through the tip. Your left hand merely cradles the tip and gently points it where you want the contents of the bag to go. Don't use your left hand to push the contents out of the bag or you run the risk of pushing the contents back out the top of the bag and all over the place.

FOLDING

Folding, as opposed to stirring, whisking, or mixing, is a controlled and gentle method of combining ingredients. Sometimes you want to keep a mixture light and airy, such as when adding ingredients to whipped egg whites or whipped cream, or you want to make sure you don't overmix a batter (for example, when adding liquids to dry ingredients for a cake or muffins), which can lead to a tough crumb. Folding is perfect for these situations because it allows you to combine ingredients while maintaining as much air and lightness as possible.

 ## dEcorating with a pastry tip

FOR A SIMPLE, PRETTY DECORATION ON A CAKE, USE A SMALL ROUND OR STAR TIP TO PIPE LITTLE BALLS OR TINY STARS OF FROSTING, ONE RIGHT NEXT TO THE OTHER, ALL AROUND THE BASE OR TOP EDGE OF A CAKE. Be quick with your movements as you pipe ball on ball (or star on star), holding the tip at a 90-degree angle to the top of the cake or a 45-degree angle to the base of the cake, and you'll be rewarded with a neat row. You can also use a star tip to make a "shell" border along the base of the cake: As you push the frosting out through the tip against the cake, flick your wrist so that you end up with a small, tapered shape reminiscent of a conch shell. Another fun decorating idea for the top of a cake is a "snail" pattern: With a star tip, make a small S shape (smaller on top and larger on the bottom, reminiscent of a swan). Then, starting at the base of the bottom hook of the S, pipe a backward S (again smaller on the top and larger on the bottom). Repeat again with a forward-facing S and then a backward S, interlocking all the way around the top of the cake.

To fold properly, don't sweep around the edge of the bowl. That creates a whirlpool of ingredients that don't really combine. The ingredients just get moved around in the vortex. Instead, using a rubber spatula, cut straight down through the center of the bowl, sweep along the bottom and up the side, give the bowl a quarter turn, and repeat until the ingredients are combined. Be sure to cut smack dab through the ingredients in the center of the bowl and go all the way to the bottom. Then, sweep up the side, scraping up all of the loose stuff along the way. Every few turns, scrape the sides of the bowl all the way around to catch any unmixed ingredients, which tend to accumulate there.

If you have a large amount of one ingredient, such as egg whites, to fold into a mixture, fold it in batches so you don't overwhelm the mixture (see Tempering, page 18). Start by folding in about one-fourth of the ingredient. Once that portion is melded with the mixture, add the rest of the ingredient in one or two batches. The goal is to combine the ingredients well with minimal vigorous action and to maintain as much lightness as you can.

FRAISAGE

To achieve flaky pastry for your pies and tarts, you need to sandwich long, flat sheets of butter within your pastry or pie dough. When the rolled-out dough pastry or pie goes into a hot oven, the liquid in the butter turns to steam, which causes the dough to puff up, creating a network of little flaky pockets within the pastry. I use a French technique called *fraisage* to achieve the sandwiched butter: Dump the dough in a mound onto a work surface. Using the palm of your hand, smear the barely mixed dough (chunks of butter should still be punctuating it) along the work surface, smooshing the butter into long streaks as you go. Smear through all of the dough, moving through each part of the mound, until the whole mess has been smeared into a cohesive mass with long streaks of butter. If the dough still seems shaggy and not well mixed, smear the whole mound again.

The trick to successful *fraisage* is to keep from fully incorporating the liquid ingredients into the dry ingredients when you first mix them together. You want the dough to be a shaggy mess when you dump it out of the bowl onto the work surface. *Fraisage* brings the unkempt mass together into a tidy packet that has long striations, rather than little pieces, of butter. These stripes will melt and turn to steam in the oven, separating the dough into a multitude of flaky layers and creating a tender, melt-in-your-mouth pastry.

SCALDING LIQUID

To *scald* is to heat a liquid to just under the boiling point, when small bubbles form around the edge of the pan and you can tell the whole pot is just about to bubble. Scalding allows you to heat the liquid as hot as possible (so it combines smoothly with other ingredients) without boiling, which would cause loss of some liquid to evaporation and throw off the proportions of the ingredients.

SLASHING BREAD

For the same reason you put on earrings, wear a belt, or button your coat, you slash bread dough before baking: it's a nice finishing touch. In other words, it's mainly an aesthetic technique. Slashing the loaf guides the expansion of the bread in the oven and helps make the bread look pretty when it emerges. If you don't slash, the bread will burst on its own every which way, a result that some bread bakers like. In fact, you'll find that many rustic loaves haven't been slashed.

To slash bread, use a sharp paring knife, a razor blade, or a professional lame. Dip it in water to keep it from dragging. Use the tip of the knife or blade, not the length of it, and use quick, strong, sure movements. There's no wrong way to arrange your slashes, but here are a few suggestions: For baguettes and long loaves, space slashes an even ½ to ¾ inch apart. For round loaves, either make four slashes to form a square, so you end up with a little hat in the middle of your bread, or make one slash down the middle of the loaf and a few diagonal slashes on either side, which should meet the slash down the middle.

SPLITTING A CAKE INTO LAYERS

To split a cake into layers, place it on a flat work surface and use a long, thin serrated knife. Working carefully and evenly, score the cake horizontally all the way around the perimeter, cutting about an inch into the cake at the point at which you want to split it. Once the entire cake is scored, place the knife into the scored groove and, using a sawing motion, slowly start cutting at the same time you rotate the cake. If you follow the groove and continue to rotate the cake, you will eventually cut all the way through. If you have a revolving cake stand or a lazy Susan, use it to make rotating the cake easier.

TEMPERING

You know how some people like to dive headfirst into a pool, and others like to inch their way into the water one toe at a time? If pastry were a swimmer, it would be in the latter group. Pastry is all about patience, and when combining two ingredients of different temperatures or textures, it's important to introduce one into the other gently, via a method called *tempering*. This is when you whisk a little bit of hot liquid into a cold mixture, then whisk in a little more and a little more, until the two are completely combined. A gradual approach is especially important when you are whisking hot liquid into raw eggs. If the eggs are not properly tempered, the hot liquid will cook them, making your final product uncomfortably reminiscent of scrambled eggs. Another example of tempering is when you gently fold a little bit of a light whipped mixture into a stiffer mixture to lighten the latter, and then add the rest of the lighter mixture. Add too much all at once and the lightness will be lost; tempering helps you preserve as much air as possible.

WHIPPING EGG WHITES

Eggs, and especially egg whites, contain so much water that they work beautifully as leaveners in recipes such as sponge cakes and angel food cakes.

Problems arise (pun intended) when you don't know how much to beat the whites and you end up overbeating them. Once they are overbeaten, the walls of the individual egg cells are stretched to the max. That means, when you put the item in the oven, even if the evaporation of the water in the whites creates tons of steam, the dessert won't rise because the cell walls are already expanded to their limit. The key is to whip them until just before they are completely whipped, so that you still have some stretch and give in the cell walls to expand in the heat of the oven. How do you know when you've overbeaten your whites? The whipped mixture goes from glossy and cloudlike to grainy and matte, liquid seeps out of the whites to the bottom of the bowl, and the whole mess starts to resemble Styrofoam. If you overshoot and whip your whites to this point, your only option is to start over with fresh whites.

If the ratio of sugar to egg whites is low (that is, you don't have a lot of sugar but you have a lot of egg whites), you want to beat the whites just until they hold a soft peak but not beyond that point. Whites that are beaten with just a little sugar will never get stiff and glossy no matter how long you whip. These whites are best gently folded into your batter, and then when they get into the oven, they will rise, rise, rise and expand your batter into a light and airy pastry. Whites with little sugar are the easiest to overwhip, since sugar adds stretchiness, allowing you to whip them much longer and stiffer. As the ratio of sugar to whites goes up, you can whip longer and get a stiffer, shinier egg white mixture.

Whenever you beat egg whites, both the bowl and whisk (or mixer attachment) must be spotlessly clean. Any speck of egg yolk or fat will weaken the walls of the whites, reducing their ability to stretch and hold the air you are trying to beat into them. If you have been beating whites for a while, say 5 minutes, and they are still sloshy and not stiffening at all, you are plumb out of luck and will have to start over.

equipment

There's no need to stock your kitchen with every gadget on the market. In fact, if all you have is a few bowls, a whisk, a wooden spoon, a rubber spatula, a baking sheet, and a couple of other pans—all items you probably already own—you can make many recipes. But certain pieces of equipment do come in handy for baking, making the process easier and the results better. Here are the items I think are important.

BAIN-MARIE

A bain-marie is a water bath. We use one all the time in pastry making to melt things, to cook things gently on the stove top, or to bake things gently in the oven. For stove-top use, you can purchase a specifically designed set of nesting saucepans, known as a double boiler, but it is unnecessary. All you need is a saucepan and a metal or other heat-resistant bowl that rests snugly on top of the pan. Simply pour water to a depth of at least 2 inches into the saucepan and bring it to a simmer (or as directed in individual recipes). Rest the bowl in the top of the pan (the bottom of the bowl should not come into contact with the water) and voilà—instant bain-marie! For a bain-marie to be used in the oven, you need a deep roasting pan that is large enough to hold whatever you are baking. Place the item, usually in a baking dish or in ramekins, in the roasting pan, place the roasting pan on the oven rack, and then carefully add hot water to the roasting pan, typically enough to come about halfway up the sides of the baking dish.

BAKING PANS

Standard-size cake pans are round and 8 or 9 inches in diameter, with 2- to 3-inch-high sides. You'll want at least two of either size, so you can make layer cakes. The sizes are some-what interchangeable: if you go with 9-inch pans, your layers will be a little thinner; if you go with 8-inch pans, you'll end up with somewhat taller cakes. Adjust the baking time accordingly by adding 6 to 8 minutes if you are baking a 9-inch cake in an 8-inch pan or by deducting 5 to 6 minutes if you are baking an 8-inch cake in a 9-inch pan. If you have cake pans of other sizes, such as 6 inches, be sure not to fill them any more than two-thirds full, or the batter will overflow the sides in the oven. I use a springform pan for baking Luscious Cheesecake (page 192), but I also include instructions on page 193 for baking it without a springform pan if you don't have one.

An oft-used baking pan in my cupboard is a 9-by-13-inch glass or metal pan with 2- to 3-inch sides. This comes in handy for all sorts of bar cookies, such as Intense Chocolate Brownies (page 148) or Brown Butter–Crispy Rice Treats (page 133).

A tin or recyclable disposable aluminum 9-by-5-inch loaf pan is great for making everything from breakfast loaf breads to pound cakes to frozen treats like French parfaits. (A tempered glass pan works, too, but things bake faster in glass, so you'll need to check your cake or quick bread about 10 minutes earlier.) You'll need a 10-inch tube pan with a removable bottom, preferably made of sturdy aluminum, for the coffee cake on page 62 or if you want to make the angel food cake on page 178. For tarts, I use a bottomless, smooth-sided 10¼-by-¾-inch tart ring. You can substitute a fluted 9½-inch tart pan with a removable bottom. A tempered-glass 9½-inch pie dish or recyclable disposable aluminum pan will work for all of the pies in this book.

BAKING SHEETS

One large baking sheet is plenty; two are nice but not necessary. The best choice is a heavy-gauge aluminum half-sheet pan measuring 18 by 13 inches, with a small lip all the way around. It is small enough to fit into home ovens but big enough to hold a decent number of cookies or meringues, a sponge cake for rolling, or a batch of scones. A 14-by-11-inch baking sheet or a 15-by-10-inch jelly-roll pan is handy for making my tiramisu (page 194).

BENCH SCRAPER

A small, straight-edged, spatula-like metal rectangle with a wooden or plastic handle, a bench scraper is handy for working with pie, tart, and bread doughs. Use it to pick up and move dough, divide dough into smaller pieces, lift items off baking sheets, or transfer chopped ingredients to a bowl. It can also be used to scrape up bits of sticky dough and the like from work surfaces. I always have a bench scraper nearby when I am working, and I constantly use it to clean and scrape.

BOWLS

Having bowls in a variety of sizes is helpful for measuring out in advance all of the ingredients you need for a recipe. (Or, you can use small storage containers for holding measured ingredients.) At the very least, you will need at least one small metal or sturdy, heat-resistant plastic bowl for holding cracked eggs and for whisking together liquid ingredients, and one medium-to-large metal bowl for folding cake batters, whipping cream, and to use as a bain-marie bowl.

BOWL SCRAPER

A thin, flexible piece of plastic about the size of your hand and the shape of a kidney bean or half-moon, a bowl scraper is nifty for scraping batters out of bowls and folding large amounts of ingredients into batters. They are also convenient for quick cleanup jobs. I always have one in my chef's coat pocket when I'm baking.

CAKE STAND

Although it isn't necessary, an elevated, revolving cake stand is convenient if you make and decorate a lot of cakes. The spinning top helps you to split cakes and to spread frosting more easily and evenly on the top and sides.

CANDY THERMOMETER

If you are making something that requires preparing a sugar syrup and you are not comfortable testing the temperature of the syrup by hand, you'll need a candy thermometer. I explain how to test the syrup without a thermometer on page 14, so if you decide to master the technique, you won't need the thermometer.

KNIVES

You will want at least one long, thin serrated knife for splitting cakes into layers and slicing bread. A paring knife is perfect for trimming fruit and helping you pop cakes out of pans. An 8-inch chef's knife is ideal for chopping chocolate, nuts, and fruit.

MEASURING CUPS AND SPOONS

For dry ingredients, you need measuring cups, usually of stainless steel or hard plastic, with cylindrical walls and a straight rim, so you can level them off easily with the back of a knife or another straight utensil. For liquid ingredients, you need measuring cups of tempered glass that look like small pitchers, with measurements of fluid ounces and sometimes milliliters printed vertically on their sides. If you get a scale (see below right), however, you won't need any of these cups because you can weigh all your ingredients except for those called for in small amounts (3 tablespoons or less). For those cases, you will need at least one set of measuring spoons.

MICROPLANE GRATER

This fine-holed rasp grater is the best and easiest tool to use for grating the zest from citrus fruits. It is also terrific for grating fresh ginger (which is much easier to do if the ginger is frozen first) and whole nutmegs.

MUFFIN TIN

Muffin tins come in all sizes, from mini (or gem) to standard to jumbo to the latest craze, muffin top. All of the muffin recipes in this book were tested with an aluminum standard 12-cup muffin tin.

PARCHMENT PAPER

Parchment paper is a staple at the bakery for two reasons: it prevents cakes and cookies from sticking to pans as they bake, and it is perfect for making piping cornets for decorating cakes.

PASTRY BAG AND TIPS

Pastry bags are great for decorating cakes and for piping out soft batters, like *pâte à choux* for cream puffs and *dacquoise* for meringue cake layers. You can use a cloth bag or a disposable plastic bag. The advantage to cloth is that you can reuse the bag over and over. The disadvantages are that the bag will get smelly if you don't clean it with bleach every time, and the bulky cloth is sometimes challenging to manipulate as you pipe. The advantage to disposable bags is that they are more flexible to manipulate, which makes piping easier. The disadvantages are that they are not environmentally friendly and they tear more easily than cloth bags. But you can (and we do) wash the plastic bags after every use, so you can use them over and over, and if you don't overfill them, they are much less likely to tear.

I like the larger 16- to 18-inch bags. Smaller ones tend to get messy quickly. As for piping tips, get one small round tip and one small star tip as starters. The round tip is exactly what you need when you're piping *pâte à choux* for shaping cream puffs or éclairs. (As you get more experienced and move on to things like a *dacquoise*, you'll need more tips in larger sizes.) A star tip is a basic decorating tip that can add pizzazz to any frosted cake.

ROLLING PINS

I like using a tapered French pin—a long, smooth, tapered wooden rod—for rolling out pie and tart doughs. It allows me to feel the dough underneath the pin, and I can maneuver the dough with the tapered ends to roll it into the shape I want. For laminated doughs, a small pin with two offset handles—a steel rod that runs from handle to handle and rotates smoothly on ball bearings—is nice. You need more strength and leverage to roll out sheets of laminated dough, and with a pin that rolls while you hold the handles, you can lean in and push down and the pin, helped by the ball bearings, will glide over the dough.

SCALE

If you want to become a great baker, this is the most important piece of equipment you can buy. You can find a decent digital scale at any kitchen store or online for fifteen or twenty dollars. Make sure you get one that goes easily from pounds to grams, because if you are going to weigh your ingredients, you should weigh in grams and kilograms, rather than ounces and pounds. The metric system is much easier to work with. It's straightforward, it allows you to scale recipes up and down with ease, and you avoid confusion with measurements such as "21 ounces," which you would have to convert in your head to "1 pound, 5 ounces." In the metric system, conversions from grams to kilograms only require moving a decimal point. Also, make sure that the scale has a tare function, which allows you to zero out the scale with each new ingredient you put on it.

Weighing your ingredients ensures that your measurements are exact, which is of primary importance in baking. Plus, it is easier and faster to weigh your ingredients than to scoop and level. Weighing eliminates much of the uncertainty in baking.

All of the recipes in this book were tested using the volume measurements given and then matching them with the corresponding weights for each ingredient. In some instances, the weights given are absolute and immutable for best results. For example, the amount of sugar, flour, butter in most every recipe is carefully measured and weighed to give you the best result. I did not round when listing the weight of butter, since it commonly comes in ½-cup sticks, which weigh 114 grams each. I did, however, round when it came to instances such as ⅓ cup sugar. This weighs 66.7 grams, but I chose to round up to 70 grams. In each case I studied whether or not rounding would make a significant difference in the final product. If the answer was no, I chose to round.

Weights for some ingredients are included as guidelines only, not hard and fast measurements. For example, when you add 1 cup sliced peaches or ½ cup chopped scallions to a recipe, the ingredient is typically included purely for flavor and does not affect the chemistry or consistency of the final product, which means exacting weights are not critical. Also, for measurements of 3 tablespoons or less, I do not give weights. It is generally easier and more accurate to measure these amounts by volume than by weight, since most scales are not sensitive to very small amounts.

SIFTER

A sifter is essential for sifting flour and other dry ingredients to make sure they are as light and aerated as possible. When a recipe calls for sifting, be sure to sift! You don't know how long your dry ingredients have been sitting on a shelf packing themselves into clumps and lumps. Sifting airs them out and lets them breathe. Once you have sifted ingredients together, always give them a stir with a spoon, as sifting doesn't do a great job of evenly combining them. To see evidence of this, try sifting together some flour with a few tablespoons of cocoa powder. You will see that even though the flour and cocoa aerate, they don't combine evenly; the cocoa stays separate. We use a drum sifter at Flour, and I have an old-fashioned rotary-handled sifter at home. Both kinds are great, and a fine-mesh sieve is a good substitute.

SPATULAS

A rubber spatula (or a silicone spatula, which can withstand very high temperatures) is indispensable in a baker's kitchen. Make sure you have one at least 12 inches long to give you enough leverage to fold and mix your batters. It is also handy for scraping the batter out of a bowl: its curved, somewhat flexible head allows you to clean out every last bit.

My favorite piece of baking equipment is the offset spatula, which has a thin, stiff yet flexible blade that bends up to meet the handle, hence the name. Offset spatulas come in all sizes and are invaluable for icing and decorating cakes and for spreading jams and fillings on tarts.

STAND MIXER AND HANDHELD MIXER

I have used the exact same KitchenAid mixer at home almost since I started baking. (I have used Cuisinart and Krups stand mixers in various other kitchens along the way.) With a stand mixer, you can have one item mixing and still have both hands free for adding other items or doing other tasks. A stand mixer also combines ingredients more thoroughly and evenly than is possible by hand. Many steps in baking—kneading bread dough, whipping eggs and cream, creaming butter and sugar—require some muscle power. Having a stand mixer makes these actions easier. You can certainly make almost any recipe in this book without a stand mixer, but it is exponentially more efficient to use one.

A handheld mixer falls somewhere between a stand mixer and mixing by hand in terms of efficiency. Because you have to use one hand to hold it, leaving only one hand free to add ingredients, scrape down the sides of the bowl, and so on, a handheld mixer can be more awkward to use. But it is definitely a step up from mixing by hand because of the power and speed it offers. If you use a handheld mixer, you will clock less time than if you are mixing by hand, but you will definitely need more time than what's necessary with a stand mixer.

WHISK

One 12-inch (from head to toe) whisk can serve multiple purposes. If possible, purchase a piano whisk, which has a slightly rounded head and 7 to 8 thin, flexible wires. You'll use it to whisk sugar into eggs, to whip cream by hand, and to whisk pastry cream and other custards that require constant attention.

WIRE RACK

A gridded wire rack is helpful for cooling baked items just out of the oven, because it allows air to circulate around them, keeping them from getting soggy. A rack is also helpful when you are topping a cake with a glaze: place the rack holding the cake over a baking sheet or small tray to catch drips.

ingredients

Use the best-quality ingredients you can when you bake. You will taste the extra expense in the final product. Here are some guidelines for ingredients frequently called for in this book.

BROWN SUGAR

All of the recipes in the book that call for brown sugar use light brown sugar with one exception: Butterscotch Pudding (page 243). If you are measuring brown sugar in a measuring cup instead of weighing it, be sure to pack the sugar into the cup to ensure you are using the correct amount.

BUTTER

Use unsalted grade A butter—*always* unsalted! Salt acts as a preservative, so I think salted butter is suspect. Who knows how long it's been in the grocery store? Unsalted butter has a much shorter shelf life, so stores are forced to buy it in smaller quantities, which means it is usually fresher. Plus, when you use salted butter, you don't know how much salt it contains, and whatever you are baking could end up too salty. Start with unsalted butter and you will be able to control the amount of salt you use.

CHOCOLATE AND COCOA POWDER

Many recipes in this book call for chocolate—milk, semisweet, bittersweet, unsweetened—and each recipe was tested with a specific type of chocolate for flavor and texture. The best advice I can give you about choosing a chocolate is to taste it before you use it. If it's waxy, gritty, chalky, or harsh, your pastry will be waxy, gritty, chalky, or harsh. Buy the best chocolate—the one with the smoothest mouthfeel and the richest flavor—you can afford. You will taste the difference in whatever you make with it.

There are two types of cocoa powder, Dutch processed and natural. They are not interchangeable in baking. Dutch-processed cocoa powder, which has been treated with an alkali that neutralizes cocoa's natural acidity, is milder in flavor and reddish-brown in color. Nonalkalized natural cocoa, which reacts with baking soda in recipes, is strong, bitter, and more intense. All of the recipes in this book use Dutch-processed cocoa powder.

CRÈME FRAÎCHE

If there is a "magic" ingredient in my baking arsenal, it's crème fraîche. Although common in France it hasn't yet swept the United States. It has a tangy, mellow flavor that is divine on its own as a topping for cobbler or pie. As an ingredient, it adds a rich flavor that is impossible to replicate with sour cream, its closest competitor. And although sour cream will technically work in recipes that call for crème fraîche, in a side-by-side taste test of pastries made with the two ingredients, there is no contest. If you want pastries that will impress, use crème fraîche.

Making crème fraîche is easy: Pour a quart of heavy cream into a bowl or other container, stir in 4 tablespoons of buttermilk, cover, and let stand at warm room temperature overnight (at least 10 hours), or until it thickens. Stir it in the morning and it should be thick and creamy. If it is still liquidy, re-cover, return it to a warm spot, and check it every hour or so until it thickens. When it has a good consistency, cover it tightly and store in the refrigerator for up to 2 weeks. To make more crème fraîche, you can just add 4 tablespoons of your previous batch to a quart of heavy cream and proceed as directed. The old crème fraîche acts as a starter to get the new batch going, and you don't need to buy more buttermilk.

EGGS

Always use large eggs, and make sure they are at room temperature unless otherwise specified. A quick way to warm up eggs from the fridge is to place them in a bowl of warm water for about 10 minutes, or hold them under a stream of hot tap water for a minute or so.

If you prefer to weigh your egg whites for these recipes, please do. If you have reserved whites from a previous recipe, just note that 1 large egg white weighs 30 grams. If you are using packaged egg whites, and decide not to weigh, follow the packaging's conversion information.

FLOUR

All of the recipes that specify all-purpose flour were tested with King Arthur brand unbleached all-purpose flour, which is milled from a mixture of soft and hard wheats. Brands of flour are all a bit different from one another, but as long as you stick to all-purpose when it's called for, you will have good results. From a baking standpoint, bleached and unbleached flour are interchangeable. Some people are sensitive to the chemicals used to bleach flour, and since I'm a relative

purist, I'd rather use unbleached flour, which is less processed and closer to its natural state than bleached flour.

The balance of the recipes call for cake flour, bread flour, or whole-wheat flour. Cake flour, which is made from soft wheat and is more finely milled than all-purpose flour, more readily absorbs fat and holds more sugar. It has a low protein content, too, which means that it doesn't have a lot of gluten, a type of protein that can make a cake tough. So cakes made with cake flour have a finer, more tender crumb. In a pinch, you can substitute ¾ cup (105 grams) unbleached all-purpose flour and 2 tablespoons cornstarch for 1 cup (120 grams) cake flour.

On the other end of the spectrum is bread flour, which is milled from hard wheat and has a high protein content, making it perfect for recipes in which you want a lot of gluten to ensure a good chewy texture, such as many yeast breads. The gluten that develops when you use bread flour also helps keep the gases produced during fermentation trapped inside the dough, so the dough will rise nicely.

Whole-wheat flour is milled from whole kernels of wheat, the outer layers of the kernel—the bran and germ—as well as the center endosperm. This results in a darker, more textured flour than white flour, which contains only the endosperm. The presence of the bran and germ also means that it has a lower protein content than white flour. Whole-wheat flour is typically too coarse for most pastry baking, but if you want to add more of it to your diet, try substituting one-fourth or one-third of the all-purpose or bread flour in a recipe with whole-wheat flour. Expect a heavier, denser crumb. I do not recommend substituting whole-wheat flour for cake flour.

FRUITS

Your fruit desserts will only be as good as your ingredients, so don't skimp and use underripe or out-of-season fruits. Use crisp apples and firm but ripe pears. Stone fruits like peaches and plums should yield to gentle pressure and have a per-fumy fragrance. Bananas should always be ripe; if they are tinged with green, *wait!*—or go buy some riper bananas. If berries don't taste delicious eaten out of hand, don't bake with them. Even the best-made pastry won't disguise a pale, under-ripe berry. The exception is the blueberry pie on page 217, which was tested with individually quick-frozen (IQF) berries. IQF blueberries allow me to bake with blueberries year-round, and not just in July, when luscious berries are plentiful.

MILK

Always use whole milk in baking, unless otherwise specified. Whole milk is rich and flavorful, and fat carries flavor, so using whole milk, rather than skim or low fat, means there will be more flavor carriers in whatever you make.

SALT

Although baking recipes often call for table salt, I always bake—and have tested all of these recipes—with kosher salt. That preference may be because of my experience working in restaurants, where kosher salt was invariably the salt of choice. It has a cleaner, milder flavor than table salt and its coarser grains allow you to control the amount you use more easily. Table salt is so fine that I find it is easy to mismeasure it. You can use table salt if you don't have kosher salt, but only use about half the amount called for. Except for bread recipes, where salt is a key ingredient that reacts with the yeast to alter the dough chemically, salt in pastries is used solely for flavoring.

SUGAR

The recipes in this book will be delicious if you use regular granulated sugar, but I like baking with superfine sugar. Superfine sugar is granu-lated sugar that has been pulverized to a finer texture. It results in lighter, fluffier creamed butter-sugar mixtures, it dissolves better in meringues, and it generally produces a finer crumb. You can buy superfine sugar, or you can make it: pulse regular granulated sugar in a food processor for 5 to 10 seconds to yield finer granules.

VANILLA BEANS AND VANILLA EXTRACT

Did you know that the vanilla bean is the pod of a specific orchid native to southern Mexico that only flowers for one day each year? Each flower must be hand-pollinated on this day to ensure that it bears its fruit, the vanilla bean, hence its hefty price! But it's worth it. Nothing compares to the fragrant, mellow character of pure vanilla. To preserve that unique quality, store beans tightly wrapped in plastic wrap in a cool, dark cupboard or in your refrigerator for up to 1 year.

The essence of the bean is found within the pod in the form of millions of tiny black specks, or seeds. To get at them, place the bean on a work surface. Holding it down at either end, poke a hole at one end with the tip of a paring knife. Lay the knife parallel to the work surface and slide it down the bean, splitting it open. With the blade of the knife, scrape along the length of the pod, collect-ing the seeds on the knife blade. If you are making custard or infusing a liquid with vanilla, throw the seeds and the pod into the liquid. If you are adding vanilla to a batter, take a small bit of the batter, smoosh the vanilla seeds into the batter until they are mixed in, and then fold the concen-trated vanilla batter into the rest of the batter.

Save the pod and use it to make vanilla sugar to use in place of regular sugar in any recipe to which you would like to impart a subtle vanilla flavor: If the pod was retrieved from a liquid, rinse and air dry it. Place it in an airtight container with about 4 cups (about 800 grams) sugar for 1 week, and the sugar will pick up the aroma of the vanilla.

Vanilla extract is a more cost-effective way to add vanilla flavor to baked goods. It is also more readily available, and it mixes easily into batters. Be sure to buy only pure vanilla extract, and not imitation vanilla flavoring.

joanne's top 12 baking tips

Throughout this book, I offer recipe-specific tips and tricks that will help you bake beautiful pastries and other baked goods every time. But some tips are so important, and so universally relevant, that they qualify for my Top 12 list. Here are a dozen keys to success that I've learned over the years.

 TIP N°: 1 Preheat the oven and make sure your oven temperature is correct

The oven must always be at the proper temperature before you start baking, so you must heat it for at least 15 minutes before you will need it. (Remember that the time it takes to heat totally depends on your oven—and yours may take longer!) You should also routinely check its accuracy with an oven thermometer to make sure the dial setting actually matches the temperature inside the oven. If your dial setting does not match the oven temperature, adjust the dial accordingly to make sure your oven is at the right temperature.

Many home bakers underestimate the importance of having the oven at the correct temperature. If you put a cake into the oven while it is still heating, instead of expanding and growing, the batter will melt and you'll end up with a hockey puck. If your oven is too hot and you put a cake into it, the excessive heat will cause a hard crust to form on the outside and the inside will remain raw. By the time the inside bakes, the outside will be charred. When baking bread, the yeast in the dough depends on a hot oven temperature to give the dough enough oomph to rise and develop an airy, light crumb. If your oven is not hot enough, the bread will deflate, rather than be springy, and will not rise to its full potential.

TIP N°: 2 "Mise" everything and read recipes carefully

When you hear a chef say "mise," he or she is referring to getting everything in order before starting a recipe. (It comes from *mise en place*, which is essentially French for "Get organized!") In order to bake well and happily, you need to approach the task like a one-act play with no dress rehearsal. Read through the entire recipe carefully, assemble all of the equipment you will need, gather together and measure all of the ingredients, heat the oven to the correct temperature—and then raise the curtain and begin the play. If you mise everything in advance, you should be able to march through the recipe step-by-step with no problem. Trouble occurs when you don't have all of the elements ready: Midway through a recipe, you realize you should have already melted the chocolate, and as you stop to do just that, your egg whites overwhip, your cream boils over, and, wah, chaos strikes. Or, your cake batter is ready to go, and as you start to pop it into the oven, you realize the oven isn't on. If you mise properly, such scenarios will never happen to you.

Along the same lines, I have found that even experienced bakers forget the cardinal rule of baking: read the recipe. Baking is not improv theater. The recipe is there to guide you in making the best pastry possible, and "winging it" is never a good idea. I've been sharing recipes since I've been baking, and people often ask how I can share so freely. It is because I know that the list of ingredients is not the key. Instead, it's how you put them all together. At Flour, it boggles my mind that the same recipe can come out so differently when it's made by different bakers, simply because some read the recipe more closely than others. The instructions in a well-written recipe have been carefully thought out, so follow them! Most baking mistakes are avoidable if you read carefully. And if you fail to do so, don't despair—read Tip No. 12.

TIP N°: 3 Weigh your ingredients

Good results in baking depend on accurate measurements, and the best way to guarantee accuracy is to weigh your ingredients. Use a scale and you won't have to worry about how you scooped your flour or packed your brown sugar, because you'll know for sure you are using the correct amount. I've scrupulously gone through these recipes and matched up the weights of ingredients with their corresponding volume measurements. Now that I have spent time testing recipes and baking with both volume and weight measurements, I am eager to get all home bakers onto the scale bandwagon. The weather, the bin in which the ingredient was stored, the measuring cup used, how tired I was—all of these factors and more contributed to inconsistencies when I tested with volume versus weight measurements. Sometimes the difference was insignificant, but other times it was enough of a discrepancy to throw off the whole recipe. If you want to guarantee that what you bake will come out great, buy a scale (see page 23). You will thank me for it.

TIP N°: 4 Measure flour carefully

I stayed up nights thinking about the flour measurements for this book. See Tip No. 3 about weighing all your ingredients, and if you follow my advice there, you can skip this tip and never worry again about whether you are using the correct amount of flour. But if you don't have a scale, you need to know how the baker who wrote the recipe you are following measured the flour. Here's why: All of the recipes in this book assume that 1 cup unbleached all-purpose flour weighs

140 grams. I measured flour for this book by first stirring it up, then dipping my measuring cup into the canister, and finally sweeping the top level with the back of a knife. If I don't aerate the flour first, however, and I just dip and sweep, then 1 cup weighs 155 grams. Or, if I spoon the flour into the cup and level it off, 1 cup weighs 125 grams. The difference between the dip-and-sweep method and the spoon-and-sweep method is 30 grams, which is almost ¼ cup flour. If the recipe you are using calls for 2 cups flour, depending on how you choose to measure, you could end up putting in an extra ½ cup or shorting the recipe by ½ cup. No wonder your cake is dry or your cookie dough is soupy!

Please note that if you decide not to weigh the ingredients for the recipes in this book, you need to aerate the flour and then use the dip-and-sweep method. I picked this method after surveying all my bakers and all my nonprofessional baking friends on how they typically measure flour if they are not weighing it, and everyone of them said they dip and sweep. Even professional bakers who know that the key to successful baking is to weigh flour will sometimes take shortcuts at home and use volume measures. Just remember that if you opt to do the same, always aerate the flour before you dip, because the flour will be packed differently in every bin.

 ## TIP N°: 5 Pay attention to the temperature of your ingredients

I am always aware of the temperature of my butter, eggs, melted chocolate, and any liquids. Temperature matters, and one ingredient at the wrong temperature can foil a recipe. For example, if you're making a flaky pie pastry or scone, the ingredients must be as cold as possible. If they are warm, the fat will combine too thoroughly with the dry ingredients when you mix them together, and you will end up with a cookie-like dough, rather than a flaky one. You want the fat to stay firm and cold and not blend completely into the dry ingredients, so that it melts in the heat of the oven, steams up, and makes the dough puff up. Beating together butter and sugar for a cake batter is another example. You want the sugar crystals to carve out numerous microscopic air pockets in the butter, so that when the batter is in the oven, the pockets will expand, ensuring a light cake. If the butter is too warm, the pockets created by the sugar will collapse and your cake will be dense. A third example is when you add a liquid, such as eggs, to creamed butter and sugar. If the liquid is a lot colder than the creamed mixture, it won't blend in well, and you'll end up with lots of tunnels and tough spots in your cake because the liquid mixed directly with the dry ingredients, rather than with the butter and sugar. Cake and cookie batters are all about the thorough emulsification of ingredients, and if you have ingredients that aren't around the same temperature, they can't emulsify. There are many more examples, such as when you mix melted chocolate or butter into other ingredients, but the bottom line is simple: Pay attention to the temperature of the ingredients specified in each recipe.

TIP N°: 6   Use salt

Wait a minute, isn't this a pastry cookbook? All the more reason to let you in on what I consider a key element in making great pastries: salt. Used in moderation, salt does for pastries exactly what it does for your beef stew, roast chicken, and lasagna—it enhances flavor. You'll notice that all of the recipes in this book call for some salt. I often conduct an experiment with new bakers, asking them to taste lemon curd before we add salt and then again after. I love watching their eyes light up when they taste how the salt brings out the brightness of the lemon and makes it taste more, well, lemony. I've found, especially with chocolate and vanilla, that salt drastically changes the way sweet flavors taste, making them less one-dimensionally sweet and more flavorful, and I encourage you to try the same experiments. Taste chocolate pudding before salt is added and then after; dip your spoon into a vanilla ice cream base before seasoning it with salt, and again after you add salt. The salt rounds out the flavors and keeps the dessert from tasting flat. It's a common ingredient, yet it is too often underutilized in the pastry kitchen.

TIP N°: 7   Toast your nuts

Toasting nuts too little or not at all is a fairly common—and easy-to-fix—baking mistake. When I go out to a restaurant or bakery and try a new pastry or dessert, I can taste whether the nuts are properly toasted. When they are, I know someone who is paying attention is in the kitchen making pastries that I want to eat. Untoasted nuts are labeled "raw" and that is exactly how they taste. Taking the time to toast nuts to a proper light golden brown color brings out their natural oils and heightens their nutty flavor. It is easy to do, too: Spread the nuts on a rimmed baking sheet and place in a preheated 350-degree-F oven for 8 to 10 minutes, or until they are fragrant and have taken on a golden brown color. To make sure they are ready, bite into a nut. For almonds and hazelnuts (which tend to require longer toasting), the interior should be medium brown. For walnuts and pecans (which toast more quickly), the interior should be light brown. In general, the firmer the nut, the longer it should be toasted to bring out its full flavor.

TIP Nº: **8** Don't overwhip

I've noticed that there are two items that beginning pastry cooks invariably over-whip: cream and egg whites. For different reasons, overwhipping either of them can lead to a poorer-quality product. First, let's talk about cream. If you grew up with ReddiWip, you know the firm, stiff, foamy stuff that comes out of the spout of the can. It looks like whipped cream and it says it is whipped cream, but it is nothing like properly whipped cream. Whipped cream should be, well, creamy. It should be light on your tongue, airy, and smooth. Overwhipping it changes the texture from something luscious to something that can mar your dessert with a stiff, lumpy mouthfeel. So don't overwhip. Just whip your cream until it holds a soft peak and still looks soft and pillowy, unless otherwise instructed. (When you're using whipped cream for decorating cakes or you are folding it into a stiff mixture like pastry cream, you need to whip it to a stiff peak.) If you go too far and it looks bumpy and rough, you can often rescue it by carefully folding in a few tablespoons of unwhipped cream. It should come back together into a smooth wonder.

If you overwhip egg whites, the walls of their cells are stretched to the max, which means they can no longer act effectively as a leavener when the pastry is baked (read more about egg whites on page 18).

TIP Nº: **9** Roll out dough properly

Watching beginners with a rolling pin reminds me of when I was a kid trying to learn how to ride a bike. At first I was tentative, nervous, and slow. But my dad kept assuring me that he was holding on (he wasn't!) and encouraging me to pedal faster with firmness and confidence. Before I knew it, I was flying around the block. Own that pin! Use it as an extension of your hands and take advantage of the strength that you and the pin have together versus the dough. Pound the dough, move it around, use the pin to coax it into place. Press down evenly and with confidence. The dough will do what you tell it to do if you approach it with the attitude that you are the boss.

People often think that rolling the pin repeatedly back and forth over the dough is good rolling. But it's not. Think about it: If you keep going back and forth over the length of the dough, you are stretching it out, but you are not working efficiently. The dough is being stretched out and then rolled right back tight. You risk working the dough needlessly and you end up rolling it more than necessary.

The proper way to roll is to position your pin at the center of the dough and firmly roll out to stretch the dough away from you. Then lift the pin, reposition it at the center of the dough, and firmly roll inward to stretch the dough toward you. Each part of the dough gets stretched in the direction you are aiming for: away from the center. Rotate the dough an eighth of a turn with every center-out-center-in roll and you will have a nice circle in no time.

TIP N°: **10** Bake tart and pie dough all the way through

Too often tarts and pies, even those with delicious filling and perfectly prepared dough, have an underbaked crust. The first thing I do when I take a bite of a tart or pie is scrutinize the crust, to see if it's golden brown or pale. An underbaked pie or tart shell is doughy and chewy and has not reached its full potential. A fully baked shell is golden brown all over, which signals that the sugars have caramelized into a deliciously nutty flavor and the pastry is crisp and flaky. When you think your shell is fully baked, try to pick it up—be careful not to break it—and peek at the bottom. If the bottom is completely browned, the shell is ready. If it is pale, the pastry will lack flavor and feel tough, even if the dough is well made. Leave it in the oven for a few minutes more, until it bakes into a sweet, nutty, golden brown container for your filling.

TIP N°: **11** Make things ahead and use your freezer

Your freezer is one of your best friends when it comes to baking. Almost every dough can be made ahead and stored in the freezer, and many pastries, especially breakfast pastries, suffer little loss of flavor or texture if you store them, unbaked and well wrapped, in the freezer. The Flour freezer is stocked to the brim with pie dough, tart dough, and unbaked scones, brioche, and certain cakes. This little trick allows us to offer dozens and dozens of freshly baked pastries to our customers without having a coterie of bakers in at midnight every night to get ready for the next day. You probably don't want to be up at the crack of dawn every time you want to serve a freshly baked breakfast treat, and you can't be tied to your kitchen all day the next time you want to make a cake. So, use the freezer to your advantage. If you always have a bit of cookie dough or tart dough on hand, you're just minutes away from a delicious dessert.

12 Have fun and relax

This should really be Tip No. 1 because it is my most important one of all. It might not seem like an insider's secret to you, but I promise you it is. Many people say that they don't bake, or that they can't bake, or that the precision required in baking is not their gig, or that baking makes them nervous. Baking needs to have its reputation overhauled! I can't tell you the number of times I've made a pastry, been pretty darn proud of it, made it again, and then again and again, only to learn later that many people avoid making it because it is thought to be rife with tricks and pitfalls. I'm sure that if I had been aware of the reputed difficulty level of such treats as brioche and croissants, I might have avoided making them as well. The best thing about baking (and cooking) is that most of the time your mistakes are edible—and usually quite enjoyable!

I mess up all the time in the kitchen. *All the time!* I've thrown away more rubbery cakes and tough pastries than I care to remember, burying them at the bottom of the trashcan to hide the evidence. I've been yelled at by more than one boss who has thrown my burnt tarts or my other disasters at me. I once cried my heart out after I slipped and dropped a wedding cake I had spent a full day making—and then promptly had to dry my tears and race around to rebake and rebuild a new one. The Chinese say, "Fall down seven times, get up eight." And this is what I do. I eat my mistakes, figure out what I could do differently the next time, and try again. For every time I have messed up, I have brought joy and happiness many times over to a customer, friend, family member, or even just me with a delicious, amazing dessert. I hope you will do the same, and have fun along the way.

pb + j   4.50
gRilled cheese   4.50
milk + a cookie   2.50

with love

breakfast treats

OATMEAL-MAPLE SCONES

1½ cups (210 grams) unbleached all-purpose flour

1¼ cups (125 grams) old-fashioned rolled oats (not instant or quick cooking)

1½ teaspoons baking powder

¼ teaspoon baking soda

¼ teaspoon kosher salt

½ cup (50 grams) pecan halves, toasted and chopped

½ cup (80 grams) golden raisins

½ cup (1 stick, 114 grams) cold unsalted butter, cut into 8 to 10 pieces

⅓ cup (80 grams) cold heavy cream

½ cup (160 grams) maple syrup

1 cold egg

MAPLE GLAZE

1 cup (140 grams) confectioners' sugar

3 tablespoons maple syrup

1 to 2 tablespoons water

MAKES 8 SCONES

I always order oatmeal when I go out for breakfast, and we always have boxes of instant oatmeal, packages of regular rolled oats, and canisters of steel-cut oats in the pantry at home. It's not that I like oatmeal so much, it's that, instead, I like all the things I mix into it. I especially enjoy it sweetened with copious amounts of maple syrup. I developed this recipe when I first opened Flour as a way to get that oaty-mapley fix in a scone package. The use of maple syrup as the sweetener in this scone makes the dough extra soft so you can drop these scones onto a baking sheet, rather than patting out the dough and cutting the scones with a knife or cookie cutter. I adore scones made this way. The craggy, uneven tops are browned into crunchy, addictive bits.

➡ Position a rack in the center of the oven, and heat the oven to 350 degrees F.

➡ Using a stand mixer fitted with the paddle attachment (or a handheld mixer), mix together the flour, oats, baking powder, baking soda, salt, pecans, and raisins on low speed for 10 to 15 seconds, or until combined. Scatter the butter over the top and beat on low speed for about 30 seconds, or until the butter is somewhat broken down and grape-size pieces are still visible.

➡ In a small bowl, whisk together the cream, maple syrup, and egg until thoroughly mixed. On low speed, pour the cream mixture into the flour-butter mixture and beat for 20 to 30 seconds, or just until the dough comes together. It will be fairly wet.

➡ Remove the bowl from the mixer stand. With a rubber spatula, scrape the bottom and sides of the bowl to ensure that all of the dry ingredients are mixed into the dough. Using a ⅓-cup dry-measuring cup, drop mounded scoops of the dough onto a baking sheet, forming 8 scones and spacing them 2 to 3 inches apart. (At this point, the unbaked scones can be frozen, tightly wrapped in plastic wrap, for up to 1 week. Proceed as directed, baking directly from the freezer and adding 5 to 10 minutes to the baking time.)

(continued)

➡ Bake for about 40 minutes, or until the scones are golden brown on top. Transfer to a wire rack to cool for 30 minutes.

➡ To make the maple glaze: While the scones are cooling, in a small bowl, whisk together the confectioners' sugar, maple syrup, and enough of the water to make a smooth, pourable glaze. You should have about ½ cup. (The glaze can be made ahead and stored in an airtight container at room temperature for up to 1 week.)

➡ When the scones have cooled for 30 minutes, brush the tops evenly with the maple glaze, then serve.

➡ The scones taste best on the day they are baked, but they can be stored in an airtight container at room temperature for up to 3 days. If you keep them for longer than 1 day, refresh them in a 300-degree-F oven for 4 to 5 minutes. Or, you can freeze them, wrapped tightly in plastic wrap, for up to 1 week; reheat, directly from the freezer, in a 300-degree-F oven for 8 to 10 minutes.

CLASSIC CURRANT SCONES

2¾ cups (385 grams) unbleached all-purpose flour

1½ teaspoons baking powder

½ teaspoon baking soda

¼ teaspoon kosher salt

⅓ cup (70 grams) granulated sugar

½ cup (80 grams) dried currants

½ cup (1 stick, 114 grams) cold unsalted butter, cut into 8 to 10 pieces

½ cup (120 grams) cold nonfat buttermilk

½ cup (120 grams) cold crème fraîche

1 cold egg

1 egg yolk, lightly beaten

2 tablespoons sanding sugar, pearl sugar, or granulated sugar

MAKES 8 SCONES

This is a recipe for an English pastry of Scottish origin from a Taiwanese American pastry chef. Given scones' reputation for being dry, flavorless hockey pucks, you may wonder if such a circuitous journey is worthwhile. Trust me, this one is. When you've had a scone prepared the right way, it's like true love: you know it when you see it, and if you have to ask, it's not the real thing. These are quite simple and simply delicious, with rich, buttery flavor and layers of flaky, tender pastry.

Here are a few fail-safe secrets to scone success: First, make sure you use butter straight from the refrigerator, because small pieces of very cold butter in the dough add tenderness and flakiness to the final product. The crème fraîche, buttermilk, and egg should also be cold, so they don't warm up the dough and soften the butter. Seek out real crème fraîche—no substitutions! If you can't find it at the supermarket, make your own (see page 27). Finally, if you can, enjoy your scones warm, fresh out of the oven.

⇒ Position a rack in the center of the oven, and heat the oven to 350 degrees F.

⇒ Using a stand mixer fitted with the paddle attachment (or a handheld mixer), mix together the flour, baking powder, baking soda, salt, granulated sugar, and currants on low speed for 10 to 15 seconds, or until combined. Scatter the butter over the top and beat on low speed for about 30 seconds, or until the butter is somewhat broken down and grape-size pieces are still visible.

⇒ In a small bowl, whisk together the buttermilk, crème fraîche, and whole egg until thoroughly mixed. On low speed, pour the buttermilk mixture into the flour-butter mixture and beat for 20 to 30 seconds, or just until the dough comes together. There will still be a little loose flour mixture at the bottom of the bowl.

⇒ Remove the bowl from the mixer stand. Gather and lift the dough with your hands and turn it over in the bowl, so that it starts to pick up the loose flour at the bottom. Turn over the dough several times until all of the loose flour is mixed in.

➡ Dump the dough onto a baking sheet and pat it into an 8-inch circle about 1 inch thick. Brush the egg yolk evenly over the entire top of the dough circle. Sprinkle the sanding sugar evenly over the top, then cut the circle into 8 wedges, as if cutting a pizza. (At this point, the unbaked scones can be tightly wrapped in plastic wrap and frozen for up to 1 week. Proceed as directed, baking directly from the freezer and adding 5 to 10 minutes to the baking time.)

➡ Bake for 50 to 55 minutes, or until the entire circle is golden brown. Transfer to a wire rack to cool for 30 minutes, then cut into the prescored wedges (the cuts will be visible but will have baked together) and serve.

➡ The scones taste best on the day they are baked, but they can be stored in an airtight container at room temperature for up to 3 days. If you keep them for longer than 1 day, refresh them in a 300-degree-F oven for 4 to 5 minutes. Or, you can freeze them, wrapped tightly in plastic wrap, for up to 1 week; reheat, directly from the freezer, in a 300-degree-F oven for 8 to 10 minutes.

Baker's Bite

All of the scone recipes in this chapter can be made by hand. Use a pastry cutter, two knives, or a fork to cut the butter into the dry ingredients, and a wooden spoon to mix the wet ingredients into the dry ingredients, then proceed as directed.

Same recipe, different flavors

CRANBERRY-ORANGE SCONES: This is a terrific variation to make during the holiday season. Your home will instantly smell like Thanksgiving. Omit the currants and substitute 2 tablespoons finely grated orange zest (about 1 orange) and 2 cups (200 grams) fresh cranberries, chopped. Add them to the dry mixture at the beginning of the recipe. Proceed as directed.

LEMON-GINGER SCONES

2¾ cups (385 grams) unbleached all-purpose flour

1½ teaspoons baking powder

¼ teaspoon baking soda

¼ teaspoon kosher salt

⅓ cup (70 grams) granulated sugar

½ teaspoon ground ginger

½ cup (80 grams) finely chopped crystallized ginger

2 tablespoons finely grated lemon zest (about 1½ lemons)

¾ cup plus 2 tablespoons (1¾ sticks/200 grams) cold unsalted butter, cut into 8 to 10 pieces

½ cup (120 grams) cold nonfat buttermilk

½ cup (120 grams) cold heavy cream

1 cold egg

2 tablespoons finely grated fresh ginger (about a 2-inch knob)

FRESH LEMON GLAZE

1 cup (140 grams) confectioners' sugar

2 to 3 tablespoons fresh lemon juice (1 to 1½ lemons)

MAKES 10 SCONES

An all-time favorite at Flour, these scones are rich, buttery, lemony, and filled with not one, not two, but *three* different kinds of ginger. As when making any kind of scones, it is important that the butter be straight from the refrigerator, so it is cold and firm and doesn't mix completely into the dry ingredients. Those unmixed little pieces are what will make your scones light and flaky. Don't skip the tart lemon glaze, it is easy to make and it takes the scone from delicious to truly sublime.

➡ Position a rack in the center of the oven, and heat the oven to 350 degrees F.

➡ Using a stand mixer fitted with the paddle attachment (or a handheld mixer), mix together the flour, baking powder, baking soda, salt, granulated sugar, ground ginger, crystallized ginger, and lemon zest on low speed for 10 to 15 seconds, or until combined. Scatter the butter over the top and beat on low speed for about 30 seconds, or until the butter is somewhat broken down and grape-size pieces are still visible.

➡ In a small bowl, whisk together the buttermilk, cream, egg, and grated ginger until thoroughly mixed. On low speed, pour the buttermilk mixture into the flour-butter mixture and beat for 20 to 30 seconds, or just until the dough comes together. There will still be a little loose flour mixture at the bottom of the bowl.

➡ Remove the bowl from the mixer stand. Gather and lift the dough in your hands and turn it over in the bowl, so that it starts to pick up the loose flour at the bottom. Turn the dough over several times until all of the loose flour is mixed in.

➡ Dump the dough onto a lightly floured work surface and gently roll it out about 1 inch thick. Using a 3½-inch round cookie cutter, cut out circles. Reroll the scraps and cut out more circles. You should have 10 circles. (At this point, the unbaked scones can be frozen, tightly wrapped in plastic wrap, for up to 1 week. Proceed as directed, baking directly from the freezer and adding 5 to 10 minutes to the baking time.) Place them on a baking sheet, spacing them 2 to 3 inches apart.

⇒ Bake for 40 to 45 minutes, or until the scones are a light golden brown on top. Transfer to a wire rack to cool for 10 to 15 minutes.

⇒ To make the lemon glaze: While the scones are cooling, in a small bowl, whisk together the confectioners' sugar and enough of the lemon juice to make a smooth, thick, pourable glaze. You should have about ½ cup. (The glaze can be made ahead and stored in an airtight container at room temperature for up to 1 week.)

⇒ When the scones have cooled for 10 to 15 minutes, brush the tops evenly with the lemon glaze, then serve.

⇒ The scones taste best on the day they are baked, but they can be stored in an airtight container at room temperature for up to 3 days. If you keep them for longer than 1 day, refresh them in a 300-degree-F oven for 4 to 5 minutes. Or, you can freeze them, wrapped tightly in plastic wrap, for up to 1 week; reheat, directly from the freezer, in a 300-degree-F oven for 8 to 10 minutes.

Baker's Bite

To make grating ginger easy, use a Microplane grater. It's a fantastic kitchen gadget for pastry cooks to have on hand. For this recipe, it will effortlessly shred your knob of ginger into fine pieces that will add a heavenly perfume to the scones. A helpful hint for working with fresh ginger—whether you are using a Microplane, the fine holes on a more traditional box grater, or a knife—is to freeze the ginger overnight. Freezing changes its texture, making it less fibrous, so you get marvelous results whether you are grating or mincing it.

CHEDDAR-SCALLION SCONES

1¾ cups (245 grams) unbleached all-purpose flour

½ cup (100 grams) medium-coarse yellow cornmeal

1½ teaspoons baking powder

½ teaspoon baking soda

1 teaspoon kosher salt

¼ teaspoon ground cumin

3 ounces (84 grams) Cheddar cheese, cut into ¼-inch dice (about ½ cup)

5 scallions, minced (about ½ cup/50 grams)

½ cup (1 stick/114 grams) cold unsalted butter, cut into 8 to 10 pieces

½ cup (120 grams) cold nonfat buttermilk

½ cup (120 grams) cold crème fraîche

1 cold egg

1 egg yolk, lightly beaten

MAKES 8 SCONES

As I explained earlier in the book, when I entered the world of professional cooking, I wasn't on the pastry side. My first restaurant job was as a garde manger cook, and for a year I tossed salads, poached chicken breasts, and fried shallot rings—all the while gazing longingly at the delectable desserts and beautiful plating in the pastry area. It was that perspective that taught me where my true passions lie: all I ever really wanted to do was make and eat and think about sweets. So, I decided to leave the restaurant for a baking job, and I never looked back.

A few weeks after I opened Flour, someone filled out a suggestion card and requested (demanded, actually), "Savory breakfast pastries please!" I was confused. Who in their right mind would want to eat savory pastries? But it seems I'm the odd man out on this one. Many of our customers skip sugar in the morning and reach for something with egg or cheese or breakfast meat. So, this scone was born. It is a savory riff on our currant scone, with cornmeal for texture, a handful of diced Cheddar, a scattering of chopped scallions, and a pinch of cumin for extra flavor. Even if you're a nonsavory person like me, I think you'll fall for this earthy blend of ingredients, wrapped in a buttery scone package.

➡ Position a rack in the center of the oven, and heat the oven to 350 degrees F.

➡ Using a stand mixer fitted with the paddle attachment (or a handheld mixer), mix together the flour, cornmeal, baking powder, baking soda, salt, cumin, cheese, and scallions on low speed for 10 to 15 seconds, or until combined. Scatter the butter over the top and beat on low speed for about 30 seconds, or until the butter is somewhat broken down and grape-size pieces are still visible.

➡ In a small bowl, whisk together the buttermilk, crème fraîche, and whole egg until thoroughly mixed. On low speed, pour the buttermilk mixture into the flour-butter mixture and beat for 20 to 30 seconds, or just until the dough comes together. There will still be a little loose flour mixture at the bottom of the bowl.

➡ Remove the bowl from the mixer stand. Gather and lift the dough with your hands and turn it over in the bowl, so that it starts to pick up the loose flour at the bottom. Turn the dough over several times until all of the loose flour is mixed in.

➡ Dump the dough onto a baking sheet and pat it into an 8-inch circle about 1 inch thick. Brush the egg yolk evenly over the entire top of the dough circle. Cut the circle into 8 wedges, as if cutting a pizza. (At this point, the unbaked scones can be frozen, tightly wrapped in plastic wrap, for up to 1 week. Proceed as directed, baking directly from the freezer and adding 5 to 10 minutes to the baking time.)

➡ Bake for 40 to 50 minutes, or until the entire circle is golden brown. Transfer to a wire rack to cool for 30 minutes, then cut into the prescored wedges (the cuts will be visible but will have baked together) and serve.

➡ The scones taste best on the day they are baked, but they can be stored in an airtight container at room temperature for up to 3 days. If you keep them for longer than 1 day, refresh them in a 300-degree-F oven for 4 to 5 minutes. Or, you can freeze them, wrapped tightly in plastic wrap, for up to 1 week; reheat, directly from the freezer, in a 300-degree-F oven for 8 to 10 minutes.

HEART-HEALTHY DRIED FRUIT SCONES

2½ cups (350 grams) unbleached all-purpose flour

⅓ cup (70 grams) granulated sugar

1 tablespoon baking powder

¼ teaspoon baking soda

½ teaspoon kosher salt

½ teaspoon ground cinnamon

¼ cup (40 grams) dark raisins

¼ cup (40 grams) golden raisins

¼ cup (40 grams) dried apricots, chopped

¼ cup (20 grams) dried apples, chopped

¼ cup (40 grams) dried cranberries

½ cup (50 grams) fresh or frozen cranberries or blueberries, chopped

¼ cup (40 grams) crystallized ginger, chopped

2 eggs

½ cup (120 grams) cold plain nonfat yogurt

½ cup (120 grams) cold nonfat buttermilk

¼ cup (50 grams) canola oil

SIMPLE VANILLA GLAZE

1 cup (140 grams) confectioners' sugar

¼ teaspoon vanilla extract

2 to 3 tablespoons water

MAKES 8 SCONES

The idea of low fat is akin to heresy for many bakers. We love our butter and our cream and all things rich and delightful. I've found that commercially produced low-fat items often mask the lack of fat with a surplus of sugar: "If we make these cookies ultrasweet, maybe people won't notice that they are as dry as sawdust!" These scones are the antithesis of typical low-fat grocery-store offerings. They do contain a little fat—a small amount of canola oil and a couple of eggs—but what they mostly contain is a whole lot of scrumptious dried and fresh fruits, bound together by barely sweetened dough. They are so tasty that you won't even notice the missing butter and cream. The simple glaze isn't mandatory, but it does add both appealing flavor and extra moisture.

➡ Position a rack in the center of the oven, and heat the oven to 350 degrees F. Line a baking sheet with parchment paper.

➡ In a medium bowl, stir together the flour, granulated sugar, baking powder, baking soda, salt, and cinnamon. Add the dark raisins, golden raisins, apricots, apples, dried cranberries, fresh cranberries, and ginger and stir well to distribute the fruit evenly.

➡ In a small bowl, whisk together the eggs, yogurt, buttermilk, and oil until smooth.

➡ Pour the egg mixture into the flour mixture and, using a wooden spoon or rubber spatula, fold together just until all of the dry ingredients are thoroughly mixed into the wet ingredients. The mixture will seem dry at first, as if there is too much flour. But as you continue folding gently, the flour will soon mix in and you will have a soft dough. Once that happens, stop mixing.

➡ Using a ½-cup dry-measuring cup, drop scant ½-cup mounds of dough onto the prepared baking sheet, making 8 scones total and spacing them 2 to 3 inches apart. (At this point, the unbaked scones can be frozen, tightly wrapped in plastic wrap, for up to 1 week. Proceed as directed, baking directly from the freezer and adding 5 to 10 minutes to the baking time.)

➡ Bake for 45 to 50 minutes, or until the scones are golden brown and firm along the edges and light brown in the center. Transfer to a wire rack to cool for 30 minutes.

➡ To make the vanilla glaze: While the scones are cooling, in a small bowl, whisk together the confectioners' sugar, vanilla, and enough of the water to make a smooth, pourable glaze. You should have about ½ cup. (The glaze can be made ahead and stored in an airtight container at room temperature for up to 1 week.)

➡ When the scones have cooled for 30 minutes, brush the tops evenly with the glaze, then let stand for 10 to 15 minutes to allow the glaze to set before serving.

➡ The scones taste best on the day they are baked, but they can be stored in an airtight container at room temperature for up to 3 days. If you keep them for longer than 1 day, refresh them in a 300-degree-F oven for 4 to 5 minutes. Or, you can freeze them, wrapped tightly in plastic wrap, for up to 1 week; reheat, directly from the freezer, in a 300-degree-F oven for 8 to 10 minutes.

Baker's Bite

The specific dried and fresh fruits in the ingredients list for these scones are only a guide. This is one case in baking where you can play around with amounts and combinations, so feel free to improvise with whatever you have in the house or with the fruits you like best. You'll want a total of about 2 cups fruit, and I suggest that most of the fruit be dried. Too much fresh or frozen fruit can make the dough soggy and gummy.

RASPBERRY-RHUBARB MUFFINS

3¼ cups (455 grams) unbleached all-purpose flour

½ teaspoon baking soda

4 teaspoons baking powder

½ teaspoon kosher salt

2 eggs

1 egg yolk

1⅓ cups (270 grams) sugar

½ cup plus 2 tablespoons (1¼ sticks/140 grams) butter, melted

1 cup (240 grams) milk, at room temperature

1 cup (240 grams) crème fraîche, at room temperature

2 teaspoons vanilla extract

1 cup (130 grams) fresh or frozen raspberries

1 cup (120 grams) chopped rhubarb

MAKES 12 MUFFINS

People who know me know that I'm crazy about pastry. Not just eating it or making it but truly nuts in the head about it. Certain recipes will work for me for years, and then they stop working. Some pastries call out to me day in and day out, and then suddenly I am no longer in love with them. Although the true reason for my fickleness is probably that my personal taste is evolving, I do believe that certain recipes take many months of tweaking and adjusting before you get them just right. The evolution of this muffin recipe is a perfect example. It should be simple to make a good muffin, and although we have always made delicious muffins at Flour, every few months I would decide that I needed to rework this muffin recipe to make it more tender, more moist, more amazing. I now think we have come up with the muffin recipe to end all muffin recipes. I've fine-tuned the ratio of butter to flour to liquid to fruit to a point where everything is in perfect balance. The batter couldn't be easier to put together, and it leads to endless variations (see box on page 54)—plus, it's all-out scrumptious!

➡ Position a rack in the center of the oven, and heat the oven to 350 degrees F. Butter a standard 12-cup muffin tin, coat with nonstick cooking spray, or line with paper liners.

➡ In a large bowl, sift together the flour, baking soda, baking powder, and salt. In a medium bowl, whisk together the eggs and egg yolk until thoroughly mixed. Slowly whisk in the sugar, butter, milk, crème fraîche, and vanilla until well combined. Pour the butter-sugar mixture into the flour mixture and, using a rubber spatula, fold gently just until the ingredients are combined. Gently fold in the raspberries and rhubarb until evenly distributed. The batter may seem lumpy, but don't try to smooth it out. (The batter can be made up to 1 day ahead and stored in an airtight container in the refrigerator.)

➡ Spoon the batter into the prepared cups, dividing it evenly and filling the cups to the rim (almost overflowing).

(continued)

➡ Bake for 30 to 40 minutes, or until the muffins are golden brown on top and spring back when pressed in the middle with a fingertip. Let cool in the pan on a wire rack for 20 minutes, then remove the muffins from the pan.

➡ The muffins taste best on the day they are baked, but they can be stored in an airtight container at room temperature for up 3 days. If you keep them for longer than 1 day, refresh them in a 300-degree-F oven for 4 to 5 minutes. Or, you can freeze them, wrapped tightly in plastic wrap, for up to 1 week; reheat, directly from the freezer, in a 300-degree-F oven for 8 to 10 minutes.

Same recipe, different flavors . . . .

CLASSIC BLUEBERRY MUFFINS: Omit the raspberries and rhubarb and substitute 2 cups (320 grams) fresh or frozen blueberries. Proceed as directed.

CRANBERRY-ORANGE MUFFINS: Omit the raspberries and rhubarb and substitute 2 tablespoons finely grated orange zest (about 1 orange) and 2 cups (200 grams) whole or chopped frozen cranberries. Proceed as directed.

ALMOND-APRICOT MUFFINS: Substitute 2 teaspoons almond extract for the vanilla extract. Omit the raspberries and rhubarb and substitute ½ cup (50 grams) toasted sliced almonds; and 1½ cups (230 grams) chopped fresh or (330 grams) canned apricots. Proceed as directed.

GINGER-PEACH MUFFINS: Omit the raspberries and rhubarb and substitute 4 ripe peaches (about 400 grams total), pitted and chopped; ¼ cup (40 grams) finely chopped crystallized ginger; and 2 tablespoons minced fresh ginger. Proceed as directed.

CORN MUFFINS
WITH RASPBERRY JAM

2¾ cups (385 grams) unbleached all-purpose flour

1 cup (200 grams) medium-coarse yellow cornmeal

2 teaspoons baking powder

1 teaspoon baking soda

1 teaspoon kosher salt

¼ cup (½ stick/56 grams) unsalted butter, melted

¾ cup (165 grams) packed light brown sugar

3 eggs

1 cup (240 grams) milk, at room temperature

⅓ cup (70 grams) canola oil

¾ cup (180 grams) crème fraîche, at room temperature

¾ cup (255 grams) raspberry jam

MAKES 12 MUFFINS

If you grew up like I did thinking that the best corn muffins are the ones that come from a boxed mix, then you have to try this recipe. It will change your life—well, as much as a muffin can! It has a great crumb, somewhere between tender cake and crumbly corn bread, and amazing flavor, with butter, milk, and crème fraîche all adding richness. The oil keeps it incredibly moist and the jam in the middle is a sweet surprise.

➡ Position a rack in the center of the oven, and heat the oven to 350 degrees F. Butter a standard 12-cup muffin tin, coat with nonstick cooking spray, or line with paper liners.

➡ In a large bowl, stir together the flour, cornmeal, baking powder, baking soda, and salt until well mixed. In a small bowl, whisk together the butter and sugar until it forms a thick slurry. In a second large bowl, whisk the eggs until well blended. One at a time, whisk the milk, then the oil, then the crème fraîche, and finally the butter-sugar slurry into the eggs. Pour the wet mixture into the dry mixture and fold carefully just until the dry and wet ingredients are well combined. The batter will be thick and pasty.

➡ Spoon about ¼ cup batter into each prepared muffin cup. Spoon 1 tablespoon jam on top of the batter in each cup, then top off each cup with another ¼ cup batter, making sure the cups are evenly filled. They should be filled to the rim.

➡ Bake for 25 to 28 minutes, or until the edges of each muffin are golden brown and the center springs back when pressed with a fingertip. Let cool in the pan on a wire rack for 20 minutes, then remove the muffins from the pan.

➡ The muffins taste best the day they are baked, but they may be stored in an airtight container at room temperature for up to 3 days. If you keep them for longer than 1 day, refresh them in a 300-degree-F oven for 4 to 5 minutes. Or, you can freeze them, wrapped tightly in plastic wrap, for up to 1 week; reheat, directly from the freezer, in a 300-degree-F oven for 8 to 10 minutes.

PUMPKIN MUFFINS
WITH CANDIED PEPITAS

CANDIED PEPITAS

¾ cup (170 grams) *pepitas* (pumpkin seeds)

1 egg white

¼ cup (50 grams) sugar

¾ cup (1½ sticks/170 grams) unsalted butter

2 cups (400 grams) sugar

3 tablespoons unsulfured light or dark molasses

4 eggs

¾ cup (180 grams) fresh orange juice (about 3 oranges)

1 can (16 ounces/454 grams) pumpkin puree

3 cups (420 grams) unbleached all-purpose flour

2 teaspoons baking powder

½ teaspoon baking soda

1 teaspoon kosher salt

1 teaspoon ground cinnamon

½ teaspoon ground cloves

MAKES 12 MUFFINS

These warm, earthy muffins are soft and tender and lightly scented with clove and cinnamon. We bring them out every October when we start to see pumpkins at the grocery store and our thoughts turn to Thanksgiving and all the pumpkin pies we'll soon be baking at Flour. They are a delightful way to ease into the season. The candied *pepitas*, or pumpkin seeds, add a bit of sweet crunch to a not-too-sweet muffin.

➡ To make the candied *pepitas*: Line a small tray with parchment paper. In a small bowl, stir together the *pepitas*, egg white, and sugar to make a loose slurry. Pour the seed mixture onto the prepared tray and leave out, uncovered, to dry overnight. The next day, using your fingers, break apart the *pepitas* into separate pieces. (The *pepitas* can be prepared up to 1 week in advance and stored in an airtight container at room temperature.)

➡ Position a rack in the center of the oven, and heat the oven to 350 degrees F. Butter a standard 12-cup muffin tin, coat with nonstick cooking spray, or line with paper liners.

➡ Using a stand mixer fitted with the paddle attachment (or a handheld mixer), cream together the butter, sugar, and molasses on medium speed for 2 to 3 minutes, or until the mixture is light and fluffy. Stop the mixer and scrape down the sides and bottom of the bowl with a rubber spatula.

➡ On low speed, add the eggs one at a time, beating well after each addition to combine the eggs and butter-sugar mixture thoroughly. Scrape the bottom and sides of the bowl once more. On low speed, add the orange juice and pumpkin and beat until combined. The mixture will look somewhat curdled. Don't worry. It will all come together once you mix in the flour.

➡ In a large bowl, stir together the flour, baking powder, baking soda, salt, cinnamon, and cloves until well mixed. Dump the egg mixture into the dry ingredients and fold carefully just until the dry and wet ingredients are well combined. (The batter can be made up to 2 days ahead and stored in an airtight container in the refrigerator.)

➡ Spoon the batter into the prepared muffin cups, dividing it evenly and filling the cups to the rim (almost overflowing). Sprinkle the tops evenly with the candied *pepitas*.

➡ Bake for 35 to 45 minutes, or until the muffins are golden brown on top and spring back when pressed in the middle with a fingertip. Let cool in the pan on a wire rack for 20 minutes, then remove the muffins from the pan.

➡ The muffins taste best on the day they are baked, but they can be stored in an airtight container at room temperature for up to 3 days. If you keep them for longer than 1 day, refresh them in a 300-degree-F oven for 4 to 5 minutes. Or, you can freeze them, wrapped tightly in plastic wrap, for up to 1 week; reheat, directly from the freezer, in a 300-degree-F oven for 8 to 10 minutes.

ADDICTIVE BRAN MUFFINS
WITH GOLDEN RAISINS AND "BIRD SEED"

2½ cups (200 grams) wheat bran

1¼ cups (300 grams) milk

1¾ cups (420 grams) crème fraîche

2 eggs

1 cup (160 grams) golden raisins

½ cup (110 grams) packed light brown sugar

2 tablespoons unsulfured light or dark molasses

2⅓ cups (330 grams) unbleached all-purpose flour

2 teaspoons baking powder

1 teaspoon baking soda

1 teaspoon kosher salt

¼ cup (50 grams) millet

¼ cup (40 grams) flaxseeds

¼ cup (30 grams) sunflower seeds

MAKES 12 MUFFINS

My goal with every recipe is to bake something that I end up craving, something that I keep reaching for. That's when I know the recipe is finally where I want it. I created this recipe as a healthful breakfast option that is moist, earthy, filled with fiber, and just as enticing as the rest of our more indulgent offerings. With all the bran and raisins and "bird seed," these hearty muffins are packed with goodness and, even better, impossible to resist.

➡ Position a rack in the center of the oven, and heat the oven to 350 degrees F. Butter a standard 12-cup muffin tin, coat with nonstick cooking spray, or line with paper liners.

➡ In a medium bowl, stir together the wheat bran, milk, crème fraîche, and eggs until well mixed. Put the raisins in a small bowl, cover them with hot water, and set aside. Let stand for 30 minutes to allow the bran to soak up some of the liquid and soften and the raisins to plump.

➡ After 30 minutes, add the brown sugar and molasses to the bran mixture and stir until thoroughly combined. Drain the raisins, add them to the bran mixture, and stir until well mixed. The mixture will be thick and gloppy.

➡ In a large bowl, stir together the flour, baking powder, baking soda, and salt until well mixed. Scrape the bran mixture into the dry ingredients and fold carefully just until the dry and wet ingredients are well combined. You will end up with a very thick, somewhat stiff batter that verges on being a dough.

➡ Spoon the batter into the prepared muffin cups, dividing it evenly and filling the cups to the rim (almost overflowing). In a small bowl, mix together the millet, flaxseeds, and sunflower seeds. Sprinkle the mixture evenly over the tops of the muffins.

⇒ Bake for 35 to 40 minutes, or until the muffins are golden brown on top and spring back when pressed in the middle with a fingertip. Let cool in the pan on a wire rack for 20 minutes, then remove the muffins from the pan.

⇒ The muffins taste best on the day they are baked, but they can be stored in an airtight container at room temperature for up to 3 days. If you keep them for longer than 1 day, refresh them in a 300-degree-F oven for 4 to 5 minutes. Or, you can freeze them, wrapped tightly in plastic wrap, for up to 1 week; reheat, directly from the freezer, in a 300-degree-F oven for 8 to 10 minutes.

GOOD MORNING MUFFINS

½ cup (40 grams) wheat bran

½ cup (120 grams) hot water

1 small zucchini, grated (about 1½ cups/200 grams packed)

½ cup (80 grams) raisins

½ cup (50 grams) pecan halves, roughly chopped, toasted

½ cup (60 grams) sweetened flaked coconut

1 apple, peeled, cored, and chopped (about 1 cup/120 grams)

⅔ cup (150 grams) packed light brown sugar

3 eggs

¾ cup (150 grams) canola oil

1 teaspoon vanilla extract

1½ cups (210 grams) unbleached all-purpose flour

¾ cup (75 grams) old-fashioned rolled oats (not instant or quick cooking)

2 teaspoons baking powder

½ teaspoon kosher salt

½ teaspoon ground cinnamon

MAKES 12 MUFFINS

"Morning glory" muffins used to be all the rage. They boasted a fiber-rich assortment of ingredients that was supposed to give you a good start to the day. I always liked the idea of them, but I was often disappointed at how heavy and greasy and overly sweet they could be. When I decided to put a morning glory–type muffin on the breakfast menu at Flour, I wanted it to be filled with wholesome, good-for-me ingredients but still be light, moist, and delicious. So, I adjusted the traditional roster of ingredients and then added a few of my own twists to create an updated version. It's breakfast-on-the-go and the perfect start to a good morning, indeed.

➡ Position a rack in the center of the oven, and heat the oven to 350 degrees F. Butter a standard 12-cup muffin tin, coat with nonstick cooking spray, or line with paper liners.

➡ In a medium bowl, stir together the wheat bran and hot water until the bran is completely moistened. Add the zucchini, raisins, pecans, coconut, and apple and stir until well mixed.

➡ Using a stand mixer fitted with the whip attachment, beat together the sugar and eggs on medium speed for 3 to 4 minutes, or until the mixture thickens and lightens. (If you use a handheld mixer, this same step will take 6 to 8 minutes.) On low speed, slowly drizzle in the oil and then the vanilla. Don't pour the oil in all at once. Add it slowly so it has time to incorporate into the eggs and doesn't deflate the air you have just beaten into the batter. Adding it should take about 1 minute. When the oil and vanilla are incorporated, remove the bowl from the mixer stand.

→ In a medium bowl, stir together the flour, oats, baking powder, salt, and cinnamon until well mixed. Add the flour mixture to the egg mixture and fold carefully just until the dry and wet ingredients are well combined. Then add the bran mixture and fold again just until well combined. Spoon the batter into the prepared muffin cups, dividing it evenly and filling the cups to the rim (almost overflowing).

→ Bake for 35 to 45 minutes, or until the muffins are lightly browned on top and spring back when pressed in the middle with a fingertip. Let cool in the pan on a wire rack for 20 minutes, then remove the muffins from the pan.

→ The muffins taste best the day you bake them, but they can be stored in an airtight container at room temperature for up to 3 days. If you keep them for longer than 1 day, refresh them in a 300-degree-F oven for 4 to 5 minutes. Or, you can freeze them, wrapped tightly in plastic wrap, for up to 1 week; reheat, directly from the freezer, in a 300-degree-F oven for 8 to 10 minutes.

NEW OLD-FASHIONED COFFEE CAKE

STREUSEL

3 tablespoons packed light brown sugar

⅓ cup (70 grams) granulated sugar

¾ cup (75 grams) pecan halves, toasted and chopped

¼ teaspoon ground cinnamon

¼ teaspoon ground ginger

⅛ teaspoon ground cloves

3 tablespoons cake flour

2 tablespoons (¼ stick/28 grams) unsalted butter, at room temperature

2½ cups (300 grams) cake flour

¾ teaspoon baking powder

2 teaspoons baking soda

½ teaspoon kosher salt

1½ cups (300 grams) granulated sugar

1 cup plus 2 tablespoons (2¼ sticks/256 grams) unsalted butter, at room temperature, cut into 10 or 12 pieces

3 eggs

1 egg yolk

2 teaspoons vanilla extract

¾ cup (180 grams) crème fraîche

MAKES ONE 10-INCH TUBE CAKE

Do you know the game Telephone? Friends sit in a circle and the first person whispers something into the second person's ear, then that person whispers exactly what he or she heard into the third person's ear, and so on until the "message" makes its way completely around the circle. The last person repeats out loud what he or she heard, and everyone laughs at how different the final message is from the original. The idea for this cake originally came from Rose Levy Beranbaum's *The Cake Bible,* **one of my go-to baking books. When I was developing recipes for the opening menu of Flour, I wanted a buttery, velvety traditional sour cream coffee cake. I tested at least a dozen recipes. I felt like Goldilocks: this one's too light, that one's too heavy, and this one's too sweet.** *The Cake Bible* **version was** *juuuuust* **right—or so I thought. During years of baking hundreds of these coffee cakes and continually tweaking and adjusting the recipe, I have played Telephone with the original recipe and have come up with my own take on it. It has a beautifully light and soft crumb and tastes of butter and vanilla. A crunch of pecans in the middle makes it even more scrumptious, and using crème fraîche instead of sour cream pushes its mellow, rich flavor over the top.**

➡ Position a rack in the center of the oven, and heat the oven to 350 degrees F. Butter and flour a 10-inch tube pan with a removable insert.

➡ To make the streusel: In a food processor, combine the brown sugar, ⅓ cup granulated sugar, pecans, cinnamon, ginger, cloves, 3 tablespoons flour, and butter and pulse for about 20 seconds, or until the mixture comes together roughly. Don't pulse too long. You want to chop the ingredients coarsely to make a crumbly mix. Transfer to a medium bowl and set aside. You should have about 1½ cups. Alternatively, put all of the ingredients in a medium bowl and use a pastry cutter to combine them until crumbly. (The streusel can be stored in an airtight container in the refrigerator for up to 1 week or in the freezer for up to 1 month.)

⇒ Using a stand mixer fitted with the paddle attachment (or a handheld mixer), mix together the 2½ cups flour, baking powder, baking soda, salt, and 1½ cups granulated sugar on low speed just until well mixed. Add the butter a few pieces at a time and continue to beat on low speed for 3 to 4 minutes, or until the butter is well incorporated into the dry ingredients. The mixture will look like coarse meal. If the butter is a little softer than room temperature, the mixture may come together as a soft dough.

⇒ In a small bowl, whisk together the eggs, egg yolk, vanilla, and crème fraîche until thoroughly mixed. On low speed, slowly pour about half of the egg mixture into the flour mixture and mix until combined. Turn up the mixer speed to medium and beat the batter for about 1½ minutes. The mixture will go from looking thick and clumpy and yellowish to light and fluffy and whitish. Stop the mixer once or twice during the mixing and scrape the sides and bottom of the bowl to make sure all of the ingredients are mixed in. Turn down the mixer to low speed, add the remaining egg mixture, and beat for about 30 seconds, or until combined. Again, stop once or twice during the mixing to scrape the sides and bottom of the bowl.

⇒ Spoon about 1½ cups of the batter into the bowl holding the streusel, then fold the streusel and batter together until well mixed. (This step helps keep the streusel from sinking directly to the bottom of the pan during baking.) Scrape all of the nonstreusel batter into the prepared pan and smooth the top. Then, top with the streusel batter, spreading it in an even layer and smoothing it.

⇒ Bake for about 1 hour and 10 minutes, or until the top of the cake is golden brown and bounces back when you touch it near the center. Let cool in the pan on a wire rack for at least 3 hours, or until completely cool, then carefully remove the cake from the pan.

⇒ The cake can be stored in an airtight container at room temperature for up to 2 days. Or it can be well wrapped in plastic wrap and frozen for up to 2 weeks; thaw overnight at room temperature for serving.

APPLE SNACKING SPICE CAKE

1 cup (140 grams) unbleached all-purpose flour

¾ cup (90 grams) cake flour

1½ teaspoons baking soda

½ teaspoon kosher salt

¼ teaspoon ground cinnamon

¼ teaspoon ground ginger

⅛ teaspoon ground cloves

1½ cups (300 grams) granulated sugar

¾ cup (1½ sticks/170 grams) unsalted butter, at room temperature

2 eggs

4 cups (450 grams) peeled, cored, and chopped Granny Smith apples (2 to 3 apples)

½ cup (80 grams) raisins

1 cup (100 grams) pecan halves, toasted and chopped

Confectioners' sugar for dusting

MAKES ONE 10-INCH
ROUND CAKE

I adored my fourth-grade teacher, Ms. Davis, and at the end of the school year, I wanted to bake her a cake to let her know how much I loved her. I saw a picture of an apple spice cake in a magazine and tried, with my mom's help, to make it. It didn't go well. We tried four times, each attempt more disastrous than the one before. Finally, we gave up on the from-scratch idea and made a cake from a mix. Ms. Davis proclaimed it the best cake she'd ever tasted (see why I loved her?), and while I bashfully accepted her praise, deep down I was wishing it hadn't come from a box. Years later, after I had become a professional baker, I spotted a recipe for an apple spice cake and, remembering my failed childhood attempts, decided to give it a try. The recipe worked (yay!), so I tweaked and tweaked it until the result was moist, delicious, apple-and-nut-filled perfection. I added "snacking" to the name because during all of the testing that's what I couldn't stop doing: snacking on it! It's now one of the best-sellers at Flour, and Boston pastry chef Paige Retus, whom I've admired for years, told the *Boston Globe* that it is one of her favorite desserts in town. I think Ms. Davis would approve.

⇒ Position a rack in the center of the oven, and heat the oven to 350 degrees F. Butter and flour a 10-inch round cake pan.

⇒ In the bowl of a stand mixer, sift together the all-purpose flour, cake flour, baking soda, salt, cinnamon, ginger, and cloves. (Or, sift together into a medium bowl if using a handheld mixer.) Fit the mixer with the paddle attachment. Add the granulated sugar and butter to the flour mixture and beat on medium speed for about 1 minute, or until the butter is fully incorporated into the dry ingredients. Stop the mixer several times to scrape the paddle and the sides of the bowl to make sure all of the butter is mixed in. Add the eggs and mix on low speed for 10 to 15 seconds, or until fully incorporated. Then, turn the mixer to medium-high speed and beat for about 1 minute, or until the batter is light and fluffy.

→ Using a rubber spatula, fold in the apples, raisins, and pecans. The batter will be very stiff and thick. It will look like too many apples and not enough batter, but that's okay. Scrape all of the batter into the prepared pan, then spread it evenly to fill the pan.

→ Bake for about 1 hour and 20 minutes, or until the cake feels firm when you press it in the middle and the top is dark golden brown. Let the cake cool completely in the pan on a wire rack.

→ Invert the cake onto a serving plate, lifting away the pan, and then invert the cake again so it is right-side up. Slice and plate, then dust the slices with confectioners' sugar.

→ The cake can be stored in an airtight container at room temperature for up to 3 days. Or, it can be well wrapped in plastic wrap and frozen for up to 2 weeks; thaw overnight at room temperature for serving.

FLOUR'S FAMOUS BANANA BREAD

1½ cups (210 grams) unbleached all-purpose flour

1 teaspoon baking soda

¼ teaspoon ground cinnamon

½ teaspoon kosher salt

1 cup plus 2 tablespoons (230 grams) sugar

2 eggs

½ cup (100 grams) canola oil

3½ very ripe, medium bananas, peeled and mashed (1⅓ cups mashed/about 340 grams)

2 tablespoons crème fraîche or sour cream

1 teaspoon vanilla extract

¾ cup (75 grams) walnut halves, toasted and chopped

MAKES ONE 9-INCH LOAF

I remember grocery shopping with my mom and toting home large bags of overripe bananas when we found them on special for ten cents a pound. My mom would encourage my brother, my dad, and me to "have a banana!" every time we were near the kitchen. My brother and I began to avoid the kitchen for fear of being accosted by Mom and her banana entreaties. In time, I developed this banana bread as a protection device for us. We loved it so much we sometimes found ourselves buying more bananas just to make it.

➡ Position a rack in the center of the oven, and heat the oven to 325 degrees F. Butter a 9-by-5-inch loaf pan.

➡ In a bowl, sift together the flour, baking soda, cinnamon, and salt. Set aside.

➡ Using a stand mixer fitted with the whip attachment (or a handheld mixer), beat together the sugar and eggs on medium speed for about 5 minutes, or until light and fluffy. (If you use a handheld mixer, this same step will take about 8 minutes.)

➡ On low speed, slowly drizzle in the oil. Don't pour the oil in all at once. Add it slowly so it has time to incorporate into the eggs and doesn't deflate the air you have just beaten into the batter. Adding it should take about 1 minute. Add the bananas, crème fraîche, and vanilla and continue to mix on low speed just until combined.

➡ Using a rubber spatula, fold in the flour mixture and the nuts just until thoroughly combined. No flour streaks should be visible, and the nuts should be evenly distributed. Pour the batter into the prepared loaf pan and smooth the top.

➡ Bake for 1 to 1¼ hours, or until golden brown on top and the center springs back when you press it. If your finger sinks when you poke the bread, it needs to bake a little longer. Let cool in the pan on a wire rack for at least 30 minutes, and then pop it out of the pan to finish cooling.

➡ The banana bread can be stored tightly wrapped in plastic wrap at room temperature for up to 3 days. Or, it can be well wrapped in plastic wrap and frozen for up to 2 weeks; thaw overnight at room temperature for serving.

CRANBERRY-MAPLE-PECAN BREAKFAST CAKE

MAPLE PECANS

3 tablespoons maple syrup

½ cup (50 grams) pecan halves, toasted and chopped

1⅓ cups (160 grams) cake flour

¾ cup (150 grams) granulated sugar

1 teaspoon baking powder

¼ teaspoon baking soda

½ teaspoon kosher salt

6 tablespoons (¾ stick/86 grams) unsalted butter, at room temperature cut into 6 to 8 pieces

⅓ cup (80 grams) nonfat buttermilk at room temperature

2 eggs

1 teaspoon vanilla extract

⅓ cup (110 grams) maple syrup

1 cup (100 grams) fresh or frozen cranberries, coarsely chopped

MAPLE GLAZE

½ cup (70 grams) confectioners' sugar

2 to 3 tablespoons maple syrup

MAKES ONE 9-INCH LOAF

I fell in love with this cake before I'd ever made it. I was dreaming of flavors that I crave at breakfast and came up with this combination. I worked on the recipe every day for several weeks until I hit the correct proportion of tart cranberries; crunchy, mapley nuts; and warm maple flavor. The cake is offered at Flour every year during the holiday season when cranberries are plentiful. It tastes remarkably like pancakes: the maple syrup flavor thoroughly infuses the buttery cake, so that when you bite into a piece, it is like taking a delicious bite from a short stack. Like many breakfast cakes, this one is great the day it's baked, and it continues to develop flavor into the next day or two, when it becomes ideal for slicing and toasting for an afternoon snack.

➡ Position a rack in the center of the oven, and heat the oven to 350 degrees F. Butter and flour a 9-by-5-inch loaf pan, or line the bottom and sides of the pan with parchment paper.

➡ To make the maple pecans: In a small saucepan, combine the 3 tablespoons maple syrup and pecans over medium heat and stir for 3 to 4 minutes, or until the syrup is completely absorbed by the nuts. Remove the pan from the heat, scrape the pecans onto a plate, and let cool completely. (If you leave the pecans in the saucepan, they will stick to the pan.) Set aside.

➡ Using a stand mixer fitted with the paddle attachment (or a handheld mixer), beat together the flour, granulated sugar, baking powder, baking soda, salt, and butter on medium speed for 3 to 4 minutes, or until the butter is completely incorporated into the dry ingredients. The mixture will look like coarse meal. (If you use a handheld mixer, this same step will take 5 to 6 minutes.)

→ In a small bowl, whisk together the buttermilk, eggs, vanilla, and ⅓ cup maple syrup until thoroughly mixed. Add about half of the buttermilk mixture to the butter-flour mixture and beat on medium-high speed for about 1 minute, or until the mixture is light, fluffy, and pale. Stop the mixer and scrape the sides and bottom of the bowl to make sure all of the buttermilk mixture is incorporated. On low speed, add the remaining buttermilk mixture and beat for about 30 seconds, then stop the mixer and scrape again. Turn on the mixer to medium speed and mix for another 30 seconds.

→ Using a rubber spatula, fold in the cranberries and the maple pecans. Pour the batter into the prepared pan and smooth the top.

→ Bake for 1 hour to 1 hour and 10 minutes, or until the top of the cake is golden brown and springs back when you press it in the middle. Let cool in the pan on a wire rack for at least 30 minutes.

→ To make the maple glaze: While the cake is cooling, in a small bowl, whisk together the confectioners' sugar and enough of the maple syrup to make a thick, spreadable glaze.

→ When the cake has cooled for at least 30 minutes, pop it out of the pan and place it on the rack. Spread or spoon the glaze over the top of the still-warm cake, letting the glaze dribble down the sides.

→ The cake can be stored tightly wrapped in plastic wrap at room temperature for up to 3 days.

FRENCH LEMON-POPPY POUND CAKE

2 cups (240 grams) cake flour

¾ teaspoon baking powder

½ teaspoon kosher salt

½ cup plus 3 tablespoons (1⅜ sticks/156 grams) unsalted butter, melted and cooled to slightly warm

¼ cup (60 grams) heavy cream, at room temperature

3 tablespoons finely grated lemon zest (about 2 lemons)

1 tablespoon fresh lemon juice (about ½ lemon)

3 tablespoons poppy seeds

4 eggs

1¼ cups (250 grams) granulated sugar

LEMON GLAZE

½ cup (70 grams) confectioners' sugar

1 to 2 tablespoons fresh lemon juice (½ to 1 lemon)

MAKES ONE 9-INCH LOAF

Pound cakes are traditionally made with a pound of butter, a pound of flour, a pound of sugar, and a pound of eggs, hence the name. When properly made, the result is a dense, velvety cake with a tight crumb. But the key is knowing how to make it properly. I can't tell you the number of times I've attempted a classic pound cake recipe only to pull a tough, unimpressive loaf out of the oven. When I worked at Payard, I learned a new approach to making pound cakes that borrows a page from the genoise playbook. First, you whip the eggs and sugar together until they are as light as a feather. Then, you gently fold in the flour and leavening agents. And finally, you whisk together melted butter and heavy cream and combine them, quickly and gently, with the batter. You end up with a cake with the warm, rich, buttery flavor and incredible texture you want. This is my favorite way to enjoy pound cake: laced with copious amounts of fresh lemon zest and nutty poppy seeds.

➡ Position a rack in the center of the oven, and heat the oven to 350 degrees F. Butter and flour a 9-by-5-inch loaf pan, or line the bottom and sides of the pan with parchment paper.

➡ In a medium bowl, sift together the flour, baking powder, and salt. Set aside.

➡ In a large bowl, whisk together the butter, cream, lemon zest, lemon juice, and poppy seeds. The mixture should have the consistency of a thick liquid. If the butter hardens into little lumps, heat the mixture gently until the butter melts again. Set aside.

➡ Using a stand mixer fitted with the whip attachment (or a handheld mixer), beat together the eggs and granulated sugar on medium speed for 4 to 5 minutes, or until light and fluffy and lemon colored. (If you use a handheld mixer, this same step will take 8 to 10 minutes.)

➡ Using a rubber spatula, gently fold the flour mixture into the egg mixture just until combined. Fold about one-fourth of the egg-flour mixture into the butter-cream mixture to lighten it. Then fold in the remaining egg-flour mixture just until thoroughly combined. Pour the batter into the prepared pan.

(continued)

➡ Bake for 1 hour to 1 hour and 10 minutes, or until the top of the cake is golden brown and springs back when you press it in the middle. Let cool in the pan on a wire rack for at least 30 minutes.

➡ To make the lemon glaze: While the cake is cooling, in a small bowl, whisk together the confectioners' sugar and enough of the lemon juice to make an easily spreadable, smooth glaze.

➡ When the cake has cooled for at least 30 minutes, pop it out of the pan and place it on the rack. Spread or spoon the glaze over the top of the still-warm cake, letting the glaze dribble down the sides.

➡ The cake can be stored tightly wrapped in plastic wrap at room temperature for up to 3 days.

Same recipe, different flavors . . . .

VANILLA BEAN POUND CAKE: To make a fragrant vanilla pound cake, omit the lemon zest and juice and poppy seeds from the cake batter and leave off the lemon glaze. Split ½ vanilla bean lengthwise, and scrape the seeds from the pod into the butter-cream mixture. Whisk well to distribute the seeds evenly. Proceed as directed, then lightly dust the cake with confectioners' sugar just before serving.

BASIC BRIOCHE

2¼ cups (315 grams) unbleached all-purpose flour

2¼ cups (340 grams) bread flour

1½ packages (3¼ teaspoons) active dry yeast, or 1 ounce (28 grams) fresh cake yeast

⅓ cup plus 1 tablespoon (82 grams) sugar

1 tablespoon kosher salt

½ cup (120 grams) cold water

6 eggs

1 cup plus 6 tablespoons (2¾ sticks/ 310 grams) unsalted butter, at room temperature, cut into 10 to 12 pieces

NOTE

Don't halve this recipe. There won't be enough dough to engage the dough hook of your mixer, and the dough won't get the workout it needs to become a light, fluffy bread. Don't worry about having too much: Both the dough and the baked loaves freeze well, and having a freezer filled with brioche is never a bad thing.

MAKES 2 LOAVES

I adore brioche! I was introduced to it during my stint at Payard. Every morning, just after the early-morning bake-off, the head baker in the *viennoiserie* (breakfast pastry) department sweetly presented me with a brioche treat, getting even my toughest sixteen-hour days off to a great start. This recipe, which evolved from the version I learned at Payard, is rich, fluffy, eggy, and buttery and never disappoints. To develop your brioche technique, make the brioche loaves as directed in this recipe. This gives you practice preparing and handling the dough so you can graduate to more advanced brioche confections, like Pain aux Raisins (page 76) and Brioche au Chocolat (page 78). This dough freezes beautifully for up to 1 week. Simply thaw it, covered, overnight in the refrigerator, and then proceed the next day with whichever recipe you are making.

The loaves can be sliced and served with butter and jam for breakfast, used as part of an amazing grilled cheese sandwich for lunch or as the base for canapés to accompany cocktails, or set out on the table at dinnertime.

➡ In a stand mixer fitted with the dough hook, combine the all-purpose flour, bread flour, yeast, sugar, salt, water, and 5 of the eggs. Beat on low speed for 3 to 4 minutes, or until all of the ingredients have come together. Stop the mixer as needed to scrape the sides and bottom of the bowl to make sure all of the flour is incorporated into the wet ingredients. Once the dough has come together, beat on low speed for another 3 to 4 minutes. The dough will be very stiff and seem quite dry.

➡ On low speed, add the butter one piece at a time, mixing after each addition until it disappears into the dough. Then, continue mixing on low speed for about 10 minutes, stopping the mixer occasionally to scrape the sides and bottom of the bowl. It is important for all of the butter to be mixed thoroughly into the dough. If necessary, stop the mixer occasionally and break up the dough with your hands to help mix in the butter.

➡ Once the butter is completely incorporated, turn up the speed to medium and beat for another 15 minutes, or until the dough becomes sticky, soft, and somewhat shiny. It will take some time to come together. It will look shaggy and questionable at

(continued)

the start and then eventually it will turn smooth and silky. Then, turn the speed to medium-high and beat for about 1 minute. You should hear the dough make a slap-slap-slap sound as it hits the sides of the bowl. Test the dough by pulling at it: it should stretch a bit and have a little give. If it seems wet and loose and more like a batter than a dough, add a few tablespoons of flour and mix until it comes together. If it breaks off into pieces when you pull at it, continue to mix on medium speed for another 2 to 3 minutes, or until it develops more strength and stretches when you grab it. It is ready when you can gather it all together and pick it up in one piece.

⇒ Place the dough in a large bowl or plastic container and cover it with plastic wrap, pressing the wrap directly onto the surface of the dough. Let the dough proof in the refrigerator for at least 6 hours or up to overnight. At this point, you can freeze the dough in an airtight container for up to 1 week.

⇒ If you are making a brioche treat (see pages 75 to 84) other than the loaves that follow here, continue on to that recipe.

⇒ To make two brioche loaves, line the bottom and sides of two 9-by-5-inch loaf pans with parchment, or butter the pans liberally. Divide the dough in half and press each piece into about a 9-inch square. The dough will feel like cold, clammy Play-Doh. Facing the square, fold down the top one-third toward you, and then fold up the bottom one-third, as if folding a letter. Press to join these layers. Turn the folded dough over and place it, seam-side down, in one of the prepared pans. Repeat with the second piece of dough, placing it in the second prepared pan.

⇒ Cover the loaves lightly with plastic wrap and place in a warm spot to proof for 4 to 5 hours, or until the loaves have nearly doubled in size. They should have risen to the rim of the pan and be rounded on top. When you poke at the dough, it should feel soft, pillowy, and light, as if it's filled with air—because it is! At this point, the texture of the loaves always reminds me a bit of touching a water balloon.

⇒ Position a rack in the center of the oven, and heat the oven to 350 degrees F.

⇒ In a small bowl, whisk the remaining egg until blended. Gently brush the tops of the loaves with the beaten egg.

⇒ Bake for 35 to 45 minutes, or until the tops and sides of the loaves are completely golden brown. Let cool in the pans on wire racks for 30 minutes, then turn the loaves out of the pans and continue to cool on the racks.

⇒ The bread can be stored tightly wrapped in plastic wrap at room temperature for up to 3 days (if it is older than 3 days, try toasting it) or in the freezer for up to 1 month.

Same recipe, different flavors . . . .

BLACK PEPPER BRIOCHE LOAVES: After you have divided the dough in half, knead about 1 tablespoon freshly ground black pepper into each half. Then, shape, proof, and bake as directed.

SUGAR + SPICE BRIOCHE BUNS

½ recipe Basic Brioche dough (page 73)

½ cup (100 grams) sugar

½ teaspoon ground cinnamon

¼ teaspoon ground ginger

¼ teaspoon freshly grated nutmeg

Pinch of ground cloves

Pinch of kosher salt

¼ cup (½ stick/56 grams) unsalted butter, melted

MAKES 10 BUNS

Sometimes plain brioche isn't quite enough. And sometimes brioche with all sorts of treats mixed and shaped and folded in is a little too much to start off your morning. That's when these buns are perfect. We take little squares of brioche dough, bake to a beautiful golden brown, brush with melted butter (there's never too much of that, right?), and roll them around in spiced sugar. They are a crunchy, buttery, delightful way to begin the day.

➡ Line 10 cups of a standard 12-cup muffin tin with paper liners or generously butter and flour them.

➡ On a floured work surface, press the dough into a rectangle about 10 by 5 inches. It will have the consistency of cold, damp Play-Doh and should be fairly easy to shape. Using a bench scraper or a chef's knife, cut the rectangle into 10 equal strips, each about 1 by 5 inches. Cut each strip into five 1-inch squares. You should have fifty 1-inch mini-squares of dough.

➡ Place 5 mini-squares of brioche into each prepared muffin cup. Cover the pastries lightly with plastic wrap and place in a warm spot to proof for about 1½ hours, or until the dough is puffy, pillowy, and soft.

➡ Position a rack in the center of the oven, and heat the oven to 350 degrees F.

➡ Bake for 35 to 45 minutes, or until golden brown. Let the buns cool in the pan on a wire rack for 5 to 10 minutes, or until they are cool enough to handle. Meanwhile, in a small bowl, stir together the sugar, cinnamon, ginger, nutmeg, cloves, and salt.

➡ When the buns can be handled, brush the tops with the butter. If you have used paper liners, remove the buns from the liners. One at a time, roll each warm bun in the sugar mixture to coat evenly.

➡ The buns are best served warm or within 4 hours of baking. They can be stored in an airtight container at room temperature for up to 1 day, and then warmed in a 300-degree-F oven for 5 minutes before serving.

PAIN AUX RAISINS

½ recipe Basic Brioche dough
(page 73)

1 recipe Pastry Cream (page 81)

1 cup (160 grams) golden raisins

GLAZE

1 cup (140 grams) confectioners'
sugar

2 to 3 tablespoons water

¼ teaspoon vanilla extract

MAKES 10 PASTRIES

During my days at Payard, I must have tried brioche a hundred different ways. I ate it plain, sweet, and savory; for breakfast, lunch, and dinner. Brioche was my kryptonite. Whenever I thought I was too beat to wake up at 3 A.M. for my sixteen-hour shift, I would start to wonder what sort of mouthwatering brioche treat we would make that day. That thought was enough to pull me out of my bed and into the city's dark streets to stumble my way to the patisserie. Within a few hours, I would have a fresh-out-of-the-oven brioche in hand and think, "Okay, I can do this."

Of all the brioche items I learned to make at Payard, these pastries were my favorite. They are the perfect example of the whole being more than the sum of its parts. Brioche? Delicious. Pastry cream? Mmmmm. Golden raisins? Nature's candy. All together? Sheer heaven. My favorite part of this pastry is the soft center, and at Payard I could never resist poking out a few and eating them, mangling at least two or three innocent pastries as I worked. I was teased mercilessly for the trail of holey *pains aux raisins* that surrounded my worktable. Once you try these, you'll understand.

➡ Line a baking sheet with parchment paper.

➡ On a floured work surface, roll out the dough into a rectangle about 16 by 12 inches and ¼ inch thick. It will have the consistency of cold, damp Play-Doh and should be fairly easy to roll. Position the rectangle so a long side is facing you. Spread the pastry cream evenly over the entire surface of the dough. Sprinkle the raisins evenly over the cream. Starting from the long side farthest from you and working your way down, roll up the rectangle like a jelly roll. Try to roll it tightly, so you have a nice round spiral. Even off the ends by trimming about ¼ inch from either side.

➡ Use a bench scraper or a chef's knife to cut the roll into 10 equal pieces, each about 1½ inches wide. (At this point, the unbaked pastries can be tightly wrapped in plastic wrap and frozen for up to 1 week. When ready to bake, thaw them, still wrapped, in the refrigerator overnight or at room temperature for 2 to 3 hours, then proceed as directed.)

➡ Space the pieces, cut-side down, evenly on the prepared baking sheet. Cover the pastries lightly with plastic wrap and place in a warm spot to proof for about 2 hours, or until the dough is puffy, pillowy, and soft.

➡ Position a rack in the center of the oven, and heat the oven to 350 degrees F.

➡ Bake for 30 to 40 minutes, or until the pastries are golden brown on the edges of the spiral and pale brown in the center. Let cool on the baking sheet on a wire rack for 20 to 30 minutes.

➡ To make the glaze: While the pastries are cooling, in a small bowl, whisk together the sugar, 2 tablespoons of the water, and vanilla until smooth. Add more water as needed to thin the glaze enough to make it spreadable. (The glaze can be made up to 1 week in advance and stored in an airtight container at room temperature.)

➡ Generously brush the tops of the still-warm pastries with the glaze.

➡ The pastries are best served warm or within 4 hours of baking. They can be stored in an airtight container at room temperature for up to 1 day, and then warmed in a 300-degree-F oven for 5 minutes before serving.

BRIOCHE AU CHOCOLAT

½ recipe Basic Brioche dough
(page 73)

1 recipe Pastry Cream (page 81)

4 ounces (114 grams) bittersweet
chocolate (62 to 70 percent cacao),
chopped, or bittersweet chocolate
chips (just under ⅔ cup)

1 egg

MAKES 10 PASTRIES

Brioche is pretty darn amazing just by itself, but when you add a layer of lightly sweetened vanilla cream and a generous sprinkling of dark chocolate, you've got an out-of-this-world indulgence. We make these by the dozen every day at Flour, and every day they sell out. You can shape them in advance, store them unbaked in the freezer, thaw them in the refrigerator overnight, and bake them fresh the next morning for an impressive breakfast or brunch indulgence.

➡ Line a baking sheet with parchment paper.

➡ On a floured work surface, roll out the dough into a rectangle about 20 by 10 inches and ¼ inch thick. It will have the consistency of cold, damp Play-Doh and should be fairly easy to roll. Position the rectangle so a long side is facing you. Spread the pastry cream evenly over the entire surface of the dough. Sprinkle the chocolate evenly over the bottom half (a 20-by-5-inch section) of the rectangle. Fold the top half of the rectangle completely over the bottom half, then press down gently so the halves are smooshed together.

➡ Use a bench scraper or a chef's knife to cut the filled dough into 10 pieces, each about 2 inches wide; each piece will be about 2 by 5 inches. (At this point, the unbaked pastries can be tightly wrapped in plastic wrap and frozen for up to 1 week. When ready to bake, thaw them, still wrapped, in the refrigerator overnight or at room temperature for 2 to 3 hours, then proceed as directed.)

➡ Carefully transfer the brioche to the prepared baking sheet. Cover the pastries lightly with plastic wrap and place in a warm spot to proof for about 2 hours, or until the dough is puffy, pillowy, and soft.

➡ Position a rack in the center of the oven, and heat the oven to 350 degrees F.

➡ In a small bowl, whisk the egg until blended. Gently brush the tops of the pastries with the beaten egg.

(continued)

➡ Bake for 35 to 45 minutes, or until golden brown. Let cool on the baking sheet on a wire rack for 20 to 30 minutes. The pastries tend to bake into one another in the oven, so break apart into 10 pieces.

➡ The pastries are best served warm or within 4 hours of baking. They can be stored in an airtight container at room temperature for up to 1 day, and then warmed in a 300-degree-F oven for 5 minutes before serving.

PASTRY CREAM

1¼ cups (300 grams) milk

½ cup (100 grams) sugar

¼ cup (30 grams) cake flour

½ teaspoon kosher salt

4 egg yolks

1 teaspoon vanilla extract

MAKES ABOUT 2 CUPS

➡ In a medium saucepan, scald the milk over medium-high heat (bubbles start to form around the edge of the pan, but the milk is not boiling). While the milk is heating, in a small bowl, stir together the sugar, flour, and salt. (Mixing the flour with the sugar will prevent the flour from clumping when you add it to the egg yolks.) In a medium bowl, whisk the egg yolks until blended, then slowly whisk in the flour mixture. The mixture will be thick and pasty.

➡ Remove the milk from the heat and slowly add it to the egg-flour mixture, a little at a time, whisking constantly. When all of the milk has been incorporated, return the contents of the bowl to the saucepan and place over medium heat. Whisk continuously and vigorously for about 3 minutes, or until the mixture thickens and comes to a boil. At first, the mixture will be very frothy and liquid; as it cooks longer, it will slowly start to thicken until the frothy bubbles disappear and it becomes more viscous. Once it thickens, stop whisking every few seconds to see if the mixture has come to a boil. If it has not, keep whisking vigorously. As soon as you see it bubbling, immediately go back to whisking for just 10 seconds, and then remove the pan from the heat. Boiling the mixture will thicken it and cook out the flour taste, but if you let it boil for longer than 10 seconds, the mixture can become grainy.

➡ Pour the mixture through a fine-mesh sieve into a small heatproof bowl. Stir in the vanilla, then cover with plastic wrap, placing it directly on the surface of the cream. This will prevent a skin from forming. Refrigerate for at least 4 hours, or until cold, or up to 3 days.

CRAQUELINE

CANDIED ORANGES

2 navel oranges

3 cups (600 grams) sugar

4 cups (960 grams) water

½ recipe Basic Brioche dough (page 73)

1 egg

¼ cup (50 grams) sugar

½ cup (50 grams) sliced almonds

MAKES 10 PASTRIES

Creating the menu for a place like Flour is a bit like playing pick-up sticks. You make a dizzying number of different breakfast treats, cookies, cakes, tarts, and breads, and then you hope that once you throw them out there, they will be snatched up! When I opened Flour, I didn't know if I should include *craqueline* on our menu because I wasn't sure it would sell. *Craqueline* is a French breakfast pastry, one I learned to make at Payard. Chef Payard's version, which inspired mine, is a fluffy brioche filled with chopped candied oranges and crowned with a crackly almond topping. I was worried the French name would intimidate customers (*craqueline* refers to the crunchy top, and ever since I learned how to make the pastries, I have loved to snack on the delicious top edges). Shame on me for doubting our brioche-loving customers! These have developed a loyal and vocal following. I took them off the menu for a short time, and frustrated customers immediately sent me a flurry of comment cards. We quickly brought them back—and I still snack on the edges every chance I get.

➡ To make the candied oranges: Slice the stem and blossom ends off both oranges and then slice the oranges crosswise about ¼ inch thick.

➡ In a medium nonreactive saucepan, combine the sugar and water and bring to a boil over high heat, stirring until the sugar dissolves. Add the orange slices, reduce the heat to very low, and simmer the slices in the syrup for 2 to 3 hours, or until they are translucent and the syrup is thick and very syrupy. As the slices simmer, gently stir them occasionally to move the slices on top to the bottom of the syrup. To test for doneness, remove 1 orange slice from the syrup and bite into it—careful, it will be hot! The rind should be completely soft and sweet and the syrup that clings to the slice should be very thick. Remove from the heat, cover the pan, and let cool completely. (The orange slices can be candied up to 2 weeks in advance and stored in their syrup in a covered container in the refrigerator.)

➡ Line a baking sheet with parchment paper.

➡ On a floured work surface, roll out the dough into a rectangle about 20 by 10 inches and ¼ inch thick. It will have the consistency of cold, damp Play-Doh and it should be fairly easy to roll. Position the rectangle so a long side is facing you.

➡ Remove the cooled orange slices from the syrup, scraping off as much syrup as possible (clinging syrup can make chopping the slices messy and difficult). Coarsely chop the slices. You should have about 1½ cups. Discard the syrup. Using a large spoon, spoon the chopped oranges over the top two-thirds of the rectangle, spreading them out evenly.

➡ Facing the rectangle, fold the bottom third of the dough up over the oranges to cover them about halfway, then fold the top third down, as if folding a letter. You should have a rectangle about 20 inches long and just over 3 inches wide, with candied oranges spread between layers of brioche dough.

➡ Use a bench scraper or a chef's knife to cut the filled dough into 10 pieces, each about 2 inches wide; each piece will be about 2 by 3 inches. (At this point, the unbaked pastries can be tightly wrapped in plastic wrap and frozen for up to 1 week. When ready to bake, thaw them, still wrapped, in the refrigerator overnight or at room temperature for 2 to 3 hours, then proceed as directed.)

➡ Place the pastries on the prepared baking sheet. Cover lightly with plastic wrap and place in a warm spot to proof for about 2 hours, or until the dough is puffy, pillowy, and soft.

➡ Position a rack in the center of the oven, and heat the oven to 350 degrees F.

➡ In a small bowl, whisk the egg until blended, then whisk in the sugar and almonds to make a slurry. Evenly spoon the slurry on top of each pastry, making sure to cover the entire top evenly.

➡ Bake for 35 to 45 minutes, or until the almond top is completely golden brown and the dough is golden through and through. Let cool on the pan on a wire rack for 20 to 30 minutes before serving.

➡ The pastries are best served warm or within 4 hours of baking. They can be stored in an airtight container at room temperature for up to 1 day, and then warmed in a 300-degree-F oven for 5 minutes before serving.

STICKY STICKY BUNS

GOO

¾ cup (1½ sticks/170 grams) unsalted butter

1½ cups (330 grams) packed light brown sugar

⅓ cup (115 grams) honey

⅓ cup (80 grams) heavy cream

⅓ cup (80 grams) water

¼ teaspoon kosher salt

½ batch Basic Brioche dough (page 73)

¼ cup (55 grams) packed light brown sugar

¼ cup (50 grams) granulated sugar

⅛ teaspoon ground cinnamon

1 cup (100 grams) pecan halves, toasted and chopped

MAKES 8 BUNS

Flour's addictive sticky buns have been famous in Boston for years, but they received national attention in the summer of 2007, when they starred in an episode of the Food Network show *Throwdown with Bobby Flay*. I went head-to-head with chef Flay in a sticky bun bake-off—in front of television cameras and a live audience of about one hundred customers at Flour. After we both finished baking our buns, an agonizing hour passed during which customers were quizzed about which buns they preferred, mine or Chef Flay's, and the judges did their evaluations. Flour's sticky buns won! Many people wonder if television-show judging is fixed. But the visible sweat on my brow during that hour should assure them it definitely is not. These sticky buns are quite simply the stickiest, richest, gooiest, most decadent buns you'll ever eat. We start them with a brioche dough base, fill them with sugar, pecans, and cinnamon, and then top them with copious amounts of a sticky caramel concoction called, naturally, goo. When you eat them, be sure to have plenty of napkins nearby.

⇒ To make the goo: In a medium saucepan, melt the butter over medium heat. Whisk in the brown sugar until the sugar dissolves. Remove from the heat and whisk in the honey, cream, water, and salt. Let cool for about 30 minutes, or until cooled to room temperature. You should have about 2 cups. (The mixture can be made up to 2 weeks in advance and stored in an airtight container in the refrigerator.)

⇒ On a floured work surface, roll out the dough into a rectangle about 16 by 12 inches and ¼ inch thick. It will have the consistency of cold, damp Play-Doh and should be fairly easy to roll. Position the rectangle so a short side is facing you.

⇒ In a small bowl, stir together the brown sugar, granulated sugar, cinnamon, and half of the pecans. Sprinkle this mixture evenly over the entire surface of the dough. Starting from the short side farthest from you and working your way down, roll up the rectangle like a jelly roll. Try to roll tightly, so you have a nice round spiral. Even off the ends by trimming about ¼ inch from either side.

(continued)

➡ Use a bench scraper or a chef's knife to cut the roll into 8 equal pieces, each about 1½ inches wide. (At this point, the unbaked buns can be tightly wrapped in plastic wrap and and frozen for up to 1 week. When ready to bake, thaw them, still wrapped, in the refrigerator overnight or at room temperature for 2 to 3 hours, then proceed as directed.)

➡ Pour the goo into a 9-by-13-inch baking dish, covering the bottom evenly. Sprinkle the remaining pecans evenly over the surface. Place the buns, a cut side down and evenly spaced, 2-by-4 inches, in the baking dish. Cover with plastic wrap and place in a warm spot to proof for about 2 hours, or until the dough is puffy, pillowy, and soft and the buns are touching.

➡ Position a rack in the center of the oven, and heat the oven to 350 degrees F.

➡ Bake for 35 to 45 minutes, or until golden brown. Let cool in the dish on a wire rack for 20 to 30 minutes. One at a time, invert the buns onto a serving platter, and spoon any extra goo and pecans from the bottom of the dish over the top.

➡ The buns are best served warm or within 4 hours of baking. They can be stored in an air-tight container at room temperature for up to 1 day, and then warmed in a 325-degree-F oven for 6 to 8 minutes before serving.

the next food network star

AT LEAST THREE TIMES A DAY, PEOPLE ASK ME HOW I ENDED UP ON THE FOOD NETWORK, PITTED AGAINST BOBBY FLAY ON *THROWDOWN WITH BOBBY FLAY*. On the show, Bobby surprises chefs, challenges them in their area of expertise, and tries to outdo them by making a better version of their specialty. All in front of television cameras!

In March 2007, the Food Network contacted me to ask if I was available for a few days of filming in Boston. They said they were considering a series called *The Science of Sweets* and that they wanted me to film the pilot episode. This is sort of like Publisher's Clearinghouse calling to ask if you'd be willing to come to their offices to pick up your ten-million-dollar prize: Shock gives way to elation, which then gives way to disbelief. (And then the sequence repeats.) When your mind is in the elation stage you gleefully say yes, yes, yes. After you've hung up and you're in disbelief, you wonder if *Candid Camera* crews are in the vicinity.

It all seemed legitimate when I showed up at the studio. There were actual cameras and people who seemed to know what they were doing. I spent a day saying things over and over into a camera: "Welcome to *The Science of Sweets*!" "These sticky buns will knock your socks off!" "Baking is like chemistry!" And by the end of the day I was convinced that a show was going to be filmed, though I was somewhat skeptical of the premise. (For a science and baking junkie like me, a whole series on "the science of sweets" sure sounded awesome, yet were there really that many people out there who were as interested in this stuff as I am?) But I was the pastry expert, not the marketing expert, so I went with it.

The second day the Food Network team came to the bakery and filmed me teaching an audience how to make sticky buns. Again, it was all under the pretense that I was demonstrating that baking sticky buns is full of science and wonder. All seemed normal and then . . . Bobby Flay walked in. And that's when I found out I was on *Throwdown*, and that *The Science of Sweets* was just a ruse. Too bad—if any Food Network execs are reading this, I think that idea had potential!

HOMEMADE POP-TARTS

1 recipe Pâte Brisée I (page 92)

1 egg, lightly beaten

1 cup (340 grams) raspberry jam

SIMPLE VANILLA GLAZE

1 cup (140 grams) confectioners' sugar

¼ teaspoon vanilla extract

2 to 3 tablespoons water

Rainbow sprinkles for sprinkling (optional)

MAKES 8 PASTRIES

I took the bus to elementary school every day with Linda, my best childhood friend and next-door neighbor. We always sat together in the third row and shared our breakfasts-on-the-go. Most of the time I had buttered toast or a traditional *bao* (Chinese white steamed bun)—pretty boring. Linda's mom often sent her with foil-wrapped packets of Pop-Tarts, which I could never get her to trade with me. She shared bites with me occasionally, but I longed to have my own, and I could never convince my mom to buy them. When I started baking professionally, I dreamed of all the things I would offer at my own bakery. Those childhood tarts were high on my list, and I thought if I made them from scratch, they could surpass the packaged supermarket version I remembered. I was right. The tarts we make at Flour get steady attention from both our customers and the press. Making them is similar to making ravioli, but even if you've never done that, you'll find the process quite straightforward: First, you roll out flaky, buttery dough into a big sheet and score it into rectangles. Then, you spoon jam into the rectangles, lay another sheet of pastry dough on top, and press down to make little jam pockets. Finally, you cut the pockets apart and bake them to golden brown yumminess.

➡ Position a rack in the center of the oven, and heat the oven to 350 degrees F.

➡ Remove the dough from the refrigerator and divide it in half. Press each half into a rectangle. On a lightly floured surface, roll out each half into a 14-by-11-inch rectangle. Using a paring knife, lightly score one rectangle into eight 3½-by-5½-inch rectangles (each about the size of an index card).

(continued)

➡ Brush the top surface of the entire scored rect-angle with the egg. Spoon 2 tablespoons of the jam in a mound in the center of each scored rectangle. Lay the second large dough rectangle directly on top of the first. Using fingertips, care-fully press down all around each jam mound, so the pastry sheets adhere to each other.

➡ Using a knife, a pizza roller (easier), or a fluted roller (easier and prettier), and following the scored lines, cut the layered dough into 8 rectangles. Place the rectangles, well spaced, on a baking sheet.

➡ Bake for 40 to 45 minutes, or until the tops of the pastries are evenly golden brown. Let cool on the baking sheet on a wire rack for about 30 minutes.

Same recipe, different flavors

Replace the raspberry jam with Apple, Cinnamon, and Brown Sugar Filling, and replace the Simple Vanilla Glaze with Cinnamon Glaze.

APPLE, CINNAMON, AND BROWN SUGAR FILLING

MAKES ABOUT 1 CUP

3 tablespoons unsalted butter

2 Granny Smith apples, peeled, cored, and thinly sliced (about 2 cups/240 grams)

½ cup (110 grams) packed light brown sugar

1 egg, lightly beaten

½ teaspoon ground cinnamon

⅛ teaspoon kosher salt

½ cup (70 grams) unbleached all-purpose flour

In a medium saucepan, melt the butter over high heat. Add the apples and toss around with a heat-resistant spatula for 2 to 3 minutes, or until they just start to soften. Add the sugar and continue to toss for another 3 to 4 minutes, or until the sugar has melted and mixed with the apples. Remove from the heat and transfer the apple mixture to a medium bowl. Let cool for about 30 minutes, or until no longer hot to the touch.

Add the egg, cinnamon, salt, and flour to the apple mixture and mix with a rubber spatula until they are thoroughly and evenly incorporated. Let cool completely before using.

CINNAMON GLAZE

MAKES ½ CUP

1 cup (140 grams) confectioners' sugar

2 tablespoons plus 2 teaspoons water

¼ teaspoon ground cinnamon

In a small bowl, whisk together the sugar, water, and cinnamon to make a smooth, pourable glaze. (The glaze can be made ahead and stored in an airtight container at room tempera-ture for up to 1 week.)

➡ To make the glaze: While the pastries are cooling, in a small bowl, whisk together the confectioners' sugar, vanilla, and enough of the water to make a smooth, pourable glaze. You should have about ½ cup. (The glaze can be made ahead and stored in an airtight container at room temperature for up to 1 week.)

➡ When the pastries have cooled for 30 minutes, brush the tops evenly with the glaze, then sprinkle with the rainbow sprinkles (if using). Let stand for 10 to 15 minutes to allow the glaze to set before serving.

➡ The pastries can be stored in an airtight container at room temperature for up to 2 days.

Replace the raspberry jam with Chocolate Filling, and replace the Simple Vanilla Glaze with Chocolate Glaze.

Chocolate Filling

MAKES ABOUT 1 CUP

7 ounces (200 grams) bittersweet chocolate (60 to 72 percent cacao), chopped

6 tablespoons (¾ stick/86 grams) unsalted butter

⅓ cup (80 grams) heavy cream

3 tablespoons sugar

½ teaspoon kosher salt

Place the chocolate in a small heatproof bowl over (not touching) barely simmering water in a saucepan and heat, stirring occasionally, until completely melted and smooth. Remove from the heat.

In a small saucepan, combine the butter, cream, and sugar over medium heat and heat, stirring occasionally, until the butter has melted and the sugar has dissolved. Remove from the heat.

Add the butter mixture to the chocolate and whisk together with the salt. Refrigerate for at least 1 hour, or until the mixture firms up enough to spoon into the pastry pockets. (The filling can be made ahead and stored in an airtight container in the refrigerator for up to 4 days.)

Chocolate Glaze

MAKES ½ CUP

1 cup (140 grams) confectioners' sugar

¼ cup (60 grams) water

1 ounce (28 grams) bittersweet chocolate (62 to 70 percent cacao), melted and cooled

In a small bowl, whisk together the confectioners' sugar, water, and chocolate until smooth and pourable. (The glaze can be made ahead and stored in an airtight container in the refrigerator for up to 1 week.)

PÂTE BRISÉE I

1¾ cups (245 grams) unbleached all-purpose flour

1 tablespoon sugar

1 teaspoon kosher salt

1 cup (2 sticks/228 grams) cold unsalted butter, cut into 12 pieces

2 egg yolks

3 tablespoons cold milk

MAKES ABOUT 18 OUNCES DOUGH, ENOUGH FOR 8 POP-TARTS OR ONE 9-INCH DOUBLE-CRUST OR LATTICE-TOP PIE

➡ Using a stand mixer fitted with the paddle attachment (or a handheld mixer), mix together the flour, sugar, and salt for 10 to 15 seconds, or until combined. Scatter the butter over the top. Mix on low speed for 1 to 1½ minutes, or just until the flour is no longer bright white and holds together when you clump it and lumps of butter the size of pecans are visible throughout.

➡ In a small bowl, whisk together the egg yolks and milk until blended. Add to the flour mixture all at once. Mix on low speed for about 30 seconds, or until the dough just barely comes together. It will look really shaggy and more like a mess than a dough.

➡ Dump the dough out onto an unfloured work surface, then gather it together into a tight mound. Using your palm and starting on one side of the mound, smear the dough bit by bit, starting at the top of the mound and then sliding your palm down the side and along the work surface (at Flour, we call this "going down the mountain"), until most of the butter chunks are smeared into the dough and the dough comes together. Do this once or twice on each part of the dough, moving through the mound until the whole mess has been smeared into a cohesive dough with streaks of butter.

➡ Gather up the dough, wrap tightly in plastic wrap, and press down to flatten into a disk about 1 inch thick. Refrigerate for at least 4 hours before using. The dough will keep in the refrigerator for up to 4 days or in the freezer for up to 1 month.

CROISSANTS

1 cup plus 2 tablespoons (260 grams) milk, at room temperature

1 package (2½ teaspoons) active dry yeast, or ⅔ ounce (18 grams) fresh cake yeast

2¼ cups (315 grams) unbleached all-purpose flour

⅔ cup (100 grams) bread flour

2 teaspoons kosher salt

¼ cup (50 grams) sugar

2 tablespoons (¼ stick/28 grams) unsalted butter, very soft, plus 1 cup (2 sticks/228 grams) cold unsalted butter

1 egg

MAKES ABOUT
10 CROISSANTS

A few years back, Christopher and I traveled to Paris. It was a wonderful trip—on a personal note, Christopher and I got engaged; on a pastry note, I had croissant epiphanies day after day. Every single day, no matter where we were in the city, we had crisp, buttery, delicious croissants—croissants so flaky that you had to put your hand to your mouth to protect those around you from the flying crumbs. I loved our croissants at Flour, but I viewed them with new eyes after returning from that trip. Back home in the bakery, I made it my mission to improve our croissants.

We make our croissants from scratch at Flour each day, and when I was at Payard, we did the same. You can easily buy croissant dough from a reputable source (and, to be honest, you'll save a lot in headaches and labor if you do), but making the dough yourself and getting the croissants just right is a constant (and rewarding) challenge. Every morning at Flour, I try one of our croissants to see if we have met the challenge. I'm happy to report that we consistently deliver, and with this recipe, you can, too. These croissants are messy and flaky and tender and buttery and worth every minute. Keep in mind that you'll need to start making the dough at least 2 days before you want to serve the croissants.

⇒ Using a stand mixer fitted with the dough hook (or a hand mixer), mix together the milk and yeast on low speed for 5 to 10 seconds to dissolve the yeast. Add the all-purpose flour, bread flour, salt, sugar, and the 2 tablespoons soft butter and continue to mix on low speed for 3 to 4 minutes, or until the butter is fully incorporated and the dough is smooth. Remove the dough from the mixer bowl, place it on a tray, and cover it loosely with plastic wrap. This dough block is called the *détrempe*. Place the tray in the refrigerator for at least 6 hours or up to 12 hours. The dough will firm up and the yeast will take some action and proof a bit.

⇒ At least 6 hours later, put the *détrempe* on a well-floured work surface, and then press down firmly to create about an 8-inch square. Rotate the square so that, as you face it, it looks like a baseball diamond. Use the sides of your palm to mark a 6-inch square in the middle of the diamond, creating triangular flaps at the four corners.

(continued)

➡ As best you can, roll out each of the triangular flaps into a squarish shape (about 3-inch squares). You will have to tug a bit at the edges to pull the flap into a square as you roll. When you are done, the entire piece of dough will be about 12 inches wide and tall, with a 6-inch-square lump in the middle and one squarish flap off each side of that lump. The 6-inch-square lump will be about 1 inch thick, and the four squarish flaps will be about ¼ inch thick.

➡ Place the 1 cup cold butter in the stand mixer fitted with the paddle attachment, and beat on medium speed for 15 to 20 seconds to break up the butter, yet still keep it quite cold. (Alternatively, pound the cold butter with a rolling pin to soften it and shape it into a 6-inch square.) Scrape the butter out of the bowl directly onto the 6-inch-square lump in the center of the dough, and pat it with your fingers into a square that covers the 6-inch-square lump. The butter should have about the same consistency as the dough.

➡ Fold one of the flaps up and stretch it over the butter square to cover it entirely. (The dough is quite stretchy, so you can stretch it to cover the butter completely.) Fold and stretch a second flap over the first flap, then repeat with the third and then the fourth flap. Tug at the flaps to keep them in a square that covers the butter. You will now have a butter square that is entirely encased in dough above and below. Using the palms of both hands, firmly press down on this dough package to create about an 8-inch square.

➡ When the dough package is relatively flat, switch to a rolling pin and continue to flatten the dough by pressing up and down on the package with the pin (see Baker's Bite, page 97). Roll out the dough into a rectangle about 16 by 10 inches. As you work, flour the dough and the work surface as needed to prevent the rolling pin from sticking to the dough.

➡ Position the rectangle so a long side is facing you. Using a bench scraper or a knife, score the rectangle in half vertically, to create two 10-by-8-inch rectangles. Brush any loose flour off the dough. Lift the right side of the dough and fold it in, so the right edge meets the scored line in the center. Then lift the left side of the dough and fold it in, so the left edge also meets the scored line in the center and meets the right edge, as well. Square off the folds as much as possible so the edges meet neatly, then fold the right half of the dough on top of the left half. This is called a book fold. Your dough will now be 4 inches wide, 10 inches from top to bottom, and about 2 inches thick. Rotate the dough pile clockwise 90 degrees; it will now be 10 inches wide and 4 inches from top to bottom. The process of folding and rotating is called "turning the dough."

➡ Now, roll out the dough into a rectangle about 18 inches wide and 8 inches from top to bottom. The dough might be a little sticky, so, again, be sure to flour the dough and the work surface as needed to prevent the pin from sticking. Using the bench scraper or knife, this time lightly score the rectangle vertically into thirds. Each third will be 6 inches wide and 8 inches from top to bottom. Brush any loose flour off the dough. Take the right third of the dough and flip it over onto the middle third. Then take the left third of the dough and flip that third on top of the middle and right thirds. (This is like folding a letter.) Your dough should now be about 6 inches wide, 8 inches from top to bottom, and about 2 inches thick. Rotate the dough pile clockwise 90 degrees; it will now be 8 inches wide and 6 inches from top to bottom.

➡ Place the dough on a baking sheet and cover it completely with plastic wrap, tucking the plastic under the dough as if you are tucking it into bed. Refrigerate for at least 1½ hours and no more than 3 hours.

(continued)

➡ Remove the dough from the refrigerator and place it on a well-floured work surface, with a long side of the rectangle facing you. This time roll out the dough into a rectangle about 18 inches wide and 12 inches from top to bottom. If the dough resists rolling, let it sit and relax for up to 15 minutes and roll again. Once again score it vertically into thirds, and then give it another letter fold (fold the right third onto the middle third, and fold the left third on top of that). Return the dough to the baking sheet and again cover it completely with plastic wrap. This time let it rest in the refrigerator for at least 4 hours or up to 16 hours.

➡ Line a baking sheet with parchment paper.

➡ Remove the dough from the refrigerator, and place it once again on a well-floured work surface, with a long side of the rectangle facing you. Roll it out into a long, narrow rectangle about 30 inches wide and 6 to 7 inches from top to bottom.

➡ Starting at the bottom left corner of the rectangle, make a mark along the bottom edge of the rectangle every 5 inches until you reach the bottom right corner. Then, starting at the top left corner of the rectangle, mark along the top edge exactly midway between the notches on the bottom edge. Your first notch will be 2½ inches from the left corner, and then continue to notch every 5 inches. Use a chef's knife to cut the dough rectangle into triangles by cutting on the diagonal from notch to notch. You will end up with 10 triangles and a few edge pieces of scrap.

➡ Starting at the edge, cut a 1-inch vertical slit at the center of the base of each triangle. Turn all of the triangles so the base is at the top, farthest from you, and the point is directed toward you. Pick up a triangle and hold it by its base with one hand and gently stretch it and stroke it lengthwise with your other hand to elongate it to 10 to 12 inches in length.

➡ Place the lengthened triangle on the work surface. Fan open the base at the 1-inch slit into a Y, and then roll the dough down to the point. Place the rolled triangle, point-side down, on the parchment-lined baking sheet, so the point is touching the parchment. Repeat with the remaining dough triangles, spacing the pastries 2 to 3 inches apart on the baking sheet.

➡ Cover the croissants lightly with plastic wrap and leave them in a warm place for 2 to 2½ hours, or until they are somewhat poufy and airy.

➡ In a small bowl, whisk the egg until blended. Gently brush the croissants lightly with the egg.

➡ If you are baking the croissants the same day, cover them again with plastic wrap and let them finish proofing for another 1 hour to 1 hour and 30 minutes. They will get even more poufy and jiggly when you nudge them.

➡ Position a rack in the center of the oven, and heat the oven to 400 degrees F.

➡ When the croissants are done proofing, brush them again with the beaten egg. Bake at 400 degrees F for the first 5 minutes, then turn down the oven to 350 degrees F and bake for another 25 to 35 minutes (for a total baking time of 30 to 40 minutes), or until they are golden brown all over. Let cool on the pan on a wire rack for 30 to 40 minutes. Serve warm.

➡ If you are baking the croissants the next day, after the first 2- to 2½-hour proof, brush them lightly with the beaten egg as directed, wrap them in plastic wrap and place in the refrigerator. The next morning, remove them from the refrigerator and let them sit at room temperature for 30 to 40 minutes. Then heat the oven, brush them again with the beaten egg, and bake as directed.

➡ The croissants taste best the day they are baked. They can be stored in an airtight container at room temperature overnight, and then refreshed in a 300-degree F oven for 5 to 8 minutes before serving.

Baker's Bite

When rolling out laminated dough for croissants, your goal is to keep the layers directly on top of one another. In other words, you want to preserve the layering. As you complete each turn, you will have three layers of evenly stacked dough. Rather than immediately rolling out these layers with a back-and-forth motion, first press down firmly on the dough with the pin to flatten it, and then pound the pin up and down along the length of the dough, creating ridges in the dough as you compact it. Once the dough is pressed down all over, roll the pin back and forth, smoothing out the ridges as you flatten and rolling the dough into the shape you want. By pressing down first before rolling, you preserve the layers. If you were to start rolling the dough immediately after folding it, the top layer would take all the pressure from the pin, and it would stretch it out way beyond the perimeter of the bottom layer. Using this compressing technique keeps the layers even, making for a flakier end product.

croissants by the book

MAKING CROISSANTS SEEMS EASY WHEN YOU HAVE BEEN DOING IT FOR YEARS. The challenge for me in writing this recipe was to break down all of the individual steps so that a newcomer to croissants could make them as well as I can. After literally dozens of trials in which various beginners tested and retested this recipe (the ingredients were always constant; I worked and reworked, clarified and reclarified the step-by-step instructions during the trials), I arrived at the realization that a great croissant, though certainly not unattainable for a beginner, probably benefits from both practice and some on-site instruction. I've done my best to explain each step, and if you have any familiarity with laminated dough, you won't have any problems. But if you don't, you will want to read this recipe through several times to make sure you fully understand each step. Don't be discouraged if your first attempt isn't perfect. Some of my beginning interns butchered this recipe—it was painful to watch—and their croissants baked up like lead. (Buttery, delicious lead, but still lead.) Once I walked them through the process, showing them how to complete each step, they were successful. In other words, it can be tough to learn without a teacher at your side, so read the recipe carefully before you give it a try.

VANILLA CREAM-FILLED DOUGHNUTS

1 package (2½ teaspoons) active dry yeast, or ⅔ ounce (18 grams) fresh cake yeast

⅔ cup (160 grams) milk, at room temperature

3½ cups (490 grams) unbleached all-purpose flour

1⅓ cups (270 grams) sugar

2 teaspoons kosher salt

3 eggs

7 tablespoons (⅞ stick/100 grams) butter, at room temperature, cut into 6 to 8 pieces

Canola oil for frying

VANILLA CREAM FILLING

6 tablespoons (90 grams) heavy cream

1 recipe Pastry Cream (page 81), chilled

MAKES NINE 4-INCH DOUGHNUTS

For years before I opened Flour, I had a notebook where I kept menu ideas for when I finally had my own dream bakery. It was filled with all of the pastries I had read about in cookbooks, learned to make at my jobs, and savored on my travels. When it came time to write a menu for the bakery, I realized it was impossible to include every-thing I wanted to offer. These doughnuts barely made the cut. After all, we were opening less than a block away from an outpost of the ubiquitous Dunkin' Donuts chain. These doughnuts are now a Flour best-seller. I first learned how to make doughnuts at Payard. A French pastry chef taught me how to make doughnuts that make Americans swoon, though they scarcely resemble what you get at the com-petition down the street. We only make them on Sundays, and they sell out every week.

➡ In a stand mixer fitted with the dough hook (or a hand-held mixer), combine the yeast and milk. Stir together briefly, then let sit for about 1 minute to dissolve the yeast. Add the flour, ⅓ cup (70 grams) of the sugar, the salt, and the eggs and mix on low speed for about 1 minute, or until the dough comes together. Then, still on low speed, mix for another 2 to 3 minutes to develop the dough further. Now, begin to add the butter, a few pieces at a time, and continue to mix for 5 to 6 minutes, or until the butter is fully incorporated and the dough is soft and cohesive.

➡ Remove the dough from the bowl, wrap tightly in plastic wrap, and refrigerate for at least 6 hours or up to 15 hours.

➡ Lightly flour a baking sheet. On a well-floured work surface, roll out the dough into a 12-inch square about ½ inch thick. Using a 3½- to 4-inch round biscuit cutter, cut out 9 doughnuts. Arrange them on the prepared baking sheet, cover with plastic wrap, and place in a warm spot to rise for 2 to 3 hours, or until they are about doubled in height and feel poufy and pillowy.

(continued)

⇒ When ready to fry, line with paper towels a tray or baking sheet large enough to hold the doughnuts. Pour oil to a depth of about 3 inches into a large, heavy saucepan and heat over medium-high heat until hot. To test the oil, throw in a pinch of flour. If it sizzles on contact, the oil is ready. (It should be 350 degrees F if you are using a thermometer.) Working in batches, place the doughnuts in the hot oil, being careful not to crowd them. Fry on the first side for 2 to 3 minutes, or until brown. Then gently flip them and fry for another 2 to 3 minutes, or until brown on the second side. Using a slotted spoon, transfer the doughnuts to the prepared tray and let cool for a few minutes, or until cool enough to handle.

⇒ Place the remaining 1 cup (200 grams) sugar in a small bowl. One at a time, toss the warm doughnuts in the sugar to coat evenly. As each doughnut is coated, return it to the tray to cool completely. This will take 30 to 40 minutes.

⇒ To make the vanilla cream filling: While the doughnuts are cooling, whip the heavy cream until it holds stiff peaks. Using a rubber spatula, fold it into the pastry cream. You should have about 3 cups.

⇒ When the doughnuts are completely cooled, poke a hole in the side of each one, spacing it equidistant between the top and bottom. Fit a pastry bag with a small round tip and fill the bag with the filling (see page 15). Squirt about 1/3 cup filling into each doughnut. Serve immediately.

MOM'S GRANOLA

2½ cups (270 grams) old-fashioned rolled oats (not instant or quick cooking)

1½ cups (200 grams) wheat germ

½ cup (60 grams) sweetened shredded coconut

3 tablespoons sesame seeds

⅓ cup (40 grams) sunflower seeds

½ cup (50 grams) chopped walnuts

½ cup (50 grams) sliced almonds

2 teaspoons ground cinnamon

1 teaspoon kosher salt

¾ cup (150 grams) canola oil

¾ cup (255 grams) honey

2 teaspoons vanilla extract

½ cup (80 grams) dried cranberries

MAKES ABOUT 10 CUPS

This classic granola recipe is full of hearty, earthy, nutty flavors and is simply adorned with a handful of dried cranberries. It comes from Korinn, one of the great original bakers at Flour. Every morning, she brought in a little baggie of granola for her breakfast, and we all begged her to share because it was so delicious. Finally, she brought in the recipe—which came from her mom—so that we could make our own. We tweaked it just a bit, and now we are passing it along to you. My favorite way to enjoy this granola is layered with yogurt and fresh berries.

➡ Position a rack in the center of the oven, and heat the oven to 350 degrees F. Line a baking sheet with parchment paper.

➡ In a large bowl, combine the oats, wheat germ, coconut, sesame seeds, sunflower seeds, walnuts, almonds, cinnamon, and salt and mix well. In a small bowl, whisk together the oil, honey, and vanilla. Pour the wet ingredients over the dry ingredients and mix thoroughly until the dry ingredients are evenly coated.

➡ Pour the mixture onto the prepared baking sheet and spread in an even layer. Bake for 30 to 35 minutes, or until golden brown. Stir the granola with a spatula or wooden spoon several times during baking to ensure even browning. Let cool completely, then add the cranberries and mix to distribute them evenly.

➡ The granola can be stored in an airtight container at room temperature for up to 1 week.

cookies

MILK CHOCOLATE-HAZELNUT COOKIES

¾ cup plus 1 tablespoon
(1½ sticks plus 1 tablespoon/
185 grams) unsalted butter,
at room temperature

⅔ cup (140 grams) granulated
sugar

⅔ cup (150 grams) packed light
brown sugar

2 eggs

½ teaspoon vanilla extract

1½ cups (210 grams) blanched
whole hazelnuts, toasted

1½ cups (210 grams) unbleached
all-purpose flour

1 teaspoon baking soda

¾ teaspoon kosher salt

12 ounces (340 grams) milk
chocolate, chopped into ½-inch
pieces

MAKES ABOUT 20 COOKIES

I'm an equal-opportunity sweets lover . . . with a few key exceptions. Like hazelnuts. I'm not a huge fan of the flavor, and I don't automatically think of all the delicious things I can make with hazelnuts when I'm dreaming about desserts. But I know I'm in the minority when it comes to this taste preference, and so when Nicole, Flour's head pastry chef, proposed a milk chocolate and hazelnut cookie, I hid my initial reluctance and responded, "What a great idea!" And a great idea it has been. Nicole worked on this recipe for several weeks, and now it's one of the most highly complimented cookies we make. A little ground hazelnut in the batter makes it delectably chewy, and the milk chocolate chunks melt just slightly into the dough during baking, so that the result wins over even non-hazelnut fans like me.

➡ Using a stand mixer fitted with the paddle attachment (or a handheld mixer or a wooden spoon), cream together the butter, granulated sugar, and brown sugar on medium speed for about 5 minutes, or until the mixture is light and fluffy. (This step will take about 10 minutes if using a handheld mixer or a spoon.) Stop the mixer a few times and use a rubber spatula to scrape the sides and bottom of the bowl and the paddle to release any clinging butter or sugar. Beat in the eggs and vanilla on medium speed for 2 to 3 minutes, or until thoroughly combined. Scrape the bowl and the paddle again to make sure the eggs are thoroughly incorporated.

➡ In a food processor, pulse ½ cup (70 grams) of the hazelnuts until ground to a fine powder. (Stop grinding once they are powdery; if you continue, they will become a paste.) Roughly chop the remaining 1 cup (140 grams) hazelnuts. In a medium bowl, stir together the ground and chopped hazelnuts, the flour, baking soda, salt, and chocolate. On low speed (or with the wooden spoon), slowly blend the flour mixture into the butter-sugar mixture and then mix just until the flour mixture is totally incorporated and the dough is evenly mixed.

(continued)

⇒ For the best results, scrape the dough into an airtight container and let it rest in the refrigerator overnight (or for at least 3 to 4 hours) before baking. When you are ready to bake, position a rack in the center of the oven, and heat the oven to 350 degrees F.

⇒ Drop the dough in ¼-cup balls onto a baking sheet, spacing them about 2 inches apart. Flatten each ball slightly with the palm of your hand.

⇒ Bake for 20 to 22 minutes, or until the cookies are golden brown on the edges and pale and slightly soft in the center. Let cool on the baking sheet on a wire rack for 5 to 10 minutes, then transfer the cookies to the rack to cool completely.

⇒ The cookies can be stored in an airtight container at room temperature for up to 3 days. The unbaked dough can be stored in an airtight container in the refrigerator for up to 1 week.

DOUBLE-CHOCOLATE COOKIES

4 ounces (114 grams) unsweetened chocolate, chopped, plus 2 ounces (56 grams), finely shaved

5 ounces (140 grams) bittersweet chocolate (62 to 70 percent cacao), chopped, plus 4 ounces (112 grams), chopped into ½-inch pieces

½ cup (1 stick/114 grams) unsalted butter

½ teaspoon vanilla extract

1½ cups (300 grams) sugar

4 eggs

½ cup (70 grams) unbleached all-purpose flour

¼ teaspoon baking soda

¼ teaspoon cream of tartar

¼ teaspoon kosher salt

¼ teaspoon instant espresso powder or instant coffee powder

¾ cup (75 grams) walnuts, toasted and chopped

MAKES ABOUT 15 COOKIES

There are people who love chocolate, and then there are *people who love chocolate*. This cookie is for the latter group. It is a little like a brownie, a little like fudge, and quite like the most chocolaty treat you'll ever eat. We melt unsweetened and bittersweet chocolate together and mix them into the batter, and then fold chocolate chunks into the batter, too. Walnuts are there for those who like nuts in their cookies, but you can omit them if you want only chocolate. This recipe evolved many years ago when a new baker at Flour accidentally mixed unsweetened chocolate chunks, rather than bittersweet chunks, into the batter. It was a shade too bitter for almost everyone, but the element of pure, deep chocolate flavor that the unsweetened chunks added turned on a lightbulb in our heads. We realized that unsweetened chocolate, added in moderation, was the secret ingredient that would take this cookie from very good to stellar. So we shaved some unsweetened chocolate into the final batter. Just be sure to shave it finely, as big chunks are likely to be too strong. And get ready to settle in with a few warm cookies and a big, tall glass of milk.

➡ In a heatproof bowl, combine the 4 ounces unsweetened chocolate, the 5 ounces bittersweet chocolate, and the butter. Place over (not touching) barely simmering water in a saucepan and heat, stirring occasionally, until completely melted and smooth. Remove from the heat and whisk in the vanilla. Refrigerate for at least 30 minutes.

➡ Using a stand mixer fitted with the whip attachment (or a handheld mixer), beat together the sugar and eggs on medium speed for about 5 minutes, or until light, thick, and pale yellow. (This step will take 8 to 10 minutes if using a handheld mixer.) On low speed, slowly add the chocolate mixture and mix for about 15 seconds. The mixture will not be well mixed at this point, but that's okay. You will finish combining all of the ingredients by hand.

➡ In a medium bowl, stir together the flour, baking soda, cream of tartar, salt, espresso powder, the remaining 2 ounces unsweetened chocolate, the remaining 4 ounces bittersweet chocolate, and the walnuts. Using a rubber spatula, fold the flour mixture into the sugar-butter mixture just until the flour mixture is totally incorporated and the dough is evenly mixed.

➡ For the best results, scrape the dough into an airtight container and let it rest in the refrigerator overnight (or for at least 3 to 4 hours) before baking. When you are ready to bake, position a rack in the center of the oven, and heat the oven to 350 degrees F.

➡ Drop the dough in ¼-cup balls onto a baking sheet, spacing them about 2 inches apart.

➡ Bake for about 15 minutes, or until the cookies are cracked on top and soft but not liquidy when you press them in the middle. Let cool on the baking sheet on a wire rack for 10 to 15 minutes, then transfer the cookies to the rack to cool completely.

➡ The cookies can be stored in an airtight container at room temperature for up to 3 days. The unbaked dough can be stored in an airtight container in the refrigerator for up to 1 week.

CHOCOLATE CHUNK COOKIES

1 cup (2 sticks/228 grams) unsalted butter, at room temperature

¾ cup (150 grams) granulated sugar

¾ cup (165 grams) firmly packed light brown sugar

2 eggs

½ teaspoon vanilla extract

1 cup (140 grams) unbleached all-purpose flour

1 cup (150 grams) bread flour

1 teaspoon baking soda

½ teaspoon kosher salt

9 ounces (255 grams) semisweet chocolate, chopped (about 1½ cups)

2½ ounces (70 grams) milk chocolate, chopped (about ½ cup)

MAKES ABOUT 24 COOKIES

Like many home bakers, the first time I made chocolate chip cookies I used the recipe on the back of the Toll House chocolate chips package. I was ten years old and my mom kept a careful eye on me to make sure I didn't burn down the house, but for the most part I made them myself. The cookies became a rare sweet staple in the Chang household.

Once I entered the world of professional baking, the idea of baking chocolate chip cookies from the Toll House package seemed akin to Bill Gates reading *Software for Dummies*—way too elementary. So I tested every other chocolate chip cookie recipe out there (or so it seemed). Every pastry chef has a version of this cookie that purports to be a vast improvement on the classic Toll House. Then, in 2000, I had to pick a final recipe for Flour. You know what? There's a reason why everyone loves the Toll House cookie recipe: it makes an amazingly swell cookie. I used that recipe as my starting point, but I made a few small adjustments to bring it from good to great. First, I use bread flour for some of the all-purpose flour, which gives additional heft and makes the cookie chewy, rather than flat and crispy. I stir some finely chopped milk chocolate into the dough, to add a nice caramelized note. Once the dough is made, it can be baked immediately, but for the best results, I always wait for at least a day for it to firm up in the fridge and to give the ingredients a chance to get to know one another. Believe it or not, that delay makes for a much better cookie. And finally, and most important, use the best chocolate you can. This is the key to making this recipe shine. Seek out great semisweet chocolate with a 62 to 70 percent cacao content and you will taste the difference.

➡ Using a stand mixer fitted with the paddle attachment (or a handheld mixer or a wooden spoon), cream together the butter, granulated sugar, and brown sugar on medium speed for about 5 minutes, or until the mixture is light and fluffy. (This step will take 10 minutes if using a handheld mixer or a spoon.) Stop the mixer a few times and use a rubber spatula to scrape the sides and bottom of the bowl and the paddle to release any clinging butter or sugar. Beat in the eggs and vanilla on medium speed for 2 to 3 minutes, or until thoroughly combined. Scrape the bowl and the paddle again to make sure the eggs are thoroughly incorporated.

➡ In a medium bowl, stir together the all-purpose flour, bread flour, baking soda, and salt until well mixed. Add the semisweet and milk chocolates and toss to combine. On low speed (or with the wooden spoon), slowly add the flour-chocolate mixture to the butter-sugar mixture and then mix just until the flour mixture is totally incorporated and the dough is evenly mixed.

➡ For the best results, scrape the dough into an airtight container and let it rest in the refrigerator overnight (or for at least 3 to 4 hours) before baking. When you are ready to bake, position a rack in the center of the oven, and heat the oven to 350 degrees F.

➡ Drop the dough in ¼-cup balls onto a baking sheet, spacing them about 2 inches apart. Flatten each ball slightly with the palm of your hand.

➡ Bake for 15 to 18 minutes, or until the cookies are golden brown on the edges and slightly soft in the center. Don't let them get brown through and through. Part of their appeal is the chewiness of the slightly underbaked centers. Let cool on the baking sheet on a wire rack for 5 to 10 minutes, then transfer the cookies to the rack to cool completely.

➡ The cookies can be stored in an airtight container at room temperature for up to 3 days. The unbaked dough can be stored in an airtight container in the refrigerator for up to 1 week.

Baker's Bite

As I have already noted, these cookies—and many of our other cookies—come out best when the dough has rested in the refrigerator overnight. This allows all of the liquid from the eggs and butter to absorb fully into the flour, creating a cookie with better flavor and a nicer texture.

CHUNKY LOLA COOKIES

½ cup plus 3 tablespoons
(1⅜ sticks/156 grams) unsalted
butter, at room temperature

⅔ cup (140 grams) granulated
sugar

⅔ cup (150 grams) packed light
brown sugar

2 eggs

1 teaspoon vanilla extract

1¼ cups (175 grams) unbleached
all-purpose flour

⅔ cup (70 grams) old-fashioned
rolled oats (not instant or quick
cooking)

1 teaspoon baking soda

½ teaspoon kosher salt

9 ounces (255 grams) bittersweet
chocolate (62 to 70 percent cacao),
chopped into ½-inch pieces

1¼ cups (125 grams) pecan halves,
toasted and chopped

1 cup (120 grams) sweetened
shredded coconut

MAKES ABOUT 18 COOKIES

Who is Lola? I wonder the same thing. We created this recipe at Flour after I asked our bakers what they crave most in a cookie. "I loooove coconut!" Julius exclaimed. "We don't have any cookies with pecans," Nicole lamented. "Mmmm . . . chocolate," Sarah sighed. The chorus grew louder until we finally decided to put everyone's favorites into one cookie. Developing and testing and tasting the recipe was easy. The hard part was coming up with a name. Kitchen Sink? Bakers' Collaboration? Chocolate Cookie with Nuts and Coconut and Oats? (Our creativity was running short by then.) We enlisted our customers' help with a cookie-naming contest. Whoever came up with a name for the cookie won two dozen of them. So many entries poured in that you would have thought we were giving away a January trip to the Bahamas. Some were funny, some were cute, and some were practical. In the end, we picked the name that made all of us laugh. We made up stories about Lola and the person who had entered her name. Was it an affectionate joke? Was he or she a secret admirer or a scorned lover? Was it Lola herself? We never found out. The winner claimed the prize and slipped off without sharing the story. But Chunky Lola has become one of our most popular cookies, and we hope Lola is out there somewhere basking in her Flour fame.

⇒ Using a stand mixer fitted with the paddle attachment (or a handheld mixer or a wooden spoon), cream together the butter, granulated sugar, and brown sugar on medium speed for about 5 minutes, or until the mixture is light and fluffy. (This step will take about 10 minutes if using a handheld mixer or a spoon.) Stop the mixer a few times and use a rubber spatula to scrape the sides and bottom of the bowl and the paddle to release any clinging butter or sugar. Beat in the eggs and vanilla on medium speed for 2 to 3 minutes, or until thoroughly combined. Scrape the bowl and the paddle again to make sure the eggs are thoroughly incorporated.

➡ In a medium bowl, stir together the flour, oats, baking soda, and salt. Add the chocolate, pecans, and coconut and toss to combine. On low speed (or with the wooden spoon), slowly add the flour mixture to the butter-sugar mixture and then mix just until the flour mixture is totally incorporated and the dough is evenly mixed.

➡ For the best results, scrape the dough into an airtight container and let it rest in the refrigerator overnight (or for at least 3 to 4 hours) before baking. When ready to bake, position a rack in the center of the oven, and heat the oven to 350 degrees F.

➡ Drop the dough in ¼-cup balls onto a baking sheet, spacing them about 2 inches apart. Flatten each ball slightly with the palm of your hand.

➡ Bake for 20 to 22 minutes, or until the cookies are golden brown on the edges and slightly soft in the center. Let the cookies cool on the baking sheet on a wire rack for 15 to 20 minutes, or until they are cool enough to remove with a spatula. Then transfer the cookies to the wire rack to cool completely, or enjoy them warm.

➡ The cookies can be stored in an airtight container at room temperature for up to 2 days. The unbaked dough may be stored in an airtight container in the refrigerator for up to 1 week.

OATMEAL RAISIN COOKIES

1 cup (2 sticks/228 grams) unsalted butter, at room temperature

¾ cup (150 grams) granulated sugar

1 cup (220 grams) packed light brown sugar

2 eggs

1¾ cups (245 grams) unbleached all-purpose flour

1¾ cups (175 grams) old-fashioned rolled oats (not instant or quick cooking)

1 teaspoon baking soda

1 teaspoon kosher salt

¼ teaspoon freshly grated nutmeg

¼ teaspoon ground cinnamon

1½ cups (240 grams) raisins

MAKES ABOUT 24 COOKIES

Professional pastry chefs often overlook simple recipes. We are all out to prove that we can create magic out of butter, sugar, flour, and eggs—which we can! But sometimes we are so determined to develop intricate methods and combine esoteric ingredients to prove our prowess that we go overboard. When it comes to oatmeal raisin cookies, I've found that the best recipe is the one that allows the pure and delicious flavor of nutty oats and plump raisins to shine through. This recipe is as basic as it gets. It has a slight hint of spice from freshly grated nutmeg (this is crucial—buy a whole nutmeg, use a grater, and let the smell transport you to sipping eggnog by a roaring fire) and a little bit of ground cinnamon. But mostly it is an addictive mix of chewy cookie and sweet raisins.

➡ Using a stand mixer fitted with the paddle attachment (or a handheld mixer or wooden spoon), cream together the butter, granulated sugar, and brown sugar on medium speed for about 5 minutes, or until the mixture is light and fluffy. (This step will take 10 minutes if using a handheld mixer or a spoon.) Stop the mixer a few times and use a rubber spatula to scrape the sides and bottom of the bowl and the paddle to release any clinging butter or sugar. Beat in the eggs on medium speed for 2 to 3 minutes, or until thoroughly combined. Scrape the bowl and the paddle again to make sure the eggs are thoroughly incorporated.

➡ In a medium bowl, stir together the flour, oats, baking soda, salt, nutmeg, and cinnamon. Add the raisins and toss to combine. On low speed (or with the wooden spoon), slowly add the flour mixture to the butter-sugar mixture and then mix just until the flour mixture is totally incorporated and the dough is evenly mixed.

➡ For the best results, scrape the dough into an airtight container and let it rest in the refrigerator overnight (or for at least 3 to 4 hours) before baking. When ready to bake, position a rack in the center of the oven, and heat the oven to 350 degrees F.

➡ Drop the dough in ¼-cup balls onto a baking sheet, spacing them about 2 inches apart. Flatten each ball slightly with the palm of your hand.

➡ Bake for 20 to 22 minutes, or until the cookies are golden brown on the edges and slightly soft in the center. Be careful not to overbake. Soft, chewy centers make these cookies irresistible. Let cool on the baking sheet on a wire rack for 5 to 10 minutes, then transfer the cookies to the rack to cool completely.

➡ The cookies can be stored in an airtight container at room temperature for up to 3 days. The unbaked dough can be stored in an airtight container in the refrigerator for up to 1 week.

PEANUT BUTTER COOKIES

1 cup (2 sticks/228 grams) unsalted butter, at room temperature

1 cup (200 grams) granulated sugar

1 cup (220 grams) packed light brown sugar

2 eggs

1 teaspoon vanilla extract

1¾ cups (454 grams) chunky peanut butter

2⅔ cups (375 grams) unbleached all-purpose flour

1 teaspoon baking soda

1 teaspoon kosher salt

MAKES ABOUT 24 COOKIES

When I was midway through fourth grade, my dad was transferred from Texas to Oklahoma, and since my parents didn't want to pull my brother and me out of school, my mom, my brother, and I stayed behind until the school year ended. I had recently started reading about food and nutrition and was concerned about what my dad would do for breakfast, lunch, and dinner without my mom. I'd read that peanut butter was a great source of protein, and I was soon overcome with worry that Dad wouldn't get enough protein on his own. So I begged him to eat peanut butter on his toast for breakfast every day and have a peanut butter cookie for his snack every afternoon. I can only guess that when your nine-year-old daughter is pleading with you, your only option is to do what she says. He faithfully ate peanut butter toast every morning and took a peanut butter cookie to work every day. I wish I'd had this recipe back then to make for him. Peanut butter doesn't need much help to be delicious. These simple cookies have just the right amount of sugar and salt to bring out the best in peanut butter. They are meant to be soft and chewy, so bake them just until they are light golden brown along the edges and still pale in the center. I suggest doing what Dad still does: have one every day, in the name of good nutrition.

→ Using a stand mixer fitted with the paddle attachment (or a handheld mixer or a wooden spoon), cream together the butter, granulated sugar, and brown sugar on medium speed for about 5 minutes, or until the mixture is light and fluffy. (This step will take about 10 minutes if using a handheld mixer or a spoon.) Stop the mixer a few times and use a rubber spatula to scrape the sides and bottom of the bowl and the paddle to release any clinging butter and sugar. Beat in the eggs and vanilla on medium speed for 2 to 3 minutes, or until thoroughly combined. Scrape the bowl and paddle again to make sure the eggs are thoroughly incorporated. On medium-low speed, beat in the peanut butter for another 2 minutes, or until thoroughly combined.

In a medium bowl, stir together the flour, baking soda, and salt until well mixed. On low speed (or with the wooden spoon), slowly add the flour mixture to the butter-sugar mixture and then mix just until the dry ingredients are totally incorporated and the dough is evenly mixed.

For the best results, scrape the dough into an airtight container and let it rest in the refrigerator overnight (or for at least 3 to 4 hours) before baking. When you are ready to bake, position a rack in the center of the oven, and heat the oven to 350 degrees F.

Drop the dough in ¼-cup balls onto a baking sheet, spacing them about 2 inches apart. Flatten each ball slightly with the palm of your hand. Use a fork to create the traditional crisscross pattern on the top of each cookie.

Bake for 18 to 20 minutes, or until the cookies are golden brown on the edges and still pale and slightly soft in the center. Let cool on the baking sheet on a wire rack for 5 to 10 minutes, then transfer the cookies to the rack to cool completely.

The cookies can be stored in an airtight container at room temperature for up to 3 days. The unbaked dough can be stored in an airtight container in the refrigerator for up to 1 week.

Baker's Bite

If all of the cookies won't fit on a single baking sheet, drop the remaining cookies onto a second baking sheet and bake them when the first sheet is finished. If you have only one baking sheet, bake the first batch and then cool the baking sheet by running it under cold water before loading it with the second batch.

GINGER MOLASSES COOKIES

¾ cup (1½ sticks/170 grams) unsalted butter, melted and cooled to the touch

1 cup (220 grams) packed light brown sugar

¼ cup (80 grams) unsulphured dark molasses

1 egg

2 cups (280 grams) unbleached all-purpose flour

1 teaspoon baking soda

1 teaspoon ground ginger

½ teaspoon ground cinnamon

½ teaspoon kosher salt

¼ teaspoon ground cloves

Granulated sugar for coating

MAKES ABOUT 16 COOKIES

Not long ago, one of my bakers said to me, "You don't like spices, do you?" We were talking about our favorite gingerbread and spice cake recipes, and I hastened to correct her, because I absolutely love spices in baking. Who can resist the charms of spicy ginger, warm cinnamon, sharp mace, or festive nutmeg? What I don't like is when baked goods are smothered in spices to the point of nonrecognition. Is this apple pie I'm eating, or is it cinnamon pie laced with apples? Is this a warm piece of buttery gingerbread, or a hunk of ground ginger in cake form? It is true that when I'm working on a recipe I often reduce the amount of spice in it because I find subtlety is key to the best results. I like to let the spices play modestly in the background doing what they do best: making baked goods irresistible. These cookies have just enough ginger, cinnamon, and clove to be full of flavor—and to be spice cookies, for sure—but you'll notice that you can taste the butter, sugar, and warm spices in harmony, instead of being hit in the face with spice. It's one of the easiest cookies to put together, too.

➡ Using a stand mixer fitted with the paddle attachment (or a handheld mixer or a wooden spoon), mix together the butter, brown sugar, molasses, and egg on low speed for about 20 seconds, or until well combined.

➡ In a medium bowl, stir together the flour, baking soda, ginger, cinnamon, salt, and cloves until well mixed. Add the flour mixture to the butter-sugar mixture and stir just until the flour mixture is totally incorporated and the dough is evenly mixed.

⇒ For the best results, scrape the dough into an airtight container and let it rest in the refrigerator overnight (or for at least 3 to 4 hours) before baking. When you are ready to bake, position a rack in the center of the oven, and heat the oven to 350 degrees F.

⇒ Place some granulated sugar in a small bowl. One at a time, scoop out ¼-cup balls of the dough, place them in the sugar, and roll gently in the sugar to coat on all sides. Place the coated balls on a baking sheet, spacing them about 2 inches apart.

⇒ Bake for 16 to 18 minutes, or until the cookies are crackly on top and just barely firm to the touch. Let cool on the baking sheet on a wire rack for 5 to 10 minutes, then transfer the cookies to the rack to cool completely.

⇒ The cookies can be stored in an airtight container at room temperature for up to 3 days. The unbaked dough can be stored in an airtight container in the refrigerator for up to 1 week.

CORNMEAL-LIME COOKIES

1 cup (2 sticks/228 grams) unsalted butter, at room temperature

¾ cup plus 2 tablespoons (175 grams) granulated sugar

2 tablespoons finely grated lime zest (about 4 limes)

2 eggs

1 teaspoon vanilla extract

2 cups (280 grams) unbleached all-purpose flour

½ cup (100 grams) medium-coarse yellow cornmeal

2 teaspoons baking powder

½ teaspoon kosher salt

LIME GLAZE

1 cup (140 grams) confectioners' sugar

2 teaspoons water

2 tablespoons fresh lime juice (1 to 1½ limes)

1½ teaspoons finely grated lime zest (about 1 lime)

MAKES 14 TO 16 COOKIES

A question commonly asked of professional pastry chefs is, "Where do you get your ideas?" I assume I'm not unlike others in that my response is "Everywhere!" I'm always on the lookout for unexpected flavor combinations, a beautifully presented pastry, or an enticing description of a cake. Books, magazines, movies, television shows, and restaurants all get my mind racing. And sometimes it's as simple as a visit to another bakery and a taste of something new to me that makes me want to rush home to see if I can replicate it. That's how this cookie came to me. I picked up a cornmeal-lime cookie at my favorite bakery in New York City, Amy's Breads, along with about a dozen other treats, and that's the one I went back for the next day. It's wonderfully straightforward: rustic and buttery, with a fresh hit of lime and the appealing crunch of cornmeal. I loved it at first bite, and I knew I had to come up with a version of it for Flour. Make sure you bake the cookies until the tops are just firm to the touch and no longer, so the centers stay soft and almost cakelike. The tart lime glaze adds an addictive zing.

➡ Position a rack in the center of the oven, and heat the oven to 350 degrees F.

➡ Using a stand mixer fitted with the paddle attachment (or a handheld mixer or a wooden spoon), cream together the butter and granulated sugar on medium speed for about 5 minutes, or until light and fluffy. (This step will take 10 minutes if using a handheld mixer or a spoon.) Stop the mixer a few times and use a rubber spatula to scrape the sides and bottom of the bowl and the paddle to release any clinging butter or sugar. Add the lime zest and beat on medium speed for about 1 minute to release the lime flavor. Add the eggs and vanilla and continue to beat on medium speed for 2 to 3 minutes, or until thoroughly combined. Scrape the bowl and the paddle again to make sure the eggs are thoroughly incorporated.

⇒ In a small bowl, stir together the flour, cornmeal, baking powder, and salt. On low speed (or with the wooden spoon), slowly add the flour mixture to the butter-sugar mixture and then mix until the flour is completely incorporated and the dough is evenly mixed.

⇒ Drop the dough in scant ¼-cup balls onto a baking sheet, spacing them about 2 inches apart. Flatten each ball slightly with the palm of your hand.

⇒ Bake for about 25 minutes, or until the cookies are pale brown on the edges, still pale in the center, and just firm to the touch in the center. Be careful not to overbake the cookies and let the tops brown. Let cool on the baking sheet on a wire rack for 15 to 20 minutes, then transfer to the rack to cool to room temperature or just a bit warmer before glazing. (If you try to glaze the cookies while they are still hot, the glaze will run off.)

⇒ To make the glaze: While the cookies are cooling, in a small bowl, whisk together the confectioners' sugar, water, lime juice, and lime zest until smooth. You should have about ½ cup. (The glaze can be made up to 1 week ahead and stored in an airtight container at room temperature.)

⇒ Brush the cookies with a thin layer of the glaze, then allow the glaze to set for about 10 minutes before serving or storing.

⇒ The cookies can be stored in an airtight container at room temperature for up to 3 days. The unbaked dough can be stored in an airtight container in the refrigerator for up to 1 week.

SNICKERDOODLES

1 cup (2 sticks/228 grams) unsalted butter, at room temperature

1½ cups (300 grams) sugar, plus ½ cup (100 grams) for coating

2 eggs

2½ cups (350 grams) unbleached all-purpose flour

1 teaspoon baking soda

¼ teaspoon kosher salt

2 teaspoons cream of tartar

¼ cup (30 grams) ground cinnamon

MAKES ABOUT 24 COOKIES

Although I didn't eat many sweets when I was growing up, that didn't keep me from paging through cookbooks at the bookstore and obsessing about all of the desserts I was missing out on. This is one of the recipes that completely captivated me when I was a little girl. These simple sugar cookies were described in one cookbook as being dipped in cinnamon sugar and then baked. Once baked, the recipe heading explained, the cinnamon sugar created a crackly pattern on the cookies, and if you looked closely, you would be able to make out a face or a dog or a house pattern—a sort of man-in-the-moon effect. I was fascinated by the idea of random pictures appearing on cookies, and dreamed about making them. Their look is what initially intrigued me, but what I've grown to appreciate about them is their simplicity and pure deliciousness. Snickerdoodles are what home-baking nostalgia is all about. A fragrant sugar cookie with a crunchy cinnamon exterior will be a hit at any bake sale, in any lunch box, or, as in my household, late at night when the munchies hit.

➡ Using a stand mixer fitted with the paddle attachment (or a handheld mixer or a wooden spoon), cream together the butter and 1½ cups sugar on medium speed for about 5 minutes, or until the mixture is light and fluffy. (This step will take about 10 minutes if using a handheld mixer or a spoon.) Stop the mixer a few times and use a rubber spatula to scrape the sides and bottom of the bowl and the paddle to release any clinging butter or sugar. Beat in the eggs on medium speed for 2 to 3 minutes, or until thoroughly combined. Scrape the bowl and paddle again to make sure the eggs are thoroughly incorporated.

➡ In a medium bowl, sift together the flour, baking soda, salt, and cream of tartar. On low speed (or with the wooden spoon), slowly blend the flour mixture into the butter-sugar mixture and then mix just until the flour is totally incorporated and the dough is evenly mixed.

➡ For the best results, scrape the dough into an airtight container and let it rest in the refrigerator overnight (or for at least 3 to 4 hours) before baking. When ready to bake, position a rack in the center of the oven and heat the oven to 350 degrees F.

➡ In a small bowl, mix together the remaining ½ cup sugar and the cinnamon. Drop the dough by rounded tablespoons into the cinnamon-sugar mixture and roll to coat. Place the coated balls of dough on a baking sheet, spacing them about 3 inches apart. Flatten each ball slightly with the palm of your hand.

➡ Bake for 15 to 18 minutes, or until the cookies are golden brown on the edges and slightly soft in the center. Let cool on the baking sheet on a wire rack for 5 to 10 minutes, then transfer the cookies to the rack to cool completely.

➡ The cookies can be stored in an airtight container at room temperature up to 3 days. The unbaked dough may be stored in an airtight container in the refrigerator for up to 1 week.

COCONUT MACAROONS

PASTRY CREAM

½ cup (120 grams) milk

¼ cup (50 grams) sugar

2 tablespoons cake flour

Pinch of kosher salt

2 egg yolks

½ teaspoon vanilla extract

Two 14-ounce (400-gram) bags
sweetened shredded coconut

6 egg whites

1 cup (200 grams) sugar

Pinch of kosher salt

MAKES ABOUT 24 COOKIES

Chewy, sweet, soft, crispy—this coconut macaroon combines all of these delectable descriptors in one small package. What you get depends on where you bite into the cookie. These macaroons are fabulously easy to put together, too. You make a small batch of pastry cream, mix it with coconut, egg whites, and sugar, and you're done. When baked, the edges become crispy and caramelized while the centers stay soft. These are a perennial favorite at Flour—and at my house. I bring one home almost every other day for Christopher. One of our regular customers suggested a simple variation: adding chocolate chips. (Thanks, Doe!) That version is just as popular, and I've included the simple instructions for doing that here as well.

➡ To make the pastry cream: In a small saucepan, scald the milk over medium-high heat (bubbles start to form around the edge of the pan, but the milk is not boiling). While the milk is heating, in a small bowl, stir together the sugar, flour, and salt. (Mixing the flour with the sugar will prevent the flour from clumping when you add it to the egg yolks.) In a medium bowl, whisk the egg yolks until blended, then slowly whisk in the flour mixture. The mixture will be thick and pasty.

➡ Remove the milk from the heat and slowly add it to the egg-flour mixture, a little at a time, whisking constantly. When all of the milk has been incorporated, return the contents of the bowl to the saucepan and place over medium heat. Whisk continuously and vigorously for about 1 minute, or until the mixture thickens and comes to a boil. At first, the mixture will be very frothy and liquid; as it cooks longer, it will slowly start to thicken until the frothy bubbles disappear and it becomes more viscous. Remove from the heat and stir in the vanilla. Cover with plastic wrap, placing it directly on the surface of the cream, and let cool completely.

➡ Position a rack in the center of the oven, and heat the oven to 350 degrees F. Line a baking sheet with parchment paper or butter it.

In a large bowl, combine the coconut, egg whites, sugar, salt, and pastry cream. Stir with a wooden spoon until well combined. (The dough can be made up to 5 days in advance and stored in an airtight container in the refrigerator.)

Using a ¼-cup dry-measuring cup or large spoon, scoop the dough in rounded mounds onto the prepared baking sheet.

Bake for 25 to 35 minutes, or until the cookies are golden brown all over. Let cool on the baking sheet on a wire rack for at least 20 minutes, then transfer the cookies to the rack to cool completely.

The macaroons can be stored in an airtight container at room temperature for up to 3 days.

Same recipe, different flavors

DOE'S CHOCOLATE CHIP MACAROONS: Add 1 cup (165 grams) semisweet chocolate chips to the dough and mix until evenly distributed. Scoop and bake as directed.

HOLIDAY SUGAR COOKIES

1 cup (2 sticks/228 grams) unsalted butter, at room temperature

1½ cups (300 grams) granulated sugar

2 eggs

1 tablespoon vanilla extract

3 cups (420 grams) unbleached all-purpose flour

2½ teaspoons baking powder

½ teaspoon kosher salt

FROSTING

3¼ cups (1-pound box/454 grams) confectioners' sugar

5 to 6 tablespoons (70 to 90 grams) milk

Food coloring, as desired

MAKES ABOUT TWENTY-FOUR 2½-INCH COOKIES

I've been baking holiday cookies since long before I became a pastry chef. I found a simple recipe for sugar cookies during my first year in college, and I've been using it—gradually improving it as my baking career progressed—ever since. Some years I've made so many cookies for so many people that the dough takes up an entire shelf of my refrigerator. I end up spending long hours, night after night after work, rolling out the dough, chilling it, cutting out shapes, baking the cookies, letting them cool, and decorating them. Decorating is the fun part—I customize them for the recipients, playing with Pollockesque dribbles, carefully drawn faces on gingerbread shapes, and traditional adornments like silver candy balls on Christmas trees. The whole process takes up a lot of time, but it's part of the joy of the season, and people love getting homemade cookies as a gift.

With holiday baking, always remember to relax and enjoy it. If your decorating doesn't come out perfectly, it isn't a calamity. Holiday cookies are meant to look as if they came from your home kitchen and not from some factory that cranks out hundreds of identical Santas every day. Making holiday treats at home each year encapsulates what I love about baking: handmade simple, sweet things that bring joy to others.

➡ Using a stand mixer fitted with the paddle attachment (or a handheld mixer or a wooden spoon), cream together the butter and granulated sugar on medium speed for about 5 minutes, or until the mixture is light and fluffy. (This step will take about 10 minutes if using a handheld mixer or a spoon.) Stop the mixer a few times and use a rubber spatula to scrape the sides and bottom of the bowl and the paddle to release any clinging butter or sugar. Beat in the eggs and vanilla on medium speed for 2 to 3 minutes, or until thoroughly combined. Scrape the bowl and the paddle again to make sure the eggs are thoroughly incorporated.

➡ In a medium bowl, stir together the flour, baking powder, and salt until well mixed. On low speed (or with the wooden spoon), slowly blend the flour mixture into the butter-sugar mixture and then mix just until the flour mixture is totally incorporated and the dough is evenly mixed.

➡ Scrape the dough onto a sheet of plastic wrap, and wrap the dough in the plastic wrap, pressing down to form a disk about 8 inches in diameter and 1 inch thick. Refrigerate the dough for about 1 hour, or until it firms up enough to roll out. (At this point, the dough can be stored in the refrigerator for up to 5 days or in the freezer for up to 1 month. If the dough is frozen, thaw it overnight in the refrigerator. Let the dough sit at room temperature for about 1 hour before using, then proceed as directed.)

➡ Position a rack in the center of the oven, and heat the oven to 350 degrees F.

➡ Lightly flour a work surface, place the dough disk on the surface, and lightly flour the dough. Roll out about ¼ inch thick. Keep both the work surface and the dough floured to prevent sticking. If the dough begins to stick, sprinkle on a little more flour and keep rolling. Using a cookie cutter about 2½ inches in diameter, cut out as many cookies as possible. Place them on a baking sheet, spacing them about 2 inches apart. Gather up the scraps, reroll, and cut out more cookies. If the dough is soft and warm and difficult to roll, wrap the scraps in plastic wrap and refrigerate until firm enough to roll.

➡ Bake for 15 to 17 minutes, or until the cookies are golden brown on the edges and pale to light brown in the centers. Let the cookies cool on the baking sheet on a wire rack for about 30 minutes, or until they are cool enough to remove with a spatula. Then transfer to the wire rack to cool completely.

➡ To make the frosting: While the cookies are cooling, place the confectioners' sugar in a medium bowl and whisk in enough of the milk to make a stiff, thick icing. (If it is too thin, it will run off the cookies, so err on the stiffer side. You can always add more milk.) Divide the frosting among as many small bowls as necessary to use the food coloring to tint each batch as you like. (The plain frosting can be stored in an airtight container at room temperature for up to 1 day. Use a spoon to loosen it if it stiffens at the bottom of the container, then color as desired.)

➡ Spoon each colored frosting into a pastry bag fitted with a ¼- to ⅛-inch round tip (see page 15), or place the frostings in zippered plastic bags, and snip off a tiny corner from each bag. Decorate the cookies as desired. Let the frosting dry completely, about 8 hours, before stacking the cookies for storage.

➡ The cookies can be stored in an airtight container at room temperature for up to 4 days.

MERINGUE CLOUDS

8 egg whites

1 cup (200 grams) granulated sugar

1 cup (140 grams) confectioners' sugar

½ teaspoon kosher salt

1 cup (100 grams) sliced almonds, toasted

MAKES 8 LARGE COOKIES

I learned how to make meringue cookies while working at Bentonwood Bakery, my first baking job. We made them every other week (they keep beautifully in airtight containers), and I appreciated their simplicity in both taste and procedure. We baked them overnight in a very slow oven until they were crisp through and through. When I left Bentonwood, with all the other baking I was doing and techniques I was learning, I forgot about meringues. Years later, my now-husband, Christopher, and I spent a few weeks in Paris, and we made a point of stopping in every patisserie we passed. I never left without a beautifully packaged box of at least half a dozen assorted pastries. I often chose *rochers*, grand, poufy meringues that seemed unlike anything I had ever made. They were humongous, light as a feather, filled with almonds, and still slightly chewy inside. With a bite, they shattered into pieces. As soon we got back to Boston, I tried to re-create them. It turns out I had been making them all along. It just took a little less time in the oven to keep the meringues soft and chewy. Not everyone prefers them this way; many people like them baked through and crispy, as we made them at Bentonwood. Try them both ways to see which style you like better.

⇒ Position a rack in the center of the oven, and heat the oven to 175 degrees F. Line a baking sheet with parchment paper.

⇒ Using a stand mixer fitted with the whip attachment (or a handheld mixer), beat the egg whites on medium speed for 3 to 4 minutes, or until soft peaks form. (This step will take 6 to 8 minutes if using a handheld mixer.) The whites will start to froth and turn into bubbles, and eventually the yellowy viscous part will disappear. Keep whipping until you can see the tines of the whip leaving a slight trail in the whites. To test for the soft-peak stage, stop the mixer and lift the whip out of the whites; the whites should peak and then droop.

On medium speed, add the granulated sugar in three equal additions, mixing for 1 minute after each addition. When all of the granulated sugar has been incorporated into the egg whites, increase the speed to medium-high and beat for about 30 seconds longer.

In a small bowl, sift together the confectioners' sugar and salt. Using a rubber spatula, fold the confectioners' sugar mixture into the beaten egg whites. Then, fold in the almonds, reserving 2 tablespoons for garnish.

Use a large spoon to make baseball-size billowing mounds of meringue on the prepared baking sheet, spacing them 2 to 3 inches apart. You should have 8 mounds. Sprinkle the reserved almonds evenly on top of the meringues.

Bake for about 3 hours, or until the meringues are firm to the touch and you can remove them easily from the baking sheet without them falling apart. For meringues with a soft, chewy center, remove them from the oven at this point and let them cool. For fully crisped meringues, turn off the oven and leave the meringues in the closed oven for at least 6 hours or up to 12 hours.

The meringues can be stored in an airtight container at room temperature for up to 1 week.

Same recipe, different flavors

CHOCOLATE MERINGUE CLOUDS: Replace the almonds with 3½ ounces (100 grams) bittersweet chocolate (62 to 70 percent cacao), finely chopped (about ½ cup). Reserve about 3 tablespoons for garnish and fold the rest into the batter as directed.

ALMOND AND ANISE BISCOTTI

3 eggs

1 cup (200 grams) sugar

1 teaspoon vanilla extract

1 teaspoon anise seeds

2¼ cups (315 grams) unbleached all-purpose flour

1 teaspoon baking powder

¼ teaspoon kosher salt

1½ cups (240 grams) whole natural almonds, toasted

MAKES ABOUT 15 BISCOTTI

Italian biscotti are misunderstood cookies. *Biscotti* means "twice-cooked" in Italian, and it refers to baking the cookie dough once until it is baked through, slicing it, and then baking it again until the slices are hard and dry. The rock-hard cookies are meant to be eaten dipped in espresso or wine to soften them and infuse them with flavor (hence the traditional long shape for easy dipping). In the United States, this Italian classic has been turned into an American-style cookie. The recipes kicking around today often include butter, which admittedly adds flavor and makes the cookie easier to eat without dipping, but which also removes it from its origins. I like butter, but this is one recipe where its presence makes me cringe. So, welcome back to the original. This is a traditional recipe that includes no fat other than what is in the egg yolks. I've lightened it slightly by whipping together the eggs and sugar until airy and fluffy, to yield a more porous batter. That step produces a cookie that is a bit easier to bite into than the true original recipe, but without the sacrilegious addition of butter.

⇒ Position a rack in the center of the oven, and heat the oven to 350 degrees F. Line a baking sheet with parchment paper.

⇒ Using a stand mixer fitted with the whip attachment (or a handheld mixer), beat together the eggs, sugar, and vanilla on medium-high speed for 5 to 6 minutes, or until the mixture is light and thick and lemon colored. (This step will take 10 to 12 minutes if using a handheld mixer.) Meanwhile, place the anise seeds on a cutting board, sprinkle with a few drops of water, and chop finely. (The water will help keep the anise seeds from flying all over the place while you chop.) When the egg mixture is ready, add the anise seeds and whip for a few more seconds to distribute evenly.

⇒ In a large bowl, stir together the flour, baking powder, salt, and almonds. Pour the egg mixture into the flour mixture and, using a wooden spoon, stir for 2 to 3 minutes, or until thoroughly combined. You may need to switch to mixing the dough with your hands because it will be fairly stiff.

➡ Turn out the dough directly onto the prepared baking sheet. Pat it into a log roughly 5 inches wide, 12 inches long, and 1 inch high. It is helpful to dampen your hands with water to prevent them from sticking to the batter as you shape it.

➡ Bake for 50 to 60 minutes, or until the log is completely browned and firm. To test if it is ready, press a fingertip firmly into the middle; it should not give at all. Let the log cool on the baking sheet for about 30 minutes, or until it is cool enough to handle comfortably. Turn down the oven to 200 degrees F.

➡ Transfer the log to a cutting board. Using a serrated knife, slice the log on the diagonal into ½-inch-wide biscotti. You should get about 15 biscotti. (At this point, the biscotti can be tightly wrapped in plastic wrap and stored in the freezer for up to 1 month, then baked the second time directly from the freezer.)

➡ Return the biscotti, a cut side down, to the baking sheet and bake for 3 to 4 hours, or until the biscotti are completely baked through. To test for doneness, poke at the middle of one of the cookies; it should be rock hard. Let cool completely on the baking sheet on a wire rack.

➡ The biscotti can be stored in an airtight container at room temperature for up to 2 weeks.

Baker's Bite

Be sure to toast the almonds until they are golden brown through and through. It makes a real difference in the final taste of the biscotti. To test if the almonds are well toasted, bite into one and check the interior to make sure it is golden brown.

ALMOND MACAROONS
WITH BITTERSWEET CHOCOLATE GANACHE

3¼ cups (520 grams) blanched whole almonds

2⅔ cups (540 grams) sugar

6 egg whites

2 teaspoons almond extract

¼ teaspoon kosher salt

BITTERSWEET CHOCOLATE GANACHE

8 ounces (228 grams) bittersweet chocolate (62 to 70 percent cacao), chopped

1 cup (240 grams) heavy cream

MAKES ABOUT 20 COOKIE SANDWICHES

Part of the fun of being a pastry chef and changing jobs is learning a slew of new recipes at your latest restaurant or bakery. Although you don't always like every single one, you usually discover a few winners in the bunch. When I took the job as pastry chef at Mistral in Boston, the chef wanted me to change and improve the dessert menu, but he also had some favorites that he didn't want me to mess with. These sandwich cookies—sweet, chewy, almond treats with a shmear of chocolate holding them together—were one of the untouchables. When I left Mistral to open Flour, I thought often of these addictive little cookies. The original recipe called for almond paste, an ingredient I try to avoid because it feels somewhat like cheating to me. Why buy premade almond paste when you can easily make your own with a food processor? It is fresher, cheaper, and it tastes better. So I replaced the commercial almond paste with a homemade recipe, and reduced the amount of sugar to make the cookies less achingly sweet. The recipe makes a big batch, but I doubt that you'll complain about that once you taste them.

⇒ Position a rack in the center of the oven, and heat the oven to 350 degrees F. Line a baking sheet with parchment paper.

⇒ In a food processor, pulse the almonds until ground to a fine powder. (Stop grinding once they are powdery; if you continue, they will become a paste.) Remove about 1 cup of the ground almonds from the food processor and set aside. Add the sugar to the almonds left in the food processor and process for 10 to 15 seconds, or until the sugar is completely incorporated. Add the egg whites and continue processing for about 30 seconds, or until well combined.

⇒ Transfer the almond paste to a medium bowl, and fold in the reserved ground almonds. Fold in the almond extract and salt.

⇒ Use your hands (dampen them with cold water to keep the batter from sticking to them) or a small spoon to make walnut-size rounds of batter on the prepared baking sheet, spacing them about 2 inches apart. You should have about 40.

(continued)

⇒ Bake for 20 to 25 minutes, or until the cookies are light golden brown around the edges. Let cool completely on the baking sheet on a wire rack.

⇒ To make the ganache: While the cookies are cooling, place the chocolate in a medium heat-proof bowl. In a small saucepan, scald the cream over medium-high heat (bubbles start to form around the edge of the pan, but the cream is not boiling). Pour the hot cream over the chocolate and let it sit for 30 seconds, then slowly whisk together the chocolate and cream until the chocolate is completely melted and the mixture is smooth. Let cool to room temperature (or cooler in the refrigerator) at least 1 hour until the ganache is thick and spreadable. You should have about 1½ cups. (The ganache can be made ahead and stored in an airtight container in the refrigerator for up to 2 weeks.)

⇒ Remove the cookies from the parchment. Spread about 1 tablespoon of the ganache on the flat side of one cookie. Top with a second cookie, flat-side down. Repeat until all of the cookies are sandwiched with ganache. You may have a little ganache left over.

⇒ The cookies can be stored in an airtight container at room temperature for up to 3 days.

BROWN BUTTER–
CRISPY RICE TREATS

1 cup (2 sticks/228 grams) unsalted butter

½ vanilla bean, split lengthwise

Two 10-ounce (280-gram) bags marshmallows

½ teaspoon kosher salt

9 cups (240 grams) crispy rice cereal

MAKES 12 BARS

Baking isn't a game, but if it were, vanilla would be my ace in the hole. Many of my recipes feature vanilla flavoring in some form or another, because I love the mellow essence it brings to everything it meets. Adding real vanilla bean to well-loved childhood treats, like these bars, elevates them from nostalgic snacks to divine desserts. I also brown the butter, which renders a deeper, richer flavor than plain butter. I dreamed about having these on the Flour menu from the beginning, but somehow we never got around to making them part of our routine. Finally, Nicole, our head pastry chef, surprised me one day with a large pan of them, and we've never looked back. They have quickly become a signature item.

⇒ Butter a 9-by-13-inch baking pan, coat it with nonstick cooking spray, or line it with parchment paper.

⇒ In a large saucepan, melt the butter over low heat. As the butter melts, use the tip of a knife to scrape the seeds from the vanilla bean directly into the butter. (Reserve the pod for another use. I suggest throwing it into a container of sugar to make vanilla sugar; see page 29.)

⇒ Once the butter has melted, it will start to bubble and crackle. If you lean in and listen, it will sound like an audience of people politely clapping their hands (in anticipation of these treats!). Watch the butter carefully and you will see it slowly browning. As soon as the bubbling subsides, after about 5 minutes, the butter will be fully browned and you will need to add the marshmallows. (Be attentive, because if you don't add the marshmallows right away, the butter may burn.) Add the marshmallows and salt and stir constantly over low heat until the marshmallows are completely melted and the vanilla seeds are evenly distributed.

⇒ Remove the pan from the heat, add the cereal, and mix well with a wooden spoon to coat evenly. Turn the mixture into the prepared pan and pat into an even layer. Let cool for about 1 hour, or to room temperature, then cut into 12 pieces.

⇒ These treats can be stored in an airtight container at room temperature for up to 2 days.

HOMEMADE OREOS

1 cup (2 sticks/228 grams) unsalted butter, melted and cooled slightly

¾ cup (150 grams) granulated sugar

1 teaspoon vanilla extract

1 cup (200 grams) semisweet chocolate chips, melted and cooled slightly

1 egg

1½ cups (210 grams) unbleached all-purpose flour

¾ cup (90 grams) Dutch-processed cocoa powder

1 teaspoon kosher salt

½ teaspoon baking soda

VANILLA CREAM FILLING

½ cup (1 stick/114 grams) unsalted butter, softened

1⅔ cups (230 grams) confectioners' sugar

1 teaspoon vanilla extract

1 tablespoon milk

Pinch of kosher salt

MAKES 16 TO 18 SANDWICH COOKIES

Oreos used to be a mystery to me. The debates about splitting them and eating the filling first, eating them whole, or dunking them—none of it made any sense. My mom never bought commercial sweets, and she certainly never bought the almost-black cookies that looked burnt to her. For the same reason, they never appealed to me either— until one day when I finally bit into one at a friend's house. Wow. I tried to convince my mom that they were fantastic and that we really, really needed to buy them for after-school snacking. She refused, only saying that they looked too black to be good. Years later, I created my own version of an Oreo, made with real chocolate and bittersweet cocoa and filled with a creamy mixture of sugar, butter, and a little vanilla. It's a decidedly grown-up version of the treat I fleetingly remember. And they are delicious. Flour customers go crazy for them. At first, they expect a very sweet, vaguely chocolaty treat. Instead, they get an intense, rich chocolate cookie with a buttery vanilla cream filling— an Oreo like no other. Even Mom approves. When she visits, she always requests them for the care package I send home with her.

⇒ In a medium bowl, whisk together the butter and granulated sugar until well combined. Whisk in the vanilla and chocolate. Add the egg and whisk until thoroughly incorporated.

⇒ In another medium bowl, stir together the flour, cocoa powder, salt, and baking soda until well mixed. Using a wooden spoon, stir the flour mixture into the chocolate mixture. The dough will start to seem too floury, and you will find it easiest to switch to mixing it with your hands until it comes together. It will have the consistency of Play-Doh. Let the dough sit at room temperature for about 1 hour to firm up.

⇒ Transfer the dough to a 15-inch square sheet of parchment or waxed paper. Using your hands, shape the dough into a rough log about 10 inches long and 2½ inches in diameter. Place the log at the edge of the sheet of parchment paper, and roll the parchment around the log. With the log fully encased in parchment, roll it into a smoother log, keeping it at 2½ inches in diameter. Refrigerate for at least 2 hours, or until firm. The log may settle and sink a bit in the fridge, so reroll it every 15 minutes or so to maintain

(continued)

a nice round log. (At this point, the dough log can be well wrapped in plastic wrap and stored in the refrigerator for up to 1 week or in the freezer for up to 1 month. If the dough is frozen, thaw it overnight in the refrigerator before proceeding.)

➡ Position a rack in the center of the oven, and heat the oven to 325 degrees F. Butter a baking sheet or line it with parchment paper.

➡ Cut the dough log into ¼-inch-thick slices. Place the slices about 1 inch apart on the prepared baking sheet.

➡ Bake for 20 to 25 minutes, or until the cookies are firm to the touch. Check them frequently after 16 or 17 minutes, poking them in the middle. As soon as they feel firm to the touch, remove them from the oven. You can't judge by color because they start out black. Let cool on the baking sheet to warm or room temperature. They don't have to cool completely before you fill them, but you can't fill them while they are hot.

➡ To make the filling: While the cookies are cooling, using a stand mixer fitted with the paddle attachment (or a handheld mixer), beat the butter on low speed for about 30 seconds, or until completely smooth and soft. Add the confectioners' sugar and vanilla and beat until the mixture is perfectly smooth. Add the milk and salt and again beat until smooth. It will look like white spackle and feel about the same—like putty. You can also mix this filling by hand. Make sure the butter is very soft, and use your hands to mix and knead the sugar into the butter. You should have about 1 cup. (The filling can be stored in an airtight container at room temperature for up to 2 days or in the refrigerator for up to 2 weeks. Bring to room temperature before using.)

➡ Scoop about 1 rounded tablespoon of the filling onto the bottom of one cookie. Top with a second cookie, bottom-side down, then press the cookies together to spread the filling toward the edges. Repeat until all of the cookies are filled.

Same recipe, different flavors . . . .

Replace the Vanilla Cream Filling with Peanut Butter Cream Filling.

PEANUT BUTTER CREAM FILLING

MAKES ABOUT 1 CUP

¼ cup (½ stick/56 grams) unsalted butter, softened

¾ cup (105 grams) confectioners' sugar

½ cup (130 grams) smooth peanut butter

Pinch of kosher salt

Using a stand mixer fitted with the paddle attachment (or a handheld mixer), cream the butter on low speed for about 30 seconds, or until completely soft and smooth. Add the sugar and beat until the mixture is perfectly smooth. Add the peanut butter and salt and again beat until smooth. You can also mix this filling by hand. Make sure the butter is very soft, and use your hands to mix and knead the sugar into the butter. (The filling can be stored in an airtight container at room temperature for up to 2 days or in the refrigerator for up to 2 weeks. Bring to room temperature before using.)

HOMEMADE FIG NEWTONS

FIG JAM FILLING

2 pints (680 grams) ripe Black Mission figs (about 30 figs)

1 orange, peeled, seeded, and finely chopped

½ cup (110 grams) packed light brown sugar

1 tablespoon finely grated lemon zest (about 1 lemon)

¼ teaspoon kosher salt

1 teaspoon vanilla extract

SHORTBREAD DOUGH

1 cup (2 sticks/228 grams) unsalted butter, at room temperature

6 tablespoons (75 grams) granulated sugar

2 tablespoons confectioners' sugar

1 egg yolk

1 teaspoon vanilla extract

1 cup (140 grams) unbleached all-purpose flour

1 cup (120 grams) cake flour

½ teaspoon baking powder

½ teaspoon kosher salt

MAKES 12 COOKIES

Ah, Fig Newtons! Another typical American after-school and lunch-box treat that I was oblivious to growing up in a Chinese household, where red bean moon cakes and orange slices were our typical snack options. I knew something wasn't quite right when my friends came over after school and complained that there was nothing to eat. And no one ever wanted to trade lunch-box snacks with me. They turned up their noses at the egg tarts I toted to school and ignored the fruit platters my mom left for me in the fridge for afternoon snacking. After much pleading, Mom occasionally bought packaged cookies for my lunch so I would fit in. But I admit that I usually traded away my Fig Newtons—I wasn't a fig fan. Many years later, I ate my first fresh figs on a cooking vacation in Italy. The school was in a farmhouse that had olives, figs, and grapes growing outside as far as the eye could see. The figs were abundant, ripe, soft, and full of honey sweetness. I was amazed that this was the same fruit that was in the packaged treat I had scorned as a child. I gobbled them up day and night, and they've become one of my favorite fruits. These cookies are an homage to the luscious deliciousness of figs. Seek out the ripest—even overripe—figs you can find.

→ To make the filling: Stem the figs, cut them into quarters, and place them in a medium nonreactive saucepan. Add the orange, brown sugar, lemon zest, and salt. Place over medium heat and bring to a simmer. Reduce the heat to medium-low and simmer uncovered, stirring occasionally, for about 40 minutes, or until the figs have softened and lost their shape and the filling is jam-like. Remove from the heat, stir in the vanilla, and let cool for 1 to 2 hours, or until room temperature. (If jam is soupy, drain a bit of the excess liquid before using as a filling. The fig jam can be stored in an airtight container in the refrigerator for up to 3 days.)

→ To make the shortbread dough: Using a stand mixer fitted with the paddle attachment (or a handheld mixer or a wooden spoon), cream together the butter, granulated sugar, and confectioners' sugar on medium speed for about 5 minutes, or until the mixture is light and fluffy. (This step will take about 10 minutes if using a handheld mixer or a spoon.) Stop the mixer a few times and use

(continued)

a rubber spatula to scrape the sides and bottom of the bowl and the paddle to release any clinging butter or sugar. Beat in the egg yolk and vanilla on medium speed for 2 to 3 minutes, or until thoroughly combined. Scrape the bowl and the paddle again with a rubber spatula to make sure the egg yolk is thoroughly incorporated.

➡ In a small bowl, sift together the all-purpose flour, cake flour, baking powder, and salt. On low speed (or with the wooden spoon), slowly add the flour mixture to the butter-sugar mixture and then mix for about 15 seconds, or until the flour mixture is totally incorporated and the dough is evenly mixed. Stop the mixer and scrape the bowl again to make sure all of the flour mixture is thoroughly incorporated.

➡ Scrape the dough onto a sheet of plastic wrap, and wrap the dough entirely in the plastic wrap, pressing down to form a disk about 6 inches in diameter and 1 inch thick. Refrigerate the dough for about 30 minutes, or until it has firmed up but is still somewhat pliable. (At this point, the dough may be stored in the refrigerator for up to 5 days or in the freezer for up to 1 month. If the dough is frozen, thaw it overnight in the refrigerator. Let the dough sit at room temperature for about 20 minutes before using, then proceed as directed.)

➡ Position a rack in the center of the oven, and heat the oven to 350 degrees F.

➡ Place the dough disk on a large sheet of parchment paper. Liberally flour the dough on all surfaces, then roll out into a rectangle about 16 by 9 inches and ¼ inch thick. Don't let the dough stick to the parchment or the rolling pin. If it begins to stick, add a little more flour and continue gently rolling.

➡ Position the rectangle with a long side facing you. Spoon the cooled filling lengthwise along the center of the rectangle, in a strip about 2½ inches wide. (Try not to eat all of the jam, which, to my mind, is the hardest part of the recipe.) Lifting the edge of the parchment farthest from you, drape the top of the dough rectangle over the jam, covering the top half of it. Gently peel the parchment away from the dough. Repeat with the bottom edge of the parchment, draping the bottom of the dough over the jam. The edges of the dough rectangle should meet in the middle. Gently pinch the edges of the dough together, and then turn the rectangle over, so it is facing seam-side down. Use a pastry brush or your hands to brush any excess flour off the parchment. (At this point, the rectangle can be wrapped tightly in plastic wrap and stored in the refrigerator for up to 1 day or in the freezer for up to 2 weeks. Bake as directed directly from the refrigerator or freezer. You may need to add a few minutes to the baking time.) Lift the parchment paper with the rectangle and place together on a baking sheet.

➡ Bake for 65 to 70 minutes, or until the shortbread is entirely golden brown. A little fig juice may leak out the sides—don't let this worry you. Let cool on the baking sheet on a wire rack for at least 2 hours, or until completely cool. Using a chef's knife, cut on the diagonal into strips about 5 inches long and 1 inch wide.

➡ The cookies can be stored in an airtight container at room temperature for up to 3 days.

HOMEMADE S'MORES

MARSHMALLOW

½ cup (120 grams) water

¾ cup (150 grams) sugar

1 tablespoon light corn syrup

2 teaspoons powdered gelatin

2 egg whites

1 teaspoon vanilla extract

MILK CHOCOLATE FILLING

1 pound (454 grams) milk chocolate, chopped

¾ cup (180 grams) heavy cream

GRAHAM WAFERS

½ cup (1 stick/114 grams) unsalted butter, at room temperature

½ cup (100 grams) sugar

2 tablespoons unsulfured light or dark molasses

1 egg

2 tablespoons heavy cream

1¾ cups (290 grams) whole-wheat flour

¼ cup (35 grams) unbleached all-purpose flour

2 tablespoons medium-coarse yellow cornmeal

1 teaspoon baking powder

1 teaspoon ground cinnamon

¼ teaspoon kosher salt

Cornstarch for dusting

MAKES 16 S'MORES

People who grew up camping and spending time in the great outdoors (I was not one of them) look at me as if I'm committing some sort of blasphemy when they find out that I make s'mores in my kitchen. How, they wonder, can you improve on the perfect campfire treat? Maybe they're right, but if you're a pastry person like me and you prefer puttering around in the kitchen to roughing it in the wild, you'll fall in love with this recipe. It's actually three recipes: homemade graham crackers, homemade marshmallow, and melt-in-your-mouth milk chocolate filling. None of the recipes is difficult to make, though completing the whole recipe does require advance planning, since both the marshmallow and the chocolate filling must be made in advance. So, spread the process out over a couple days—but beware that once the s'mores are completed, they will disappear in seconds! For the best results, use a candy thermometer and a kitchen torch, both of which are widely available at cookware shops and kitchen-supply stores.

→ To make the marshmallow: Butter a 9-by-13-inch baking pan, then dust with cornstarch, tapping out the excess.

→ In a small saucepan, combine ¼ cup (60 grams) of the water, the sugar, and the corn syrup and stir gently with a small rubber spatula until the sugar is dissolved. Place over high heat, bring to a boil, and cook, without stirring, until the syrup registers 265 degrees F on a candy thermometer (the hard-ball stage; see Cooking Sugar, page 13).

→ While the sugar syrup is coming up to temperature, in a small bowl, sprinkle the gelatin over the remaining ¼ cup (60 grams) water and set aside to soften. Using a stand mixer fitted with the whip attachment (or a handheld mixer), beat the egg whites on medium speed for 3 to 4 minutes, or until they hold soft peaks.

➡ When the sugar syrup is ready, remove from the heat. On low speed, slowly drizzle the syrup into the egg whites, drizzling it down the side of the bowl to keep it from hitting the whip and spattering. Then plop the softened gelatin and the vanilla in the whites and beat on low speed for 6 to 7 minutes, or until the mixture cools and changes from off-white and foamy to bright white and fluffy.

➡ Transfer the beaten whites to the prepared pan and, using the spatula, spread them in an even layer. Cover lightly with plastic wrap, and leave at room temperature for at least 8 hours or up to 1 day.

➡ To make the chocolate filling: Line a 9-by-13-inch baking pan with parchment paper.

➡ Place the chocolate in a medium heatproof bowl. Place over (not touching) barely simmering water in a saucepan and heat, stirring occasionally, until completely melted and smooth. Remove from the heat, add the cream, and whisk slowly until thoroughly combined.

➡ Pour the chocolate mixture into the prepared pan and, using a rubber spatula, spread in an even layer. Cover the pan lightly with plastic wrap and refrigerate for at least 8 hours or up to 5 days. When ready to use, invert the pan onto a work surface, lift off the pan, and peel the parchment paper off the chocolate.

➡ To make the graham wafers: Using a stand mixer fitted with a paddle attachment (or a hand-held mixer or a wooden spoon), cream together the butter, sugar, and molasses for 2 to 3 minutes, or until light and fluffy. (This step will take 5 to 7 minutes if using a handheld mixer or a spoon.) Stop the mixer a few times and use a rubber spatula to scrape the sides and bottom of the bowl and the paddle to release any clinging butter or sugar. Add the egg and cream and beat for 1 minute, or until thoroughly combined. Scrape the bowl and paddle again to make sure the egg is thoroughly incorporated.

➡ In a small bowl, stir together the whole-wheat flour, all-purpose flour, cornmeal, baking powder, cinnamon, and salt until well mixed. On low speed, slowly blend the flour mixture into the butter-sugar mixture and then beat for 1 to 2 minutes, or until the flour mixture is totally incorporated and the dough is evenly mixed.

➡ Scrape the dough onto a piece of plastic wrap, and wrap the dough in the plastic wrap, pressing down to form a disk about 8 inches in diameter and 1 inch thick. Refrigerate the dough for at least 30 minutes, or until it is firm to the touch. (At this point, the dough can be stored in the refrigerator for up to 3 days or in the freezer for up to 1 month. If the dough is frozen, thaw it overnight in the refrigerator. Let the dough sit at room temperature for about 20 minutes before using, then proceed as directed.)

➡ Position a rack in the center of the oven, and heat the oven to 350 degrees F. Line a baking sheet with parchment paper.

➡ On a well-floured work surface, roll out the dough into a 16-inch square. You may have to knead the dough a little to soften it enough so that it rolls out more easily. Using a sharp knife and a ruler, cut the dough into 32 rectangles (4 rectangles by 8 rectangles), each 2 by 4 inches. (Divide the dough first into quarters, then divide each quarter into quarters, and then divide each of those quarters in half.) Transfer the rectangles to the prepared baking sheet, spacing them about 1 inch apart.

➡ Bake for 15 to 20 minutes, or until the wafers are golden brown and firm to the touch. Let cool completely on the baking sheet on a wire rack. (The wafers can be stored in an airtight container at room temperature for up to 5 days.)

(continued)

⇒ Place 16 graham wafers on a flat work surface. Dust the top surface of the marshmallow with a little cornstarch to prevent the knife from sticking to it, then use a chef's knife to cut the marshmallow into 16 pieces, each about 2 by 3 inches. Carefully lift the marshmallows out of the pan, and place 1 marshmallow on each graham wafer. If you have a kitchen torch, use it to toast the top of the marsh-mallow lightly to a golden brown. If you don't have a torch, preheat the broiler, place the cookies on a baking sheet, and place the sheet under the broiler just until the marshmallows turn brown and toasty. Be careful and quick, as they toast in an instant.

⇒ Using a small sharp knife, cut the chocolate fill-ing into 16 pieces, each about 2 by 3 inches. Place a piece of chocolate on top of each marshmallow. Top the chocolate with another graham wafer and press down. These are best served when the marshmallows are still warm from toasting, though you could wait a few hours before serving. Defi-nitely serve them the same day you make them.

BLACK SESAME LACE COOKIES

7 tablespoons (⅞ stick/100 grams) unsalted butter, at room temperature

½ cup (100 grams) granulated sugar

7 tablespoons (100 grams) packed light brown sugar

½ cup (70 grams) unbleached all-purpose flour

⅓ cup (80 grams) fresh orange juice (about 1½ oranges)

3 tablespoons black sesame seeds

MAKES 24 COOKIES

Before I opened Flour, I was lucky to get some local press about my new bakery and café. Just prior to opening day, the *Boston Globe* interviewed me for a cookie story and featured a bigger-than-life-size photo of my hand holding one of these lacy sesame cookies. They are gorgeous, but the ironic thing was that I didn't intend them as a selling point for Flour. A baking sheet of them just happened to be near me when the photographer asked for a prop. I'd been using the cookies for years in my restaurant work to garnish ice cream and sorbet desserts, and I wasn't planning to make them at Flour, because they seemed too brittle and delicate for the rough-and-tumble world of chocolate chip cookies and oatmeal scones. But when our doors opened, practically every other customer who walked in asked about the scrumptious-looking cookie in the newspaper and wanted to order one. We tried making them for a while, but, as I had suspected, they didn't hold up well stacked with the other cookies on our counter. Ever so slowly, we phased them out and customers eventually forgot about them.

But they are fantastic for making at home! This is a wonderfully easy recipe made with ingredients that you probably already have in the kitchen, except for the black sesame seeds. Seek them out—you can find them in most Asian grocery stores and specialty food shops—because they contrast beautifully with the golden brown cookie and add a distinctive flavor. Serve them as I did during my restaurant days, with a bowl of ice cream or sorbet.

➡ Using a stand mixer fitted with the paddle attachment (or a handheld mixer or a wooden spoon), cream the butter until creamy and light, about 2 minutes. Add the granulated sugar and brown sugar and continue to beat on medium speed for about 1 minute, or until combined. Turn down the speed to low and add the flour and mix until well combined. Slowly drizzle in the orange juice and mix for about 30 seconds; the mixture will look a little broken, which is okay. Mix in the sesame seeds.

➡ Transfer the batter to an airtight container and refrigerate for at least 4 hours or for up to 1 week.

(continued)

➡ When ready to bake the cookies, position a rack in the center of the oven, and heat the oven to 350 degrees F. Line a very flat baking sheet with parchment paper. (This batter spreads like crazy, so you have to use an extremely flat baking sheet in order for the cookies to bake in circles and not amoeba-like shapes.)

➡ Pinch off rounded tablespoon-size balls of dough and place on the prepared baking sheet, spacing them at least 3 inches apart to allow for spreading.

➡ Bake for 16 to 18 minutes, or until the cookies are completely golden brown throughout. Let cool completely (they must be firm to the touch) on the baking sheet on a wire rack. Gently remove the cookies from the parchment.

➡ The cookies can be stored, in layers separated with sheets of parchment paper or waxed paper, in an airtight container at room temperature for up to 3 days.

ROSEMARY SHORTBREAD

1 cup (2 sticks/228 grams) unsalted butter, at room temperature

½ cup (110 grams) packed light brown sugar

1 egg yolk

1 teaspoon finely chopped fresh rosemary

1½ cups (210 grams) unbleached all-purpose flour

½ cup (65 grams) cornstarch

¾ teaspoon kosher salt

½ teaspoon baking powder

MAKES 12 TO 15 COOKIES

Crumbly and delicate, these shortbread cookies are infused with subtle rosemary flavor. They are stealth cookies: They don't look like much, they don't sound fancy shmancy, and you probably don't expect them to become your new favorite cookie. But they will sneak up on you. I find that after I eat one, I keep going back again and again to have "just another bite," and before I know it, I've eaten three or four. They melt in your mouth, and they are especially appealing served with espresso after an Italian dinner. They are also nice to have on hand unbaked in the freezer for when guests drop by unexpectedly.

⇒ Using a stand mixer fitted with the paddle attachment (or a handheld mixer or a wooden spoon), cream the butter on medium speed for about 2 minutes, or until light and pale. (This step will take 3 to 4 minutes if using a handheld mixer and about 5 minutes if using a spoon.) Add the sugar and beat on medium speed for 3 to 4 minutes, or until light and fluffy. Stop the mixer a few times and use a rubber spatula to scrape the sides and bottom of the bowl and the paddle to release any clinging butter or sugar. On low speed, add the egg yolk and rosemary and beat for about 1 minute, or until thoroughly combined.

⇒ In a small bowl, sift together the flour, cornstarch, salt, and baking powder. On low speed, slowly add the flour mixture to the butter-sugar mixture and then mix just until the flour mixture is totally incorporated and the dough is evenly mixed. Stop the mixer several times to scrape the bowl and the paddle to free any trapped flour mixture.

⇒ Scrape the dough onto a piece of plastic wrap, and wrap the dough in the plastic wrap, pressing down to form a disk about 8 inches in diameter and 1 inch thick. Refrigerate the dough for about 20 minutes, or until it is firm enough to roll out.

⇒ Position a rack in the center of the oven, and heat the oven to 325 degrees F.

⇒ On a floured work surface, roll out the dough into a rectangle about 12 by 10 inches and ¼ inch thick. Using a sharp knife, cut the dough into 12 to 15 uniform pieces—rectangles, triangles, or cookie-cutter shapes—and arrange them on a baking sheet, spacing them about 2 inches apart. (At this point, the cookies can be tightly wrapped and frozen for up to 2 weeks. Bake as directed directly from the freezer. You may need to add a few minutes to the baking time.)

⇒ Bake for 18 to 20 minutes, or until the cookies are medium golden brown all the way through. Let cool on the baking sheet on a wire rack for 15 to 20 minutes, then transfer to a wire rack to cool completely.

⇒ The cookies can be stored in an airtight container at room temperature for up to 4 days.

Baker's Bite

When I chop fresh rosemary, I use a trick I picked up from the savory side of the kitchen. I add a teaspoon of sugar to the rosemary leaves, which helps me chop them finer and prevents them from sticking to the knife.

INTENSE CHOCOLATE BROWNIES

5½ ounces (155 grams) unsweetened chocolate, chopped

2½ ounces (70 grams) bittersweet chocolate (62 to 70 percent cacao), chopped

¾ cup plus 2 tablespoons (1¾ sticks/200 grams) unsalted butter, melted

5 eggs

2 cups (400 grams) sugar

1¼ cups (175 grams) unbleached all-purpose flour

½ teaspoon baking powder

½ teaspoon kosher salt

MAKES 16 BROWNIES

I've always been perplexed by the age-old brownie question: should they be cakey or fudgy? The thing is, if I want a piece of chocolate cake, I pull out the mixer and the cake flour and make a chocolate cake. And if fudge is what I have a hankering for, I grab the candy thermometer and make fudge! What I want when I'm craving a brownie lies somewhere in between: not as light and fluffy as a cake, not as dense and candylike as fudge, but something moist and deep and dark and rich. These decadent, chocolaty brownies are exactly that. As with most chocolate desserts, the quality of the chocolate and the cacao percentage dictate how rich and deep the chocolate flavor will be, so I urge you to buy the best chocolate you can afford.

In this recipe, the eggs and sugar are whipped before the rest of the ingredients are added, which helps the brownies bake off with the perfect texture: moist and rich and not too dense. In addition, they are slightly underbaked, which makes the standard baking doneness test of "until a knife inserted in the middle comes out clean" moot. When you test these brownies, you want the knife to have wet crumbs clinging to it to ensure they have the correct level of fudginess. If the knife comes out completely clean, the batter has baked through and the brownies will be cakelike. That's not a bad thing, but if you taste these when they are baked to perfection—somewhere between cake and fudge— I think you'll agree that's the way to go.

➡ Position a rack in the center of the oven, and heat the oven to 325 degrees F. Butter and flour a 9-by-13-inch baking pan.

➡ Place the unsweetened chocolate and bittersweet chocolate in a medium heatproof bowl. Place over (not touching) barely simmering water in a saucepan and heat, stirring occasionally, until completely melted and smooth. Remove from the heat and whisk in the butter until well mixed. Let cool slightly.

➡ Place the eggs in a stand mixer fitted with the whip attachment (or use a handheld mixer). On low speed, slowly beat in the sugar for about 1 minute total, or until frothy and somewhat thick. Using a rubber spatula, fold in the chocolate mixture.

➡ In a medium bowl, sift together the flour, baking powder, and salt. Using the spatula, gently fold the flour mixture into the egg-chocolate mixture until thoroughly combined. (If the bowl you used for the egg-chocolate mixture is too small for folding, transfer the mixture to a larger bowl and then fold in the flour mixture.) Scrape the batter into the prepared pan and spread in an even layer with the spatula (the batter will be thick).

➡ Bake for 30 to 35 minutes (but check every few minutes starting at 20 minutes to make sure the brownies don't overbake), or until a knife slipped into the center of the pan comes out with a few wet crumbs on it. If the knife comes out with liquid batter on it, the brownies need more time in the oven; if the knife comes out with nothing on it, the brownies are probably a bit overbaked and no longer fudgy, but they will still be delicious. Let cool in the pan on a wire rack for at least 2 hours, or until completely cool. (Because these are so moist, they need time to cool and firm up enough to cut.) Cut into 16 bars.

➡ The brownies can be stored in an airtight container at room temperature for up to 3 days. Or, they can be well wrapped in plastic wrap and frozen for up to 2 weeks; thaw at room temperature for 3 to 4 hours.

RASPBERRY CRUMB BARS

RICK'S SHORTBREAD

1½ cups (3 sticks/342 grams) unsalted butter

½ cup (100 grams) granulated sugar

3 tablespoons confectioners' sugar

2 egg yolks

1 teaspoon vanilla extract

1¼ cups (175 grams) unbleached all-purpose flour

1½ cups (180 grams) cake flour

¾ teaspoon baking powder

¾ teaspoon kosher salt

1½ cups (510 grams) raspberry jam (with seeds)

¼ cup (35 grams) confectioners' sugar

MAKES 9 BARS

The best compliment I ever received about these melt-in-your-mouth bars came from Rick Katz, the first pastry chef I worked for and one of my pastry idols. Getting a job in his bakery changed my life. After a few months in his kitchen, I knew I wanted to follow in his footsteps. He was detail oriented, incredibly passionate, and cared only about making sure our pastries were all amazing and perfect. To this day, when making a new pastry I ask myself, would Rick like this? His shortbread recipe (see page 152) has a mix of regular and confectioners' sugar, as well as a combination of all-purpose and cake flour. This is typical of his recipes. He always adjusts his ingredients just so to create the best product possible.

Shortly after we opened Flour, every time Rick came to visit, my heart would pound as he sampled our cookies, tarts, cakes, and pastries. One day, after he had tasted his way through most of the menu, he asked me for the recipe for these raspberry bars, which his wife had specifically requested that he make for her birthday. I had to laugh when I presented him with this ultrasimple recipe—because it was mainly *his* recipe! He had taught me how to make the delicate, buttery shortbread when I was working for him. I simply used that shortbread as a base, spread a generous amount of tart-sweet raspberry jam on top, and then crumbled more of the shortbread for the topping. It's an addictive treat that anyone would be excited to receive as a birthday gift.

➡ To make the shortbread: Using a stand mixer fitted with the paddle attachment (or a handheld mixer or a wooden spoon), cream together the butter, granulated sugar, and confectioners' sugar on medium speed for about 5 minutes, or until the mixture is light and fluffy. (This step will take about 10 minutes if using a handheld mixer or a spoon.) Stop the mixer a few times and use a rubber spatula to scrape the sides and bottom of the bowl and the paddle to release any clinging butter or sugar. Beat in the egg yolks and vanilla on medium speed for 2 to 3 minutes, or until thoroughly combined. Scrape the bowl and the paddle again with a rubber spatula to make sure the egg yolks are thoroughly incorporated.

➡ In a medium bowl, sift together the all-purpose flour, cake flour, baking powder, and salt. On low speed (or with the wooden spoon), gradually add the flour mixture to the butter-sugar mixture and then mix for about 15 seconds, or until the flour mixture is totally incorporated and the dough is evenly mixed. Stop the mixer and scrape the bowl again to make sure all of the flour mixture is thoroughly incorporated.

➡ Scrape the dough onto a sheet of plastic wrap. Remove one-fourth of the dough to a separate sheet of plastic wrap. Wrap the remaining three-fourths of the dough entirely in the plastic wrap, pressing down to form a disk about 8 inches in diameter and 1 inch thick. Refrigerate the dough disk for about 30 minutes, or until the dough has firmed up but is still somewhat pliable. Pat the reserved one-fourth of the dough into a small disk, wrap in the plastic wrap, and place in the freezer for at least 2 hours, or until hard. (At this point, the small dough portion can be stored in the freezer for up to 1 month. The larger dough disk can be stored in the refrigerator for up to 5 days or in the freezer for up to 1 month. If the larger dough disk is frozen, thaw it overnight in the refrigerator, then let it sit at room temperature for about 20 minutes before using.)

➡ Position a rack in the center of the oven, and heat the oven to 350 degrees F.

➡ Lightly flour the 8-inch dough disk and two large sheets of parchment paper. Place the dough between the sheets of parchment, and roll it out into a rectangle about 13 by 9 inches and ¼ to ⅓ inch thick. Carefully peel off the top sheet of parchment. (Place the whole thing in the fridge for a few minutes if the dough sticks to the parchment.) Trim the edges so the rectangle has fairly neat sides. Transfer the bottom sheet of parchment with the dough to a baking sheet. Trim the parchment so that it fits the baking sheet.

➡ Bake for about 20 minutes, or until the shortbread is light brown—about the same color as maple wood. Remove the shortbread from the oven (leaving the oven set at 350 degrees F), let cool for 10 to 15 minutes, and then spoon the raspberry jam on top of the still-warm shortbread. Spread it in an even layer with the spoon or with a rubber spatula, covering the surface. If the jam is stiff, put it in a small bowl and stir it with a wooden spoon to smooth it out and loosen it up before you put it on the shortbread. The heat of the shortbread should soften the jam enough to make it spreadable.

➡ Remove the smaller dough disk from the freezer and, using the large holes on a box grater, grate it into large flakes. Evenly sprinkle the dough flakes over the jam.

➡ Return the baking sheet to the oven and bake for another 20 to 25 minutes, or until the top is lightly browned. Let cool completely on the baking sheet on a wire rack.

➡ When cooled, sift the confectioners' sugar evenly over the top. Trim the edges again, then cut into 9 bars.

➡ The bars can be stored in an airtight container at room temperature for up to 5 days.

LEMON LUST BARS

1 cup (2 sticks/228 grams)
unsalted butter, at room
temperature

6 tablespoons (75 grams)
granulated sugar

2 tablespoons confectioners' sugar

1 egg yolk

1 teaspoon vanilla extract

1 cup (140 grams) unbleached
all-purpose flour

1 cup (120 grams) cake flour

½ teaspoon baking powder

½ teaspoon kosher salt

SUPER LEMON CURD

2 cups plus 2 tablespoons
(500 grams) fresh lemon juice
(14 to 16 lemons)

½ cup (1 stick/114 grams) unsalted
butter

¼ cup (60 grams) heavy cream

8 eggs

4 egg yolks

2 cups (400 grams) granulated
sugar

1 teaspoon kosher salt

1 teaspoon vanilla extract

MAKES 9 LARGE BARS

If you like lemon, you won't be able to stop eating these bars. The shortbread base is delicate and buttery, yet strong enough to be loaded with tart, lemony curd. I don't hold back with the curd. It has a touch of butter and cream to round out the lemon flavor and enough lemon to make your lips pucker . . . in a good way! Many lemon bar recipes feature a lemon base that is poured directly onto a short-bread crust and then cooked in the oven. For this recipe, you cook an intensely lemony curd on the stove top until it is thick and puddinglike. Then you spread the curd on top of the shortbread crust and bake the bars. This allows you to add much more curd, because it is already thick-ened and cooked through. When we first opened Flour, my mom (who worked at our front counter for many months and who is not a lemon fan) was shocked at the number of people who bought these and then came back to buy more. "Are you sure you want those?" she would ask incredulously whenever someone requested them. She couldn't believe that people really wanted that much lemon. Cut these into smaller squares for an afternoon tea.

➡ To make the shortbread: Using a stand mixer fitted with the paddle attachment (or a handheld mixer or a wooden spoon), cream together the butter, granulated sugar, and confectioners' sugar on medium speed for about 5 minutes, or until light and fluffy. (This step will take about 10 minutes if using a hand-held mixer or a spoon.) Stop the mixer a few times and use a rubber spatula to scrape the sides and bottom of the bowl and the paddle to release any clinging butter or sugar. Beat in the egg yolk and vanilla on medium speed for 2 to 3 minutes, or until thoroughly combined. Scrape the bowl and paddle again with a rubber spatula to make sure the egg yolk is thoroughly incorporated.

➡ In a medium bowl, sift together the all-purpose flour, cake flour, baking powder, and salt. On low speed (or with the wooden spoon), slowly add the flour mixture to the butter-sugar mixture and then mix for about 15 seconds, or until the flour mixture is totally incorporated and the dough is evenly mixed. Stop the mixer and scrape the bowl again to make sure all of the flour mixture is thoroughly incorporated.

➡ Scrape the dough out onto a sheet of plastic wrap, and wrap the dough in the plastic wrap, pressing down to form a disk 6 to 7 inches in diameter and 1 inch thick. Refrigerate the dough for about 30 minutes, or until it has firmed up but is still somewhat pliable. (At this point, the dough can be stored in the refrigerator for up to 5 days or in the freezer for up to 1 month. If the dough is frozen, thaw it overnight in the refrigerator, then let it sit at room temperature for about 20 minutes before using.)

➡ To make the lemon curd: While the dough is chilling, in a medium nonreactive saucepan, combine the lemon juice, butter, and cream. Place over medium-high heat and heat to just below a boil. Meanwhile, in a medium heatproof bowl, whisk together the eggs and egg yolks until blended, then slowly whisk in the granulated sugar until combined. Remove the lemon juice mixture from the heat and gradually whisk a little of it into the sugar-egg mixture. Continue whisking the hot liquid into the eggs, a little at a time, until all of it has been incorporated.

➡ When all of the lemon juice mixture has been incorporated, return the contents of the bowl to the saucepan, and return the saucepan to medium heat. Cook, stirring continuously with a wooden spoon and making sure to scrape the bottom of the pan frequently to prevent the eggs from scrambling, for 5 to 8 minutes, or until the mixture thickens and coats the spoon thickly. To test, draw your finger along the back of the spoon; the curd should hold the trail for a second or two before it fills.

➡ Remove the lemon curd from the heat and strain through a fine-mesh sieve into a medium bowl or pitcher. Whisk in the salt and vanilla. (The lemon curd can be made up to 4 days in advance and stored in an airtight container in the refrigerator. If using chilled curd, add 5 to 6 minutes to the baking time.)

➡ Position a rack in the center of the oven, and heat the oven to 350 degrees F.

➡ Lightly flour the dough disk and two large sheets of parchment paper. Place the dough between the sheets of parchment, and roll it out into a rectangle 9 by 11 inches and about ¼ inch thick. Carefully peel off the top sheet of parchment. (Place the whole thing in the fridge for a few minutes if the dough sticks to the parchment.) Transfer the bottom sheet of parchment with the dough to a 9-by-11-inch baking pan or baking dish with at least 2-inch-high sides. Press the dough to fit the bottom of the pan, and allow the parchment to come up the sides of the pan. The dough needs to be about the same thickness all around, but it does not have to be smooth.

➡ Bake for about 20 minutes, or until the shortbread is light brown—about the same color as maple wood. Remove from the oven (leave the over set at 350 degrees F), pour the lemon curd on top, and smooth the filling evenly over the shortbread with a rubber spatula.

➡ Bake for another 15 to 20 minutes, or until the curd has set and jiggles like firm Jell-O. Let cool to room temperature in the pan on a wire rack, then refrigerate for at least 4 hours or up to overnight to allow the curd to set. If refrigerating overnight, lightly drape plastic wrap over the top to keep any refrigerator smells from seeping into your lemon bars.

➡ Gently tug the parchment on all sides to loosen the shortbread from the pan, then slide it out onto a cutting board. Trim the edges of the shortbread, then cut into 9 bars.

➡ The bars can be stored in an airtight container in the refrigerator for up to 2 days.

GRANOLA BARS

GRANOLA JAM

1 cup (80 grams) dried apples

1 cup (160 grams) dried cranberries

1 cup (160 grams) dried apricots

⅓ cup (70 grams) granulated sugar

2 cups (480 grams) water

1 cup (100 grams) walnut halves

1¾ cups (245 grams) unbleached all-purpose flour

1½ cups (150 grams) old-fashioned rolled oats (not instant or quick cooking)

⅔ cup (150 grams) packed light brown sugar

⅔ cup (80 grams) sweetened shredded coconut

1 teaspoon kosher salt

¼ teaspoon ground cinnamon

1 cup (2 sticks/228 grams) unsalted butter, at room temperature, cut into 8 to 10 pieces

6 tablespoons (128 grams) honey

3 tablespoons flaxseeds

3 tablespoons sunflower seeds

3 tablespoons millet

MAKES 12 BARS

Every so often, a Flour customer puts a request for more healthful items in our suggestion box . . . please! It's not that Flour is full of unhealthful items—I think our baked goods are healthful, in moderation—but we are a bakery, after all, which means that many of our offerings are necessarily indulgent. We came up with this bar as an option for customers seeking a good-for-you snack. You make a granola of oats, nuts, coconut, and honey for the base. Add a fruity filling made by blending a dried-fruit compote into a sweet, chunky jam. And finish off the bar with more of the granola base mixed with a handful of sunflower seeds, flaxseeds, and millet. The bars stay moist for several days and actually get better with age (I like them best after 2 or 3 days). We make huge trayfuls of these at Flour, and one of my favorite ways to snack at the bakery is to raid the pans after the bars have been cut for serving and enjoy a plateful of edge trimmings.

➡ To make the jam: In a medium saucepan, combine the apples, cranberries, apricots, granulated sugar, and water and bring to a boil over high heat. Remove from the heat and let sit for about 1 hour. Transfer to a food processor and pulse 8 to 10 times, or until a chunky jam forms. (The jam can be made in advance and stored in the refrigerator in an airtight container for up to 5 days or in the freezer for up to 1 month.)

➡ Position a rack in the center of the oven, and heat the oven to 350 degrees F. Spread the walnuts on a baking sheet and toast for about 10 minutes, or until lightly toasted and fragrant. Transfer to a plate and let cool.

➡ Leave the oven set at 350 degrees F. Line a 9-by-13-inch baking pan with parchment paper.

➡ In the food processor, combine the walnuts, flour, oats, brown sugar, coconut, salt, cinnamon, and butter and pulse about 15 times, or until the mixture is evenly combined. Dump the mixture into a medium bowl and drizzle the honey on top. Work in the honey with your hands until the mixture comes together.

(continued)

➡ Press about two-thirds of the mixture into the bottom of the prepared pan. Place the remaining one-third of the mixture in the refrigerator.

➡ Bake for 30 to 40 minutes, or until light golden brown throughout. Remove the pan from the oven, spoon the granola jam on top, and spread in an even layer with the spoon or with a rubber spatula, covering the surface. Remove the reserved granola mixture from the refrigerator, and break it up with your fingers into a small bowl. Add the flaxseeds, sunflower seeds, and millet and stir to combine. Sprinkle the mixture, like a crumb topping, evenly over the jam.

➡ Return the pan to the oven and bake for 50 to 60 minutes, or until the top is golden brown. Let cool in the pan on a wire rack for 2 to 3 hours, or until cool enough to hold its shape when cut. Cut into 12 bars.

➡ The bars can be stored in an airtight container at room temperature for up to 1 week.

HOMEMADE DOG BISCUITS

2 cups (280 grams) unbleached all-purpose flour

1 cup (165 grams) whole-wheat flour

1 cup (200 grams) medium-coarse yellow cornmeal

1 cup (140 grams) bulgur

½ cup (100 grams) nonfat dry milk

1½ tablespoons kosher salt

1 teaspoon active dry yeast

1¼ cups (300 grams) chicken, beef, or vegetable stock

MAKES ABOUT 24 BISCUITS

Boston's South End, where the original Flour is located, takes its pups seriously! There are two dog bakeries here (you read that right) and a dedicated dog park. We bought a dog bowl for Flour's patio before we bought chairs and tables. Obviously, we had to make something for our canine-crazed clientele. Everything we sell at Flour is made from scratch, and that includes our dog biscuits. These are hearty and full of grains and flavors dogs like. Sometimes when we have bacon drippings, we add them to the chicken stock for added appeal. Dogs drool over these, and I love that we make the dogs that come to Flour as happy as their people!

➡ Position a rack in the center of the oven, and heat the oven to 300 degrees F.

➡ In the bowl of a stand mixer fitted with a paddle attachment (or a large bowl if using a handheld mixer or a wooden spoon), stir together the all-purpose flour, whole-wheat flour, cornmeal, bulgur, dry milk, and salt until well mixed. In a small bowl, stir the yeast into the stock.

➡ On low speed, add the stock mixture to the flour mixture and beat for 2 to 3 minutes, or until a stiff dough forms.

➡ Liberally dust a work surface with flour. Gather the dough, place it on the floured surface, and press down on it until it is about 1 inch thick. Use cookie cutters to cut out various shapes, or cut the dough into rectangles 3 to 4 inches long and 1 inch wide. Arrange the cutouts on a baking sheet. Gather up the scraps, reroll, cut out more biscuits, and add to the baking sheet.

➡ Bake for 45 minutes, or until the biscuits start to brown lightly and feel firm. Turn off the oven and leave the biscuits in the closed oven for at least 8 hours or up to 12 hours.

➡ The biscuits can be stored in an airtight container at room temperature for up to 2 months.

cakes

CLASSIC CARROT CAKE
WITH CREAM CHEESE FROSTING

2 eggs

1 cup (220 grams) packed light brown sugar

¾ cup (150 grams) canola oil

3 tablespoons nonfat buttermilk

½ teaspoon vanilla extract

1 cup plus 2 tablespoons (160 grams) unbleached all-purpose flour

½ teaspoon baking powder

½ teaspoon baking soda

½ teaspoon kosher salt

½ teaspoon ground cinnamon

¼ teaspoon ground ginger

2 cups (260 grams) tightly packed shredded carrots

½ cup (80 grams) raisins

½ cup (50 grams) walnuts, toasted and chopped

CREAM CHEESE FROSTING

12 ounces (340 grams) cream cheese, left at room temperature for 4 hours

½ cup (1 stick/114 grams) unsalted butter, at room temperature

1⅔ cups (230 grams) confectioners' sugar

CANDIED CARROT STRIPS (OPTIONAL)

1 small carrot

1 cup (200 grams) granulated sugar

¾ cup (180 grams) water

MAKES ONE 8-INCH, 2-LAYER CAKE (SERVES 8 TO 10) OR 12 CUPCAKES

People often ask me why I switched from being a four-star-restaurant pastry chef to making pastries in a bakery. If I could give them only one example of why, it would be a slice of this carrot cake. Restaurant desserts are like the popular kids in high school: beautiful, dressed up, suave, well put together on the outside . . . and on the inside sometimes they are truly wonderful and sometimes they still need a little more work. Bakery pastries, on the other hand, don't hide inside a fancy exterior. You can't gussie up a cookie or a scone or a slice of cake. What you see is what you get, so whatever you get had better be pretty darn good on its own. Like this carrot cake. It is the best version of carrot cake I've ever eaten: incredibly moist crumb; loads of shredded carrots, raisins, and toasted walnuts; and a sweet-but-not-too-sweet cream cheese frosting. One bite and you'll know why it always gets voted "most popular"—based on its taste alone.

➡ Position a rack in the center of the oven, and heat the oven to 350 degrees F. Butter and flour an 8-inch cake pan (or line a standard 12-cup muffin tin with paper liners).

➡ Using a stand mixer fitted with the whip attachment (or a handheld mixer), beat together the eggs and brown sugar on medium-high speed for 3 to 4 minutes, or until the mixture is light and thick. (This step will take 8 to 10 minutes if using a handheld mixer.) In a small bowl or pitcher, whisk together the oil, buttermilk, and vanilla. On low speed, slowly pour the oil mixture into the egg-sugar mixture. This should take about 30 seconds.

➡ In a small bowl, sift together the flour, baking powder, baking soda, salt, cinnamon, and ginger. Using a rubber spatula, fold the flour mixture into the egg-sugar mixture. When most of the flour mixture has been incorporated, add the carrots, raisins, and walnuts and continue to fold until the batter is homogeneous. Pour the batter into the prepared cake pan (or divide evenly among the prepared muffin cups).

➡ Bake the cake for about 1 hour and 20 minutes (or the cupcakes for about 50 minutes), or until the top is golden brown and springs back when pressed in the middle with a fingertip. Let cool completely in the pan on a wire rack.

(continued)

To make the frosting: While the cake is baking, put the cream cheese in the stand mixer fitted with the paddle attachment, and beat on medium speed for about 1 minute, or until smooth. If you have forgotten to take the cream cheese out of the refrigerator 4 hours in advance, you can soften it in a microwave on medium power for 30 seconds. Add the butter and continue to beat for another 1 minute. Scrape the sides and bottom of the bowl and add the confectioners' sugar. Beat for 1 more minute, or until well mixed. You should have about 3½ cups.

Cover the frosting and refrigerate for 2 to 3 hours before using to allow it to firm up enough to pipe and spread. (The frosting can be made up to 5 days in advance and stored in an airtight container in the refrigerator.)

To make carrot strips (if using): Peel the carrot with a vegetable peeler. Then, using the peeler, press firmly to cut lengthwise paper-thin strips from the carrot. Depending on the size of the carrot, you should have 6 to 10 long strips.

In a small saucepan, combine the granulated sugar and water and bring to a boil over high heat, stirring to dissolve the sugar. Add the carrot strips and boil for 10 seconds. Remove from the heat and let the strips cool completely in the syrup. (The strips can be stored in the syrup in an airtight container in the refrigerator for up to 5 days.)

Remove the cake from the pan and split it into two layers (see Splitting a Cake into Layers, page 18). Place the bottom layer, cut-side up, on a cake plate. Spoon about half of the frosting onto the layer and, using an offset spatula, spread it evenly to the edges. Place the top layer, cut-side down, on top and press down to adhere. Spoon on about 1 cup of the frosting and spread it over the top and down the sides of the cake. This is the crumb coat (see page 13), which will keep any loose crumbs from migrating to the surface of the finished cake. Spoon the remaining frosting on top of the cake, and spread it evenly across the top and down the sides. If using the carrot strips for decoration, lift the cooled strips from the syrup and blot gently to remove the excess syrup. Coil the strips into little spirals and place them whimsically on the cake.

(If you have baked cupcakes, remove them from the muffin tin. Fit a pastry bag with a ½-inch star tip and fill the bag with the frosting [see page 15], then pipe the frosting onto the cupcakes. Or, spread the frosting on the cupcakes with an icing spatula.)

The cake (or cupcakes) can be stored in an airtight container in the refrigerator for up to 3 days. It is best served a little cooler than room temperature, so remove it from the refrigerator about 2 hours before serving. (It's delicious straight from the fridge, too, so don't worry if you forget to pull it out in time.)

Baker's Bite

Softening the cream cheese in the microwave might sound like a strange step, but I've learned that if the cream cheese is at all cool, it will get lumpy when you try to combine it with the butter. Just 30 seconds in the microwave (or about 4 hours on a countertop) ensures that the cream cheese, butter, and sugar will blend together seamlessly to create the silkiest, creamiest frosting ever.

MIDNIGHT CHOCOLATE CAKE
WITH MILK CHOCOLATE BUTTERCREAM

½ cup (60 grams) Dutch-processed cocoa powder

1 ounce (28 grams) unsweetened chocolate, finely chopped

1 cup (240 grams) boiling water

1¾ cups plus 2 tablespoons (225 grams) cake flour

½ teaspoon kosher salt

1 teaspoon baking soda

1½ cups (330 grams) packed light brown sugar

1 cup (2 sticks/228 grams) unsalted butter, cut into pieces, at room temperature

¼ cup (60 grams) crème fraîche

2 eggs

2 egg yolks

MILK CHOCOLATE BUTTERCREAM

12 ounces (340 grams) milk chocolate, finely chopped

½ cup (120 grams) heavy cream

1½ cups (300 grams) granulated sugar

3 egg whites

3 cups (6 sticks/681 grams) unsalted butter, at room temperature, cut into 2-inch chunks

1½ teaspoons vanilla extract

¼ teaspoon kosher salt

MAKES ONE 8-INCH, 3-LAYER CAKE (SERVES 8 TO 12)

This is the chocolate cake to end all chocolate cakes: moist, velvety, and melt-in-your-mouth-tender, with deep, pure chocolate flavor and a smooth, silky frosting that tastes like the best milk chocolate bar has been melted down, whipped up, and spread all over. I baked my way through dozens of cookbooks, combining the best qualities of each recipe, and this cake was born. It's the easiest method for mixing a cake that I know. The batter holds for up to a day, so if you are short on time, you can make the batter one day and bake it the next. This cake has been on the Flour menu since opening day, and it has always been a best-seller.

➡ Position a rack in the center of the oven, and heat the oven to 350 degrees F. Butter and flour an 8x3 inch cake pan.

➡ In a small heatproof bowl, combine the cocoa powder and unsweetened chocolate. Pour the boiling water on top, then whisk until the mixture is completely combined and smooth. Let cool to room temperature, about 4 hours at room temperature or 1 hour in the refrigerator, whisking every 15 minutes if refrigerated.

➡ Using a stand mixer fitted with the paddle attachment (or a handheld mixer), mix together the flour, salt, baking soda, and brown sugar on low speed for about 10 seconds, or until mixed. On low speed, add the butter and continue to beat for 30 to 40 seconds, or until the butter is thoroughly combined and the mixture resembles dough.

➡ In a small bowl, whisk together the crème fraîche, eggs, and egg yolks until well mixed. On low speed, slowly pour the egg mixture into the butter-flour mixture and mix to combine. Turn up the mixer speed to medium-high and beat for 2 minutes, or until fluffy and light. Stop the mixer a few times and scrape the sides and bottom of the bowl to make sure the egg mixture is thoroughly incorporated. Turn down the mixer speed to low and slowly pour in the cooled chocolate mixture. Mix for about 10 seconds to combine. Scrape the sides and bottom of the bowl, and then mix on medium speed for about 30 seconds, or until the chocolate mixture is thoroughly incorporated. Pour the batter into the prepared pan.

➡ Bake for 1 hour and 20 minutes to 1½ hours, or until the top springs back when pressed in the middle with a fingertip. Let cool completely in the pan on a wire rack.

➡ To make the buttercream: While the cake is cooling, place the milk chocolate in a small heat-proof bowl. In a small saucepan, scald the cream over medium-high heat (bubbles start to form around the edge of the pan, but the cream is not boiling). Pour the cream over the chocolate and let sit for about 1 minute, then slowly whisk the chocolate and cream together until the chocolate is completely melted and the mixture is smooth. Let sit at room temperature for about 1 hour, or until cool. (Or, refrigerate until cool, about 30 minutes, whisking every 10 minutes.)

➡ In a small heatproof bowl, whisk together the sugar and egg whites to make a thick slurry. Place the bowl over (not touching) simmering water in a saucepan and heat, whisking occasionally, for 3 to 4 minutes, or until the mixture is hot to the touch.

➡ Remove from the heat and scrape the mixture into the bowl of the stand mixer fitted with the whip attachment (or use a hand-held mixer). Whip on medium-high speed for 6 to 8 minutes, or until the mixture becomes a light, white meringue and is cool to the touch. Turn down the speed to low and add the butter, a few chunks at a time. The mixture will look chunky and funky and curdled at first, but don't worry. Increase the mixer speed to medium and watch the whole thing come together! It will be smooth and silky in 2 to 3 minutes.

➡ Change to the paddle attachment and add the cooled chocolate mixture, vanilla, and salt. Beat on medium speed, stopping to scrape the bowl once or twice to loosen any butter clinging to the sides, for about 1 minute, or until the whole mixture comes together in a smooth buttercream. You should have about 5 cups. (Use immediately, or transfer to an airtight container and store at room temperature for up to 1 day, then beat again with the paddle attachment until smooth before

using. Or, store in an airtight container in the refrigerator for up to 1 week, then bring to room temperature and paddle again for a few minutes until smooth before using.)

➡ Remove the cooled cake from the pan. Using a long, serrated knife, trim the top to level it (it will have rounded a bit in the oven; the trimmed scraps make great nibbles). Then split the cake into three layers (see Splitting a Cake into Layers, page 18). Place the bottom layer, cut-side up, on a cake plate or cake pedestal (if you have a revolving cake stand, use it). Spoon about 1½ cups of the buttercream on top and use an offset spatula to spread it evenly to the edges.

➡ Carefully place the second layer on top, spoon about 1½ cups of the buttercream on top, and again spread it evenly to the edges. Place the third layer, top-side down, on top, spoon about 1 cup of the buttercream on top, and spread it over the top and down the sides of the cake, smoothing the buttercream as well as you can and covering the entire cake with a thin layer. This is the crumb coat (page 13), which will keep any loose crumbs from migrating to the surface of the finished cake.

➡ Spoon the remaining frosting on top of the cake, and spread it evenly across the top and down the sides. This is the finishing layer of frosting. If desired, spoon any remaining frosting into a pastry bag fitted with a small round or star tip and pipe a decorative line along the top and/or bottom edge of the cake (see page 16).

➡ The cake can be stored in an airtight container at room temperature for up to 2 days.

Baker's Bite

If a recipe calls for a specific amount of boiling water, boil more than the amount of water you need and then measure out the amount needed for the recipe. In the case of this cake, bring more than 1 cup water to a boil and then measure out 1 cup (240 grams). If you boil only 1 cup, you won't have enough because you will lose some to evaporation.

YELLOW BIRTHDAY CAKE
WITH FLUFFY CHOCOLATE GANACHE FROSTING

1½ cups (3 sticks/342 grams) unsalted butter, at room temperature

2 cups (400 grams) granulated sugar

3 eggs

3 egg yolks

1 teaspoon vanilla extract

3 cups (360 grams) cake flour

1 teaspoon baking powder

½ teaspoon baking soda

½ teaspoon kosher salt

1 cup (240 grams) nonfat buttermilk

FLUFFY CHOCOLATE GANACHE FROSTING

12 ounces (340 grams) semisweet chocolate, finely chopped

1 cup (240 grams) heavy cream

1 cup (2 sticks/228 grams) unsalted butter, at room temperature

1 cup (140 grams) confectioners' sugar

¼ teaspoon kosher salt

½ teaspoon vanilla extract

MAKES ONE 8-INCH,
2-LAYER CAKE
(SERVES 8 TO 12)

I know some people aren't too keen on making a big deal of birthdays. But I'm not one of them. I get excited about birthdays—mine and everyone else's—and I always try to make a knockout cake for the birthday girl or boy, even when it's me. Before I became a professional pastry chef, Betty Crocker and Duncan Hines were my best friends at birthday time. But they can't come close to a scrumptious yellow cake with chocolate frosting (in my opinion, the ultimate birthday-cake combo) made from scratch. This cake has it all. It's a simple butter cake made with buttermilk, which adds a deliciously subtle tang to the final product. When you compare a cake made with milk to a cake made with buttermilk, you taste the difference. The buttermilk adds a level of specialness that you can't quite pinpoint, but it is definitely there. The fluffy frosting combines rich chocolate ganache with butter and confectioners' sugar to make a spreadable wonder. You may have a little extra frosting, but you won't mind.

(continued)

➡ Position a rack in the center of the oven, and heat the oven to 350 degrees F. Butter and flour two 8-inch round cake pans.

➡ Using a stand mixer fitted with the paddle attachment (or a handheld mixer), cream together the butter and granulated sugar on medium speed for 3 to 4 minutes, or until light and fluffy. (This step will take 8 to 10 minutes if using a handheld mixer.) Stop the mixer a few times and use a rubber spatula to scrape the sides and bottom of the bowl and the paddle to release any clinging butter or sugar.

➡ In a small bowl, whisk together the eggs, egg yolks, and vanilla just until combined. On low speed, slowly pour the egg mixture into the butter mixture and mix just until incorporated. Scrape the bowl and paddle again, then beat on medium speed for 20 to 30 seconds, or until the mixture is homogeneous.

➡ In a medium bowl, sift together the flour, baking powder, baking soda, and salt. On the lowest speed, add about one-third of the flour mixture to the egg-butter mixture and mix just until barely combined. Immediately pour in about half of the buttermilk and continue to mix on the lowest speed until the buttermilk is almost thoroughly incorporated. Stop the mixer and scrape the sides and bottom of the bowl well. Again on the lowest speed, add about half of the remaining flour mixture and mix just until barely combined. Add the rest of the buttermilk and mix just until combined. Be careful not to overmix.

➡ At this point, it is best to finish the mixing by hand. Remove the bowl from the mixer stand and, using the rubber spatula, fold in the remaining flour mixture just until the batter is homogeneous. As you fold, be sure to incorporate any batter clinging to the sides and bottom of the bowl. Divide the batter evenly between the prepared cake pans.

➡ Bake for 40 to 50 minutes, or until the tops are golden brown and the cakes spring back when pressed in the middle with a fingertip. Let cool completely in the pans on wire racks. (The cooled cakes can be tightly wrapped in plastic wrap and stored in the freezer for up to 1 week. Thaw at room temperature, still wrapped tightly in plastic wrap.)

➡ To make the ganache frosting: While the cake layers are cooling, put the chocolate in a medium heatproof bowl. In a small saucepan, scald the cream over medium-high heat (bubbles start to form around the edge of the pan, but the cream is not boiling). Pour the hot cream over the chocolate and let sit for about 1 minute, then slowly whisk together the chocolate and cream until the chocolate is completely melted and the mixture is smooth. Let sit at room temperature for 1 to 2 hours, or until completely cool. (Or, refrigerate the ganache until cool, about 30 minutes, whisking every 10 minutes.)

➡ Fit the stand mixer with the paddle attachment (or use a handheld mixer) and beat the butter on medium-low speed for 10 to 15 seconds, or until smooth. Add the confectioners' sugar, salt, and vanilla and continue to beat on medium-low speed for about 2 minutes, or until the mixture is fluffy and smooth. Stop the mixer a few times and use a rubber spatula to scrape the bowl and the paddle to release any clinging butter or sugar. On medium speed, add the cooled ganache and beat for about 2 minutes, or until completely combined. Stop to scrape the sides and bottom of the bowl. Turn up the mixer speed to medium-high and beat for about 1 minute, or until the frosting lightens in color and thickens. You should have about 4 cups. (Use the frosting the day you make it, or cover and store in the refrigerator for up to 1 day, then bring to room temperature and paddle again for a few minutes until smooth before using.)

➡ Remove the cooled cakes from their pans. (Be sure they are completely cool. If they are even the slightest bit warm, the frosting will melt and you will have a mess.) Using a long, serrated knife, trim the top of each cake to level it (the layers will have rounded a bit in the oven; the trimmed scraps make great nibbles). Place one cake layer on a cake plate or cake pedestal (if you have a revolving cake stand, use it). Spoon about 1 cup of the frosting on top and use an offset spatula to spread it evenly to the edges.

➡ Carefully place the second cake layer, top-side down (so the even, sharp edges will be on the top of the finished cake), on top. Spoon about 1 cup of the frosting on top and spread it over the top and down the sides of the cake, smoothing the frosting as well as you can and covering the entire cake with a thin layer. This is the crumb coat (see page 13), which will keep any loose crumbs from migrating to the surface of the finished cake. Spoon a heaping cup of frosting on top of the cake, and spread it evenly across the top and down the sides. This is the finishing layer of frosting. If desired, spoon any remaining frosting into a pastry bag fitted with a small round or star tip and pipe a decorative line along the top and/or bottom edge of the cake (see page 16).

➡ The cake can be stored in an airtight container at room temperature for up to 2 days.

RED VELVET CAKE
WITH CREAMY VANILLA FROSTING

¾ cup (1½ sticks/170 grams) unsalted butter, at room temperature

2¼ cups (450 grams) sugar

3 eggs

2 egg yolks

3¾ cups (450 grams) cake flour

1½ teaspoons baking powder

1½ teaspoons baking soda

1½ teaspoons kosher salt

½ cup (60 grams) Dutch-processed cocoa powder

¾ cup (180 grams) nonfat buttermilk

¾ cup (180 grams) crème fraîche

⅓ cup (80 grams) red food coloring

2 teaspoons vanilla extract

CREAMY VANILLA FROSTING

2 cups (480 grams) milk

½ cup (70 grams) unbleached all-purpose flour

2 cups (400 grams) sugar

2 cups (4 sticks/454 grams) unsalted butter, at room temperature, cut into 2-inch cubes

2 teaspoons vanilla extract

¼ teaspoon kosher salt

MAKES ONE 8-INCH, 2-LAYER CAKE (SERVES 10 TO 12)

When I opened Flour, we were one of the few bake-from-scratch bakeries in town, and customers flooded us with requests for specialty cakes and pastries. They frequently waxed nostalgic about childhood desserts and begged us to replicate them. We often said yes, because it was a way for us to try a new dessert *and* make a customer happy—a win-win in our book. One of the most common requests was for red velvet cake. Even though I grew up in Texas, and this was purportedly a Southern cake, I had never heard of it. It is a chocolate cake covered in smooth vanilla frosting, and it gets its deep red color from copious amounts of food coloring. We are natural ingredient snobs at Flour and avoid artificial colors and flavors like the plague, but we make an exception for this popular cake. It is soft, tender, and lightly chocolaty, and it pairs beautifully with the creamy rich frosting. Plus it's bright red! Even we have to admit that's a lot of fun.

→ Position a rack in the center of the oven, and heat the oven to 350 degrees F. Butter and flour two 8-inch round cake pans.

→ Using a stand mixer fitted with the paddle attachment (or a handheld mixer), cream together the butter and sugar for 2 to 3 minutes, or until light and fluffy. (This step will take 6 to 8 minutes if using a handheld mixer.) Stop the mixer a few times and use a rubber spatula to scrape the sides and bottom of the bowl and the paddle to release any clinging butter or sugar.

→ In a small bowl, whisk together the eggs and egg yolks until mixed. On low speed, slowly pour the eggs into the butter-sugar mixture and mix to combine. Scrape the bowl again, then beat on medium speed for 1 to 2 minutes, or until the eggs are thoroughly incorporated.

→ In a medium bowl, sift together the flour, baking powder, baking soda, salt, and cocoa powder. In a small bowl, whisk together the buttermilk, crème fraîche, food coloring, and vanilla just until combined. On the lowest speed, add about one-third of the flour mixture to the egg-butter mixture and mix just until combined. Immediately pour in about half of the buttermilk mixture and continue to mix on the lowest speed until the buttermilk mixture is almost thoroughly incorporated. Stop the mixer and scrape the sides and bottom of the bowl well. Again on the lowest speed, add about half of the remaining flour mixture and mix just until barely combined. Add the rest of the buttermilk mixture and mix just until combined. Be careful not to overmix.

➡ At this point, it is best to finish the mixing by hand. Remove the bowl from the mixer stand and, using the rubber spatula, fold in the remaining flour mixture just until the batter is homogeneous. As you fold, be sure to incorporate any batter clinging to the sides and bottom of the bowl. Divide the batter evenly between the prepared cake pans.

➡ Bake for 50 to 55 minutes, or until the cakes spring back when pressed in the middle with a fingertip. Let cool completely in the pans on wire racks. (The cooled cakes can be tightly wrapped in plastic wrap and stored in the freezer for up to 1 week. Thaw at room temperature, still wrapped tightly in plastic wrap.)

➡ To make the frosting: While the cake layers are cooling, in a medium saucepan, whisk together the milk and flour to combine, place over medium heat, and heat, whisking constantly, for 3 to 4 minutes, or until the mixture starts to thicken and becomes pasty. Once it is visibly thicker, count to 30 while continuously whisking. Remove from the heat and scrape into the bowl of the stand mixer. Let it sit, uncovered, for about 1 hour, or until it cools to room temperature, whisking it every 10 minutes or so to help it cool.

➡ Fit the mixer with the paddle attachment (or use a handheld mixer). On low speed, slowly add the sugar to the cooled milk-flour mixture and mix until combined. Continuing on low speed, add the butter, a cube at a time, until all of the butter has been incorporated, then mix in the vanilla and salt.

➡ Turn up the speed to medium and mix for 6 to 8 minutes. The frosting will look curdled and clumpy at first but will gradually start to look creamy. When the frosting is completely smooth

and silky, it is ready. You should have about 5 cups. (Use immediately, or cover and leave at room temperature for up to 8 hours, then beat vigorously with a wooden spoon until smooth before using. Or, store in an airtight container in the refrigerator for up to 1 week. If you refrigerate it, you will need to beat it again for a long time [10 to 12 minutes] to bring it back to a silky consistency. For the best result, remove it from the refrigerator up to 8 hours in advance, so it doesn't separate when you beat it.)

➡ Remove the cooled cakes from their pans. Using a long, serrated knife, trim the top of each cake to level it (the layers will have rounded a bit in the oven; the trimmed scraps make for great nibbling). Place one cake layer on a cake plate or cake pedestal (if you have a revolving cake stand, use it). Spoon about 1½ cups of the frosting on top and use an offset spatula to spread it evenly to the edges.

➡ Carefully place the second cake layer, top-side down (so the even, sharp edges will be on the top of the finished cake), on top. Spoon about 1½ cups of the frosting on top and spread it over the top and down the sides of the cake, smoothing the frosting as well as you can and covering the entire cake with a thin layer. This is the crumb coat (see page 13), which will keep any loose crumbs from migrating to the surface of the finished cake. Spoon a heaping cup of frosting on top of the cake, and spread it evenly across the top and down the sides. This is the finishing layer of frosting. Spoon any remaining frosting into a pastry bag fitted with a small round or star tip and pipe a decorative line along the top and/or bottom edge of the cake (see page 16).

➡ The cake can be stored in an airtight container at room temperature for up to 2 days.

NUTMEG-SPICE CAKE
WITH CREAMY RUM BUTTERCREAM

¼ cup (½ stick/56 grams) unsalted butter, at room temperature

¼ cup (50 grams) canola oil

1½ cups (300 grams) sugar

1 teaspoon vanilla extract

3 eggs

2 cups (280 grams) unbleached all-purpose flour

1 teaspoon baking powder

½ teaspoon baking soda

1 teaspoon freshly grated nutmeg

¼ teaspoon ground cinnamon

¼ teaspoon ground ginger

¼ teaspoon ground cloves

½ teaspoon kosher salt

1 cup (240 grams) nonfat buttermilk, at room temperature

CREAMY RUM BUTTERCREAM

1½ cups (300 grams) sugar

6 egg whites

1½ cups (3 sticks/336 grams) unsalted butter, at room temperature, cut into 2-inch chunks

1 teaspoon vanilla extract

¼ teaspoon kosher salt

¼ to ⅓ cup (60 to 80 grams) dark rum

MAKES ONE 8-INCH, 2-LAYER CAKE (SERVES 8 TO 10)

One of the things I enjoy most about being in the baking business—besides baking, of course—is being surrounded by people who are passionate about what they do. It's not uncommon at Flour for one of the bakers to end his or her shift and then remain in the kitchen concocting some delicious pastry for his or her own party or event. That's how this cake came about. Shira, one of the head bakers at F2, spent many afternoons working on a layered spice cake for her best friend's wedding. I kept snacking on the trimmings and thinking that it was too bad that the Flour menu was too full to add another cake. When I needed to come up with a new dessert for Myers+Chang, the Asian restaurant I own with Christopher, I realized it was the perfect place to feature this cake. Asian desserts typically feature ginger, but nutmeg is another beloved spice, especially because, according to Asian lore, it is an aphrodisiac. Add some buttercream jazzed up with rum and you have a dessert worthy of a wedding reception, a dinner party, or any special occasion.

⇒ Position a rack in the center of the oven, and heat the oven to 350 degrees F. Butter and flour two 8-inch round cake pans, or line with parchment paper.

⇒ Using a stand mixer fitted with the paddle attachment (or a handheld mixer), beat together the butter and oil on medium speed for about 1 minute, or until well combined. On medium speed, slowly add the sugar and vanilla and beat for 2 minutes, or until the mixture is light and fluffy. Stop the mixer a few times and use a rubber spatula to scrape the sides and bottom of the bowl and the paddle to release any clinging butter or sugar. Add the eggs one at a time, beating after each addition until combined. Stop the mixer and scrape the bowl again as needed.

⇒ In a medium bowl, sift together the flour, baking powder, baking soda, nutmeg, cinnamon, ginger, cloves, and salt. On low speed, add about one-third of the flour mixture to the egg-butter mixture and mix until just barely combined. Pour in half of the buttermilk and mix until almost thoroughly incorporated. Stop the mixer and scrape the sides and bottom of the bowl well. Again on low speed, add about half of the remaining flour mixture and mix just until barely combined. Add the remaining buttermilk and mix until well incorporated. Stop the mixer and scrape the sides and bottom of the bowl again. Add the remaining flour mixture and mix until completely incorporated. Divide the batter evenly between the prepared cake pans.

⇒ Bake for 30 to 40 minutes, or until the cakes spring back when pressed in the middle with a fingertip. Let cool completely in the pans on wire racks. (The cooled cakes can be tightly wrapped in plastic wrap and stored in the freezer for up to 1 week. Thaw at room temperature, still wrapped tightly in plastic wrap.)

⇒ To make the buttercream: While the cake layers are cooling, in a small heatproof bowl, whisk together the sugar and egg whites to make a thick slurry. Place the bowl over (not touching) simmering water in a saucepan and heat, whisking occasionally, for 6 to 8 minutes, or until the mixture is hot to the touch. It will thin out a bit as the sugar melts.

⇒ Remove from the heat and scrape the mixture into the bowl of the stand mixer fitted with the whip attachment (or use a hand-held mixer). Whip on medium-high speed for 6 to 8 minutes, or until the mixture becomes a light, white meringue and is cool to the touch. Turn down the speed to low, add the butter, one chunk at a time, and mix for 2 to 3 minutes. The mixture will look curdled at first, but don't worry. Increase the mixer speed to medium and beat for 2 to 3 minutes. The buttercream will be smooth. Add the vanilla, salt, and ¼ cup rum and whip for another 1 to 2 minutes, or until the rum is completely incorporated. Taste the buttercream and whip in a little more rum, if desired. You should have about 5 cups. (Use within 30 minutes, or transfer to an airtight container and store at room temperature for up to 3 days, then beat with the stand mixer fitted with the paddle attachment until smooth before using. Or, store in an airtight container in the refrigerator for up to 2 weeks, then bring to room temperature and paddle for a few minutes until smooth before using. If you paddle the frosting straight from the refrigerator, it will separate, then come together, and it may take 10 to 12 minutes for it to become smooth and silky.)

⇒ Remove the cooled cakes from their pans. Using a long, serrated knife, trim the top of each cake to level it (the layers will have rounded a bit in the oven; the trimmed scraps make great nibbles). Place one cake on a cake plate or pedestal (if you have a revolving cake stand, use it). Spoon 1½ cups of the buttercream on top and use an offset spatula to spread it evenly to the edges.

⇒ Carefully place the second cake layer, top-side down (so the even, sharp edges will be on the top of the finished cake), on top. Spoon on about 1 cup of the buttercream and spread it over the top and down the sides of the cake, smoothing the buttercream as well as you can and covering the entire cake with a thin layer. This is the crumb coat (see page 13), which will keep any loose crumbs from migrating to the surface of the finished cake. Spoon up to 1½ cups buttercream on top of the cake, and spread it evenly across the top and down the sides. This is the finishing layer of frosting. Spoon any remaining frosting into a pastry bag fitted with a small round or star tip and pipe a decorative line along the top and/or bottom edge of the cake (see page 16).

⇒ The cake can be stored in an airtight container at room temperature for up to 2 days.

LEMON-RASPBERRY CAKE
WITH LEMON BUTTERCREAM

6 tablespoons (¾ stick/86 grams) unsalted butter, at room temperature

6 tablespoons (75 grams) canola oil

1⅓ cups (270 grams) sugar

2 teaspoons vanilla extract

1 tablespoon finely grated lemon zest (about 1 lemon)

3 cups (360 grams) cake flour

1 tablespoon baking powder

½ teaspoon kosher salt

1 cup (240 grams) milk, at room temperature

6 egg whites

LEMON CURD

1 cup (240 grams) fresh lemon juice (6 to 7 lemons)

¼ cup (½ stick/56 grams) unsalted butter

2 tablespoons heavy cream

4 eggs

2 egg yolks

1 cup (200 grams) sugar

½ teaspoon kosher salt

½ teaspoon vanilla extract

BUTTERCREAM

1½ cups (300 grams) sugar

¾ cup (180 grams) water

4 eggs

2 egg yolks

3 cups (6 sticks/681 grams) unsalted butter, at room temperature, cut into 1-inch chunks

¼ teaspoon kosher salt

½ cup (120 grams) fresh lemon juice (3 to 4 lemons)

½ cup (120 grams) water

¾ cup (150 grams) sugar

1 pint (260 grams) raspberries

MAKES ONE 9-INCH,
3-LAYER CAKE
(SERVES 10 TO 12)

Nothing says "spring" quite like this cake—but that doesn't stop it from being a best-seller at Flour year-round. It's a thrill for me to think of how many weddings, anniversaries, christenings, birthdays, Mother's Day celebrations, graduations, and showers have included this cake. And no wonder: With its light, fluffy sponge cake soaked with a sweet-tart lemon syrup, layers of lemon buttercream and lemon curd, and fresh raspberries scattered within and on top, this cake (please excuse my pastry chef humor here) takes the cake!

➡ Position a rack in the center of the oven, and heat the oven to 350 degrees F. Butter and flour three 9-inch round cake pans, or line with parchment paper.

➡ Using a stand mixer fitted with the paddle attachment (or a handheld mixer), cream together the butter, oil, and 1 cup (200 grams) of the sugar for 2 to 3 minutes, or until light and fluffy. (This step will take 4 to 5 minutes if using a handheld mixer.) Stop the mixer a few times and use a rubber spatula to scrape the sides and bottom of the bowl and the paddle to release any clinging butter or sugar. Beat in the vanilla and lemon zest.

➡ In a medium bowl, sift together the flour, baking powder, and salt. On low speed, add about one-third of the flour mixture to the butter-sugar mixture and mix until incorporated. Add about half of the milk and continue to mix on low speed until incorporated. Stop the mixer and scrape the sides and bottom of the bowl well. Add half of the remaining flour mixture and mix until incorporated. Add the rest of the milk and mix until incorporated. Stop the mixer again and scrape the sides and bottom of the bowl well. Add the remaining flour mixture and mix on low speed until incorporated. Remove the bowl from the mixer stand and transfer the batter to a large bowl.

➡ Clean the mixer bowl well (make sure absolutely no batter remains in it) and fit the mixer with the whip attachment. Place the egg whites in the bowl and beat on medium speed for 3 to 4 minutes, or until they hold soft peaks. (This step will take 6 to 7 minutes if using a handheld mixer.) The whites will start to froth and turn into bubbles, and eventually the yellowy viscous part will disappear. Keep whipping until you can see the tines of your whip leaving a slight trail in the whites. To test for the soft-peak stage, stop the mixer and lift the whip out of the whites; the whites should peak and then droop.

➡ On medium speed, slowly add the remaining ⅓ cup (70 grams) sugar and whip for 1 to 2 minutes, or until the whites are glossy and shiny and hold a peak when you slowly lift the whip straight up and out of the whites.

➡ Using the rubber spatula, gently fold about one-third of the whipped egg whites into the batter to lighten it. Then gently fold in the remaining egg whites. Scrape the sides of the bowl to catch any loose whites. Divide the batter evenly among the prepared cake pans.

➡ Bake for 25 to 30 minutes, or until each cake layer begins to pull away from the sides of the pan and the top starts to get a little golden but is still pale and it springs back when pressed in the middle with a fingertip. Let cool in the pans on wire racks until cool enough to remove from the pans, at least 30 minutes. The cakes should be warm but not hot, and should pop out of the pans easily without falling apart. Invert the cakes onto the racks, peel off the parchment (if used), and let cool for about 2 hours, or until completely cool. (The cooled cakes can be tightly wrapped in plastic wrap and stored in the freezer for up to 1 week. Thaw at room temperature, still wrapped tightly in plastic wrap.)

➡ To make the lemon curd: While the cake layers are baking, in a medium nonreactive saucepan, combine the lemon juice, butter, and cream. Place over medium-high heat and heat to just under a boil. In a medium heatproof bowl, whisk together the eggs and egg yolks until blended, then slowly whisk in the sugar until combined. Remove the lemon juice mixture from the heat and gradually whisk a little of it into the sugar-egg mixture. Continue whisking the hot liquid into the sugar-egg mixture, a little at a time, until all of it has been incorporated.

➡ When all of the hot liquid has been incorporated, return the contents of the bowl to the saucepan, and return the saucepan to medium heat. Cook,

stirring continuously with a wooden spoon and scraping the bottom of the pan frequently to prevent the eggs from scrambling, for 5 to 8 minutes, or until the mixture thickens and coats the spoon thickly. To test, draw your finger along the back of the spoon; the curd should hold the trail for a second or two before it fills.

➡ Remove the curd from the heat and strain it through a fine-mesh sieve into a bowl. Whisk in the salt and vanilla. You should have about 2 cups. Cover tightly and refrigerate for 1 to 2 hours, or until cold. (The curd can be made up to 5 days in advance and stored in an airtight container in the refrigerator.)

➡ To make the buttercream: In a small saucepan, stir together the sugar and water. Place over high heat, bring to a boil, and cook, without stirring, for 3 to 4 minutes, or until the syrup registers 238 degrees F on a candy thermometer (the softball stage; see Cooking Sugar, page 13). Meanwhile, fit the stand mixer with the whip attachment (or use a handheld mixer) and beat together the eggs and egg yolks on medium speed for 3 to 4 minutes, or until pale and light.

➡ When the syrup is ready, remove from the heat. On low speed, slowly add the syrup into the eggs, drizzling it down the side of the bowl to keep it from hitting the whip and spattering. Turn up the speed to medium and whip for 6 to 8 minutes, or until the mixture turns light and fluffy, is pale, and is cool to the touch. Turn down the speed to low and add the butter, a few chunks at a time. Increase the mixer speed to medium and continue to whip for 4 to 5 minutes. The mixture will break and look curdled at first, but don't worry. It will soon become smooth and silky.

➡ Add the salt and whip until completely combined. You should have about 6 cups. (Use within 30 minutes, or cover and leave at room temperature for up to 8 hours, and then beat vigorously with a wooden spoon until smooth before using. Or, transfer to an airtight container and store in the refrigerator for up to 5 days, then bring to room

(continued)

temperature and beat with the stand mixer fitted with the paddle attachment for a few minutes until smooth before using.)

➡ In a small saucepan, combine the lemon juice, water, and sugar and bring to a boil over high heat, stirring to dissolve the sugar. Remove from the heat and let cool to room temperature. This syrup will be used for moistening the cake layers.

➡ Scoop about 3 cups of the buttercream into a medium bowl, add about ½ cup of the lemon curd, and whisk together until well combined. This will be used to fill the cake. Set aside the remaining buttercream for frosting the cake and set aside about ⅓ cup curd for finishing off the top.

➡ Remove the cooled cakes from their pans. Using a long, serrated knife, trim the top of each cake to level it (the layers will have rounded a bit in the oven; the trimmed scraps make great nibbles). Place one layer on a 9-inch cardboard cake round (and place this on a revolving cake stand, if you have one), or place directly on a cake plate. Brush the layer generously with about one-third of the lemon syrup.

➡ Spoon about 1 cup of the curd–buttercream mixture onto the cake layer and use an offset spatula to spread it evenly to the edges. Spoon about ½ cup of the curd-buttercream mixture into a pastry bag fitted with a ½-inch round tip (see page 16) and pipe a layer of it around the perimeter to form a "flood layer" (see Baker's Bite). (Alternatively, use a small offset spatula to spread and push some of the curd-buttercream mixture from the middle of the cake up around the edge to create a crater of sorts.) Carefully spread about half of the nonreserved lemon curd on top of the buttercream. Sprinkle half of the raspberries evenly on top of the curd.

➡ Carefully place a second layer on top of the raspberries and press down lightly so the cake adheres to the curd and the raspberries settle into the curd and curd-buttercream layers. Brush this second layer with half of the remaining lemon syrup, then spoon on another 1 cup of the curd-buttercream mixture, spreading it to the edges.

Repeat the flood layer, then spread the rest of the nonreserved curd on top of the buttercream. Set aside a few pretty raspberries for garnishing the top, then sprinkle the remaining raspberries evenly over the curd layer. Carefully place the third layer, top-side down (so the even, sharp edges will be on the top of the finished cake), on top. Brush the remaining lemon syrup over the top. At this point the cake needs to firm up in the refrigerator before you finish it. Place it in the refrigerator for at least 1 hour, or up to 2 days, wrapped in plastic wrap.

➡ After the cake has firmed up, spoon about 1 cup of the reserved plain buttercream on top of the cake and spread it over the top and down the cake sides, smoothing the buttercream as well as you can and covering the entire cake with a thin layer. This is the crumb coat (see page 13), which will keep any loose crumbs from migrating to the surface of the finished cake. Refrigerate the cake once again for about 30 minutes to set the crumb coat.

➡ Spoon about 1½ cups plain buttercream on top of the cake and spread it evenly across the top and down the sides. This is the finishing layer of frosting. Spread the reserved ⅓ cup curd on the top of the cake, spreading it in a very thin layer. Spoon any remaining buttercream in a pastry bag fitted with a small round or star tip and pipe a decorative line along the top and/or the bottom edge of the cake. Garnish the top of the cake with the reserved raspberries.

➡ The cake can be stored in an airtight container in the refrigerator for up to 2 days.

Baker's Bite

When building up the layers in this cake, the ooziness of the lemon curd and the insistent tendency of the raspberries to burst open into a juicy puddle will leave you with a leaking, seeping mess of a cake unless you build what we at Flour call the "flood." This is essentially a small wall of buttercream that you pipe around the perimeter of the internal buttercream layers, before you spoon in the lemon curd and berries. Once the cake is refrigerated, the buttercream firms up and keeps the curd and berries from running out.

WHITE COCONUT CAKE
WITH COCONUT FROSTING

2¼ cups (270 grams) cake flour

1¼ cups (250 grams) sugar

2 teaspoons baking powder

½ teaspoon kosher salt

¾ cup (1½ sticks/170 grams) unsalted butter, at room temperature, cut into 2-inch pieces

6 egg whites

1 cup (240 grams) coconut milk

2 cups (240 grams) sweetened shredded coconut

1 vanilla bean, split lengthwise

COCONUT FROSTING

1½ cups (300 grams) sugar

6 egg whites

1½ cups (3 sticks/342 grams) unsalted butter, at room temperature, cut into 2-inch chunks

1 teaspoon vanilla extract

¼ teaspoon kosher salt

⅔ cup (160 grams) coconut milk

MAKES ONE 8-INCH,
2-LAYER CAKE
(SERVES 8 TO 10)

With its super-tender crumb and fluffy, snow-white frosting, this gorgeous white cake will become a go-to recipe for all coconut lovers—and all cake lovers, too. Rich coconut milk turns up in both the cake batter and the buttercream, and because I'm a firm believer in layering flavors, a generous amount of shredded coconut is mixed into the batter, as well. And then the entire thing is embellished with even more coconut. It keeps well for up to 3 days, but because it's so hard to resist, I've never had it around for more than a day.

→ Position a rack in the center of the oven, and heat the oven to 350 degrees F. Butter and flour two 8-inch round cake pans, or line with parchment paper.

→ Sift the cake flour into the bowl of a stand mixer fitted with the paddle attachment (or into a large bowl if using a handheld mixer). Add the sugar, baking powder, and salt and beat on low speed for a few seconds to combine. Add the butter pieces and beat on low speed for 45 seconds to 1 minute, or until the mixture is coarse and crumbly.

→ In a medium bowl, combine the egg whites, coconut milk, and 1 cup (120 grams) of the shredded coconut and whisk until thoroughly mixed. Use the tip of a knife to scrape in the seeds from the vanilla bean into the coconut milk mixture. Whisk until the vanilla seeds are well dispersed. (Reserve the pod for another use. You can slip it into a container of sugar to make vanilla sugar; see page 29.)

→ Add about half of the coconut milk mixture to the flour mixture and beat on medium-high speed for about 1 minute, or until combined. Stop the mixer and scrape the sides and bottom of the bowl well. Add the rest of the coconut milk mixture and beat on medium speed for 20 to 30 seconds, or until the batter is well mixed, light, and fluffy. Divide the batter evenly between the prepared cake pans.

→ Bake for 35 to 45 minutes, or until the tops are firm and golden brown and spring back when pressed lightly in the middle with a fingertip. Let cool completely in the pans on a wire rack.

⇒ To make the frosting: While the cakes are cooling, in a small heatproof bowl, whisk together the sugar and egg whites to make a thick slurry. Place the bowl over (not touching) simmering water in a saucepan and heat, whisking occasionally, for 6 to 8 minutes, or until the mixture is hot to the touch. It will thin out a bit as the sugar melts.

⇒ Remove from the heat and scrape the mixture into the bowl of the stand mixer. Fit the mixer with the whip attachment and whip on medium-high speed for 6 to 8 minutes, or until the mixture becomes a light, white meringue and is cool to the touch. Turn down the speed to low and add the butter, a few chunks at a time. Increase the speed to medium and mix for 4 to 5 minutes, or until the butter is thoroughly incorporated and the frosting is smooth and glossy. It will look curdled at first, but don't worry. Keep whipping and it will come together.

⇒ Add the vanilla extract, salt, and coconut milk and whip for another 1 to 2 minutes, or until the coconut milk is thoroughly incorporated and the frosting is smooth. You should have about 5½ cups. (Use within 30 minutes, or transfer to an airtight container and store at room temperature for up to 1 day, then beat with the stand mixer fitted with the paddle attachment until smooth before using. Or, store in an airtight container in the refrigerator for up to 2 weeks, then bring to room temperature and paddle again for 6 to 8 minutes until smooth before using.)

⇒ Remove the cooled cakes from their pans. Using a long, serrated knife, trim the top of each cake to level it (the layers will have rounded a bit in the oven; the trimmed scraps make great nibbles). Place one cake layer on a cake plate or cake pedestal (if you have a revolving cake stand, use it). Spoon about 2 cups of the frosting on top and use an offset spatula to spread it evenly to the edges.

⇒ Carefully place the second cake layer, top-side down (so the even, sharp edges will be on the top of the finished cake), on top. Spoon on about 1 cup of the frosting and spread it over the top and down the sides of the cake, smoothing the frosting as well as you can and covering the entire cake with a very thin layer of it. This is the crumb coat (see page 13), which will keep any loose crumbs from migrating to the surface of the finished cake. Place the cake in the refrigerator for about 20 minutes to firm up the crumb coat.

⇒ Beat the remaining frosting (about 2½ cups) briefly with a wooden spoon to keep it creamy. Spoon it on the cake (if desired, reserve a small amount for piping a decorative border) and spread it evenly across the top and down the sides. This is the finishing layer of frosting. Press the remaining 1 cup (120 grams) shredded coconut evenly onto the top and sides of the cake, covering the cake completely. (It helps to tilt the cake with one hand and press the coconut with your other hand.) As you work, hold the cake over a plate or bowl to catch the falling bits of coconut, so you can reuse them. Spoon any remaining frosting into a pastry bag fitted with a small round tip and pipe a decorative line along the top and/or bottom edge of the cake (see page 16).

⇒ The cake can be stored in an airtight container in a cool place for up to 3 days.

Baker's Bite

Coconut milk commonly comes in 13½-ounce (384-gram) and 14-ounce (400-gram) cans. Either size yields enough for both the cake and the frosting.

TOASTED COCONUT ANGEL FOOD CAKE

1 cup (120 grams) sweetened shredded coconut

12 egg whites

⅛ teaspoon kosher salt

Pinch of cream of tartar

1 teaspoon water

1 teaspoon vanilla extract

1½ cups (300 grams) sugar

1 cup (100 grams) sifted cake flour (sift flour before measuring)

MAKES ONE 10-INCH CAKE (SERVES 8 TO 10)

Making my first angel food cake represented a turning point in my budding baking career. In my first postcollege job as a management consultant, I found myself spending all my free time teaching myself how to bake. I lived in a studio apartment with a kitchen the size of a closet and with little in the way of baking equipment. The more I read and the more I baked, the more I became desperate for a stand mixer. With a mixer, I could jump into the world of meringue cakes and cookies, sponge cakes, chiffon cakes, and bread doughs. I was trying to pay down all my student loans, however, so buying one was out of the question. But finally, when faced with an irresistible recipe for an angel food cake, I broke down and bought a stand mixer, and I have never looked back!

I was completely captivated by the idea of this classic fluffy cake made with only egg whites, sugar, and flour, perfectly named for its white, airy interior. Angel food cakes can be made by hand, but every recipe I read suggested a stand mixer for whipping the egg whites. If you want to do it by hand, be prepared for some wrist fatigue. I've adapted the classic recipe to include toasted coconut, which adds sweetness and richness that makes the cake even more delightful. For best results, leave the cake inverted until ready to serve; this ensures the lightest possible crumb. When it is time to slice it, use a serrated knife so you don't compress it.

→ Position a rack in the center of the oven, and heat the oven to 350 degrees F.

→ Spread about ½ cup (60 grams) of the coconut on a baking sheet and toast for 6 to 8 minutes, or until lightly golden. Transfer to a plate to cool.

→ Using a stand mixer fitted with the whip attachment (or a large metal bowl and a balloon whisk), beat together the egg whites, salt, cream of tartar, water, and vanilla on medium speed for 2 to 3 minutes, or until soft peaks form. The whites will start to froth and turn into bubbles, and eventually the yellowy viscous part will disappear. Keep whipping until you can see the tines of your whip leaving a slight trail in the whites. To test for the soft-peak stage, stop the mixer and lift the whip out of the whites; the whites should peak and then droop.

→ On medium speed, add ¾ cup (150 grams) of the sugar to the egg whites, a few tablespoons at a time, whipping after each addition for 10 seconds or so before adding more. It should take at least 1 minute to add the sugar. When the sugar has been incorporated, turn up the speed to medium-high and beat for 2 to 3 minutes, or until the whites are glossy and shiny and hold a peak when you slowly lift the whip straight up and out of the whites.

→ Add the remaining ¾ cup (150 grams) sugar to the sifted flour. Carefully sprinkle the flour mixture and the toasted coconut on top of the whites. Using a rubber spatula, gently and quickly fold them into the whites until thoroughly combined. Scrape the batter into an ungreased angel food cake pan or tube pan with a removable base about 10 inches in diameter. Use the spatula or a spoon to even the top of the batter. Then sprinkle the remaining untoasted coconut evenly on top of the batter.

→ Bake for 30 to 40 minutes, or until the top is a light golden brown and the coconut is nicely toasted. Immediately remove the cake from the oven and turn the cake pan upside down. This ensures that the cake does not deflate and compact onto itself, and because the cake pan is not greased, the cake won't fall out. Leave the cake upside down for at least 2 hours, or until cooled to room temperature. (If you're using a tube pan instead of a traditional angel food cake pan, invert the pan over the neck of a full wine bottle so there is space between the top of the cake and the counter and steam can escape.)

→ Turn the cake pan right-side up, and run a knife around the inside edge of the pan and of the tube to loosen the cake. Pop out the removable pan base along with the cake, and then run a knife between the cake and the base to loosen the cake. Turn the base so the tube is upside down, and carefully and quickly remove the cake. Turn the cake right-side up on a cake plate.

→ The cake can be stored in an airtight container at room temperature for up to 1 day, but it is lightest and fluffiest on the day it is baked.

BOOZY RUM CAKE

8 eggs, separated

1⅓ cups (270 grams) sugar

½ cup (120 grams) fresh orange juice (about 2 oranges)

2 cups (240 grams) cake flour

Pinch of kosher salt

RUM CREAM

2 cups (480 grams) milk

¾ cup (150 grams) sugar

6 tablespoons (45 grams) cake flour

¼ teaspoon kosher salt

6 egg yolks

1 teaspoon vanilla

½ cup (120 grams) heavy cream

3 tablespoons light or dark rum

1 teaspoon finely grated orange zest

RUM SYRUP

½ cup (120 grams) light or dark rum

1 cup (200 grams) sugar

1 cup (240 grams) water

1 cinnamon stick

Pinch of ground cloves

Pinch of kosher salt

RUM WHIPPED CREAM

1½ cups (360 grams) heavy cream

3 tablespoons sugar

1 tablespoon cornstarch

1 tablespoon plus 1 teaspoon light or dark rum

MAKES ONE 9-INCH,
4-LAYER CAKE
(SERVES 10)

I originally developed this cake as a restaurant dessert. After I left Mistral to open Flour, Jamie Mammano, my chef at Mistral, asked if I would continue to create desserts for him that his pastry prep staff could execute until he found a replacement for me. This cake was perfect: it's one of those desserts that tastes a lot more complicated than it is to make. For the restaurant, individual ramekins of an easy-to-make sponge cake were filled with basic pastry cream flavored with rum and topped with a fluff of whipped cream. It works even better as a whole cake. The sponge cake lives up to its name: it soaks up copious amounts of rum syrup (scented with a little cinnamon and clove). The rum cream may seem too runny and almost too soft to be a layer within the cake, but don't worry. After you assemble the layers and rum cream, the whole cake goes into the refrigerator overnight so all of the elements can meld and flavor one another. The next day, you finish off the cake with lightly sweetened, boozed-up whipped cream. It's spectacular and it's spectacularly delicious.

➡ Position a rack in the center of the oven, and heat the oven to 350 degrees F. Butter and flour two 9-inch round cake pans, or line with parchment paper.

➡ Using a stand mixer fitted with the whip attachment (or a handheld mixer), beat together the egg yolks, ⅔ cup (140 grams) of the sugar, and the orange juice on high speed for at least 6 minutes, or until thick and voluminous. (This step will take about 12 minutes if using a handheld mixer.) Transfer to another bowl and set aside.

➡ Clean the mixer bowl and the whip attachment (they must be spotlessly clean) and fit the mixer with the whip attachment. Place the egg whites in the bowl and and beat on medium speed for 1 to 2 minutes, or until they hold soft peaks. The whites will start to froth and turn into bubbles, and eventually the yellowy viscous part will disappear. Keep whipping until you can see the tines of your whip leaving a slight trail in the whites. To test for the soft-peak stage, stop the mixer and lift the whip out of the whites; the whites should peak and then droop.

On medium speed, slowly add the remaining ²/₃ cup (130 grams) sugar and whip for 1 to 2 minutes, or until the whites are glossy and shiny and hold a peak when you slowly lift the whip straight up and out of the whites.

Using a rubber spatula, gently fold about one-third of the whipped whites into the yolk mixture to lighten it. Then gently fold in the remaining whites. Sift the flour and salt over the top of the mixture and fold in gently. Divide the batter evenly between the prepared pans.

Bake for 30 to 35 minutes, or until the tops are light golden brown and they spring back when pressed in the middle with a fingertip. Let cool in the pans on wire racks for about 10 minutes. Run a paring knife around the edge of each cake to loosen it from the pan sides, and invert each cake onto a rack. Gently peel off the parchment (if used), and allow the cakes to cool completely.

To make the rum cream: While the cakes are baking and cooling, in a medium saucepan, scald the milk over medium-high heat (bubbles start to form around the edge of the pan, but the milk is not boiling). While the milk is heating, in a small bowl, stir together the sugar, flour, and salt. (Mixing the flour with the sugar will prevent the flour from clumping when you add it to the egg yolks.) In a medium bowl, whisk the egg yolks until blended, then slowly whisk in the flour mixture. The mixture will be thick and pasty.

Remove the milk from the heat and slowly add it to the egg-flour mixture, a little at a time, whisking constantly. When all of the milk has been incorporated, return the contents of the bowl to the saucepan and place over medium heat. Whisk continuously and vigorously for about 3 minutes, or until the mixture thickens and comes to a boil. At first, the mixture will be very frothy and liquid; as it cooks longer, it will slowly start to thicken until the frothy bubbles disappear and it becomes more viscous. Once it thickens, stop whisking every few seconds to see if the mixture has come to a boil. If it has not, keep whisking vigorously. As

soon as you see it bubbling, immediately go back to whisking for just 10 seconds, and then remove the pan from the heat. Boiling this pastry cream will thicken it and cook out the flour taste, but if you let it boil for longer than 10 seconds, it can become grainy.

Pour the pastry cream through a fine-mesh sieve into a small heatproof bowl. Stir in the vanilla, then cover with plastic wrap, placing it directly on the surface of the cream. This will prevent a skin from forming. Refrigerate for at least 4 hours, or until cold, or up to 3 days.

Just before you are ready to assemble the cake, fit the stand mixer with the whip attachment (or use a handheld mixer) and whip the heavy cream until it holds stiff peaks. Whisk in the rum and orange zest. Whisk the chilled pastry cream to smooth it out, then use a folding motion with the whisk to incorporate the rum-flavored cream until thoroughly combined. You should have about 3 cups.

To make the rum syrup: In a small saucepan, combine the rum, sugar, water, cinnamon stick, cloves, and salt and bring to a boil over high heat. Remove from the heat and let cool for about 2 hours, or until room temperature. Strain through a fine-mesh sieve into a bowl. (The rum syrup can be made up to 1 week in advance and stored in an airtight container in the refrigerator.)

Using a long, serrated knife, trim the top of each cake to level it (the layers will have rounded a bit in the oven; the trimmed scraps make great nibbles). Then split each cake into two layers (see Splitting a Cake into Layers, page 18), so you have 4 layers total. Place one layer on a 9-inch cardboard cake round (and place this on a revolving cake stand, if you have one), or place directly on a cake plate. Brush the layer generously with about one-fourth of the rum syrup. Spread about one-fourth of the rum cream evenly over the layer. It will be fairly liquid and soft, so don't worry if a little seeps over the side.

(continued)

⇒ Carefully place a second layer on top, and brush with one-third of the remaining rum syrup. Spread one-third of the remaining rum cream evenly over the layer. Repeat with a third cake layer and top with half of the remaining syrup and cream. Top with the fourth cake layer and soak with the remaining syrup. Spoon the rest of the rum cream over the top and use an offset spatula to spread it evenly over the top and down the sides, smoothing it as well as you can and covering the entire cake with a thin layer. Immediately wrap the cake with plastic wrap, pressing the wrap directly onto the cake. If the cake is leaning to one side, straighten it up within the plastic wrap. Refrigerate for at least 8 hours or for up to overnight.

⇒ To make the rum whipped cream: Fit the stand mixer with the whip attachment (or use a handheld mixer) and whip together the cream, sugar, cornstarch, and rum until soft peaks form. You should have about 3 cups. (The whipped cream can be prepared up to 1 hour in advance, covered, and stored in the refrigerator.)

⇒ Spoon the whipped cream on top of the cake and use the offset spatula to spread it evenly over the top and sides.

⇒ The cake can be stored in an airtight container in the refrigerator for up to 3 days.

VEGAN LOW-FAT CHOCOLATE CAKE

1½ cups (210 grams) unbleached all-purpose flour

½ cup (100 grams) granulated sugar

⅓ cup (40 grams) Dutch-processed cocoa powder

2 teaspoons instant espresso powder, or 1 tablespoon instant coffee powder

1 teaspoon baking soda

¼ teaspoon kosher salt

1 cup (240 grams) water

¼ cup (50 grams) canola oil

1 teaspoon vanilla extract

2 tablespoons unsulfured light or dark molasses

Confectioners' sugar for dusting

MAKES ONE 6-INCH CAKE (SERVES 6 TO 8)

There was a time, early on in my career, when I believed that if something was low in fat, it must be dry and tasteless. Then I realized that some of my favorite desserts—Häagen-Dazs mango sorbet, angel food cake, *rochers* (those billowy, almondy, chewy-yet-crispy meringue cookies that I discovered while bakery hopping in France)—are naturally low in fat. The beauty of this recipe is that if you don't tell anyone, they probably won't guess that it is low-fat. It also happens to be vegan. It tastes incredibly rich, is super-moist, and its bittersweet chocolate flavor is highlighted by the espresso powder. As a bonus, it isn't too sweet, unlike so many low-fat dessert offerings. It is very easy to prepare and a great recipe for beginning bakers.

⇒ Position a rack in the center of the oven, and heat the oven to 350 degrees F. Butter and flour a 6-inch round cake pan.

⇒ In a medium bowl, stir together the flour, granulated sugar, cocoa powder, espresso powder, baking soda, and salt. In another medium bowl, whisk together the water, oil, vanilla, and molasses. Pour the liquid mixture into the flour mixture and mix together with a wooden spoon until the batter is smooth and homogeneous. Pour the batter into the prepared pan.

⇒ Bake for 50 to 55 minutes, or until the cake springs back when lightly pressed in the middle with a fingertip. Let cool in the pan on a wire rack for about 1 hour. Then invert the pan onto the rack, lift off the pan, turn the cake right-side up, and let cool completely.

⇒ Just before serving, dust the top with confectioners' sugar.

⇒ The cake can be stored in an airtight container at room temperature for up to 2 days.

MOLTEN CHOCOLATE CAKES

10 ounces (280 grams) bittersweet chocolate (62 to 70 percent cacao), chopped

1 cup (2 sticks/228 grams) unsalted butter, melted

8 eggs

¾ cup (150 grams) sugar

½ teaspoon kosher salt

1 teaspoon vanilla extract

MAKES 6 INDIVIDUAL CAKES

Molten chocolate cakes were all the rage on restaurant menus throughout the country during the 1990s—and for good reason. There are many versions, and most feature a moist chocolate cake that releases a river of warm chocolate when you cut into it. What molten chocolate cake aficionados will be surprised to learn is how easy these cakes are to make at home. You can make the batter in advance and then simply pop the cakes into the oven about 30 minutes before you want to serve them, making them an ideal dinner-party dessert. The only tricky part is knowing exactly when to pull the cakes out of the oven. You want the batter to firm up into cake everywhere except for the very center, which should be soft and squishy. Once you remove them from the oven, they need to sit for a few minutes so everything can settle, then you must flip them quickly upside down onto serving dishes. They should stand up straight and tall and have the faintest bit of wiggle in them when you nudge them. When the diner cuts into the cake with a fork, it will slowly break open to reveal a soft, creamy chocolate center. Chocolate is the star of the show here, so buy the best.

➡ Position a rack in the center of the oven, and heat the oven to 400 degrees F. Generously butter six 10- or 12-ounce straight-sided, ovenproof coffee mugs, or coat them with nonstick cooking spray. Pour a small handful of sugar into a mug, turn the mug on its side and rotate it to coat the inside with sugar, and then dump the excess sugar into the next mug. Continue until all of the buttered mugs are coated with sugar.

➡ Place the chocolate in a small heatproof bowl. Place over (not touching) barely simmering water in a saucepan and heat, stirring occasionally, until completely melted and smooth. Remove from the heat and whisk in the butter until well mixed.

→ Using a stand mixer fitted with the whip attachment (or a handheld mixer), beat the eggs on low speed for a few seconds to break them up. Turn up the speed to medium and slowly add the ¾ cup (150 grams) sugar. When all of the sugar is incorporated, continue to beat for 6 to 8 minutes, or until the mixture is thick and pale. Add the salt and vanilla and beat for a few seconds to incorporate.

→ Pour the chocolate-butter mixture into the eggs and beat on medium speed for 1 minute, or until combined. Remove the bowl from the mixer stand and whisk vigorously by hand to make sure all of the chocolate is fully incorporated into the egg-sugar mixture. The mixture will deflate somewhat but should still be frothy.

→ Divide the batter evenly among the prepared mugs, filling them to within at least 1 inch of the rim. (At this point, the mugs can be covered tightly with plastic wrap and stored in the refrigerator for up to 1 day.) Place all of the mugs on a single baking sheet to make transporting them easier.

→ Bake for 20 to 26 minutes (on the shorter side if the batter is fresh, on the longer side if the batter has been refrigerated). The key to making these cakes is to bake them so that they are set on the outside but still a little gooey in the very middle. To test for doneness, press each cake (which will have risen to the rim of the mug) all along the edge, which should feel firm, and then poke your finger into the center, which should be gooey, rather than set. That gooey center should be no more than the size of the quarter. Remove the cakes from the oven, and let them sit for 3 to 4 minutes to settle a little bit.

→ Run a paring knife around the inside edge of a mug to loosen the cake. As you go along, use the very tip of the knife to nudge the bottom of the cake up from the bottom of the mug. Place a small dessert plate upside down on top of the mug. Carefully invert the mug and the plate together onto a firm surface. Wiggle the mug around and carefully pull it straight up from the cake. If you have run your knife completely around the sides and bottom part of the mug, the cake should gently slide out. (If it doesn't slide out, re-invert the mug and run your knife around the edge and bottom once again.) Unmold the remaining cakes the same way, then serve the cakes immediately.

CHOCOLATE CUPCAKES
WITH CRISPY MAGIC FROSTING

2 ounces (56 grams) unsweetened chocolate, chopped

¼ cup (30 grams) Dutch-processed cocoa powder

1 cup (200 grams) granulated sugar

½ cup (1 stick/114 grams) unsalted butter

⅓ cup (80 grams) water

½ cup (120 grams) milk

1 egg

1 egg yolk

½ teaspoon vanilla extract

1 cup (140 grams) unbleached all-purpose flour

1 teaspoon baking powder

½ teaspoon baking soda

½ teaspoon kosher salt

CRISPY MAGIC FROSTING

⅔ cup (140 grams) granulated sugar

2 egg whites

1½ cups (3 sticks/342 grams) unsalted butter, at room temperature, cut into 2-inch chunks

1⅔ cups (230 grams) confectioners' sugar

¼ teaspoon kosher salt

2 tablespoons milk

1 tablespoon vanilla extract

MAKES 12 CUPCAKES

In Amanda Hesser's lovely book *Cooking for Mr. Latte*, she shares an appealing recipe for chocolate cake that she calls Dump Cake. Okay, maybe the name isn't so appealing, but after years of making cakes that involve folding two-thirds of this into one-eighth of that and timing the mixer for one minute and fourteen seconds, I was quite taken with the idea of making a cake that simply requires dumping this into that and you're done. I've started with her recipe, added some cocoa, and removed some egg and liquid. The result is a wonderfully chocolaty, moist cupcake that is one of the most popular items at the bakery. Do what we do to best enjoy the cupcake: Pop off the top half of the cupcake, put the bottom half on top of the frosted top, and voilà! You have a cupcake sandwich that gives you cupcake and frosting in each bite. The Crispy Magic Frosting forms a delicate sugary crust as it rests and it's so easy, it's magic!

⇒ Position a rack in the center of the oven, and heat the oven to 350 degrees F. Butter and flour a standard 12-cup muffin tin, or line with paper liners.

⇒ In a small heatproof bowl, combine the chocolate and cocoa powder. In a small saucepan, heat the granulated sugar, butter, and water over medium-high heat, whisking occasionally, for 3 to 4 minutes, or until the butter is melted and the sugar is dissolved. Pour the hot butter-sugar mixture over the chocolate-cocoa mixture and whisk until the chocolate is completely melted and the mixture is homogeneous.

⇒ Whisk the milk, egg, egg yolk, and vanilla into the chocolate mixture until thoroughly combined.

⇒ In a bowl, stir together the flour, baking powder, baking soda, and salt until well mixed. Dump the flour mixture on top of the chocolate mixture. Whisk until the dry ingredients are totally mixed into the chocolate mixture. Let the batter sit for at least 1 hour at room temperature, or transfer to an airtight container and store in the refrigerator for up to 3 days. (This allows the liquid to be totally absorbed into the batter, so the batter thickens up a bit and isn't so soupy.)

(continued)

➡ Spoon the batter into the prepared muffin cups, dividing it evenly and filling the cups to the rim. Bake for about 30 minutes, or until the tops spring back when pressed with a fingertip. Let cool completely in the pan on a wire rack.

➡ To make the frosting: While the cupcakes are cooling, in a small heatproof bowl, whisk together the granulated sugar and egg whites to make a thick slurry. Place the bowl over (not touching) simmering water in a saucepan and heat, whisking occasionally, for 3 to 5 minutes, or until the mixture is hot to the touch. It will thin out a bit as the sugar melts.

➡ Remove from the heat and scrape the mixture into the bowl of a stand mixer fitted with a whip attachment (or use a handheld mixer). Whip on medium-high speed for 6 to 8 minutes, or until the mixture becomes a light, white meringue and is cool to the touch. Turn down the speed to medium, add the butter, a few chunks at a time, and beat for 3 to 4 minutes, or until the butter is thoroughly incorporated. Add the confectioners' sugar, salt, milk, and vanilla and continue to beat on medium speed until the mixture is smooth and satiny. You should have about 3½ cups. (Use immediately, or transfer to an airtight container and store at room temperature for up to 3 days, then beat with the stand mixer fitted with the paddle attachment for a few minutes until smooth before using. Or, store in an airtight container in the refrigerator for up to 2 weeks, then bring to room temperature and paddle for a few minutes until smooth before using.)

➡ Remove the cupcakes from the muffin tin. Fit a pastry bag with a small round or star tip and fill the bag with the frosting (see page 15), then pipe the frosting onto cupcakes. Or, spread the frosting on the cupcakes with an icing spatula.

➡ The cupcakes taste best on the day they are baked, but they can be stored in an airtight container at room temperature for up to 2 days.

OLD-FASHIONED PINEAPPLE UPSIDE-DOWN CAKE

1 pineapple

1¾ cups (350 grams) sugar

½ cup (120 grams) water

6 tablespoons (¾ stick/86 grams) softened unsalted butter, plus ½ cup (1 stick/114 grams), melted and cooled

1 cup (140 grams) unbleached all-purpose flour

1 teaspoon baking powder

¼ teaspoon kosher salt

2 eggs, at room temperature

3 egg yolks, at room temperature

1 teaspoon vanilla extract

MAKES ONE 9-INCH CAKE (SERVES 10)

My first (and for a long time, my last) experience with pineapple upside-down cake was in my elementary school cafeteria, where it was often a dessert choice, along with red and green Jell-O cubes, fruit cocktail, and chocolate pudding. Since I rarely was allowed sweets at home, I took full advantage at school and always gobbled up whatever I was handed. I remember a jarringly sweet and artificial-tasting thick piece of cake topped with pale, skinny canned pineapple rings and maraschino cherries. This cake hardly resembles the one from my childhood memory, and that's a good thing. Fresh pineapple is cut into thick slices and braised in a buttery vanilla-scented caramel until it soaks up the rich syrup and lets some of its tart juices seep into the caramel. Both fruit and caramel are arranged in the bottom of a cake pan, and a simple butter cake batter is poured on top. The pineapple perfumes the entire cake as it bakes in the oven. When you invert the cake, the rich syrup melts into the cake and you end up with a gooey, buttery caramelized cake topped with luscious fruit.

➡ Using a serrated knife, peel, halve, and core the pineapple, then cut into ¾-inch-thick slices. Cut the slices in half.

➡ Put ¾ cup (150 grams) of the sugar in the bottom of a medium saucepan. Add the water and gently swirl the pan to moisten the sugar; if necessary, poke your fingers around the bottom of the pan to make sure all of the sugar is moistened with water. Place the pan over high heat and leave it undisturbed until the contents come to a rolling boil. Then continue to boil rapidly without moving the pan until the sugar syrup starts to caramelize. This will take 3 to 4 minutes: the sugar syrup will boil furiously; then as it thickens, it will boil more languidly; and then you will see some of the syrup start to color and darken around the edge of the pan.

(continued)

➡ When you see color in the pan, gently swirl the pan in a circular motion so the sugar caramelizes evenly, and then keep swirling gently until the caramel is a medium golden brown. Turn down the heat to low and whisk in the 6 tablespoons butter; be careful, as the caramel may sputter and steam. Carefully add the pineapple and stir until it is coated with the caramel. Don't worry if some of the caramel hardens; it will reliquefy as it continues to cook. Turn up the heat to medium-high and bring to a boil. Then turn down the heat to medium-low and simmer for 8 to 12 minutes, or until the pineapple turns golden brown. The pineapple will release juice and liquefy the caramel. Using a fork, transfer the pineapple to a plate. Continue to boil the remaining liquid on medium-high heat for 2 to 3 minutes, or until thick and syrupy.

➡ Position a rack in the center of the oven, and heat the oven to 350 degrees F. Generously butter a 9-inch round cake pan.

➡ Add all of the pineapple and the caramel syrup to the prepared pan, arranging the pineapple in concentric circles and covering as much of the bottom of the pan as possible. Cut the pineapple quarters into smaller pieces to fill in any gaps, and double layer the pineapple if there is extra.

➡ In a medium bowl, sift together the flour, baking powder, and salt. In a large bowl, whisk together the eggs and egg yolks until blended, then slowly whisk in the remaining 1 cup (200 grams) sugar, the vanilla, and the 1/2 cup melted butter. Using a rubber spatula, fold the flour mixture into the egg mixture just until well combined.

➡ Pour the batter evenly over the pineapple in the cake pan. Tap the pan gently on a countertop to get rid of any air bubbles in the batter and to make sure the batter fills in any crevices in the pineapple and settles into the bottom of the pan.

➡ Bake for 50 to 60 minutes, or until the top is golden brown and springs back when pressed in the middle with a fingertip. Let cool in the pan on a wire rack for about 30 minutes, or until cool enough to handle.

➡ Place a serving plate upside down on top of the cake pan, then holding the pan and the plate tightly together, carefully invert them. Lift off the cake pan. If some of the pineapple sticks to the pan, remove it and replace it in its place on top of the cake. Let the cake cool for at least another 30 minutes, then serve warm or at room temperature.

➡ The cake can be stored in an airtight container at room temperature for up to 2 days.

LUSCIOUS CHEESECAKE

48 graham crackers (12 full cracker sheets; 168 grams)

6 tablespoons (¾ stick/86 grams) unsalted butter, melted

2 tablespoons granulated sugar

1½ pounds (680 grams) cream cheese, at room temperature

1½ cups (300 grams) vanilla sugar (see page 29)

4 eggs

3 tablespoons fresh lemon juice (about 1½ lemons)

2 teaspoons vanilla extract

½ teaspoon kosher salt

⅓ cup (70 grams) crème fraîche or sour cream

MAKES ONE 9-INCH CAKE (SERVES 8 TO 12)

There are as many different kinds of cheesecakes as there are dieters who have sworn off them. (But what fun is that?) New York style, ricotta, rich and dense, fluffy and airy—the list goes on. This one is simply luscious, hence the name. It's not fancy, so if you're looking for a chocolate-orange-with-raspberry-swirl-type thing, this isn't for you. But if you're looking for a cheesecake with perfectly balanced flavor and a light, creamy texture that you can't stop eating, you're on the right page.

It starts with a traditional graham cracker crust (use store-bought grahams or the homemade version on page 140). Cream cheese is blended with eggs, vanilla sugar, and a hefty dollop of crème fraîche; lemon lends subtle brightness and salt heightens the tangy taste of the cream cheese and highlights the lemon and vanilla flavors. And that's it. It is a terrific example of how the best pastries are often simple recipes done right. I like serving each slice with a spoonful of sliced strawberries.

⇒ Position a rack in the center of the oven, and heat the oven to 350 degrees F. Generously butter the bottom and sides of a 9-inch springform pan or coat it with nonstick cooking spray, then line the bottom with parchment paper.

⇒ In a food processor, pulse the graham crackers until they are ground to crumbs. Use 2 to 3 tablespoons of the crumbs to dust the sides of the prepared pan. Add the butter and granulated sugar to the crumbs and process until the mixture comes together. Press the crumb mixture evenly onto the bottom of the prepared pan.

⇒ Bake the crust for 15 minutes, or until lightly browned. Set aside on a wire rack. Turn down the oven to 325 degrees F.

⇒ While the crust is baking, clean the bowl of the food processor, or fit a stand mixer with the paddle attachment. Process the cream cheese or beat on medium speed for at least 1 minute, or until smooth. Add the vanilla sugar and process or beat for 10 to 15 seconds, or until combined. Stop and scrape the sides and bottom of the bowl. Add the eggs and process or beat for 1 to 2 minutes, or until well mixed. Add the lemon juice, vanilla extract, salt, and crème fraîche and process or beat for 1 to 2 minutes longer. Scrape the sides and bottom of the bowl once again, then process or beat on medium speed for 15 to 20 seconds, or until smooth and thoroughly mixed. Pour the mixture into the baked crust.

➡ Place the springform pan in a deep roasting pan, and place the roasting pan on the oven rack. Pour hot water into the roasting pan to reach about halfway up the sides of the cake pan. (The water bath allows the cheesecake to bake slowly and gently, which leads to a smoother cake.)

➡ Bake for 1½ hours, or until the sides of the cheesecake are set and the center wobbles just a bit when the cake pan is jiggled. Turn off the oven and leave the cake in the closed oven for 1 hour longer. (This keeps the cheesecake from cracking when you remove it from the oven.)

➡ Remove the cheesecake from the oven, and let it cool on a wire rack at room temperature for about 1 hour, then place the cheesecake in the refrigerator for 3 to 4 hours before serving. To serve, remove the pan sides, place the cheesecake, still on the pan bottom, on a serving plate. Slice and serve, sliding each wedge off the parchment onto a dessert plate.

➡ The cheesecake can be stored in an airtight container in the refrigerator for up to 3 days.

Baker's Bite

If you don't have a springform pan, you can still make this cheesecake. Use a 9-inch round cake pan instead and prepare it the same way. Once the cheesecake has cooled at room temperature for 1 hour, wrap the cake in the pan in plastic wrap and place in the freezer overnight. Remove from the freezer, unwrap, and warm the bottom of the cheesecake by placing the cake pan directly over very, very low heat on the stove top for about 1 minute. Run a paring knife around the edge of the cake to loosen it from the pan sides, then turn the pan upside down. Rap the pan firmly against a countertop until the cake pops out of the pan. Peel the parchment off the bottom of the cake. Turn the cake right-side up on a cake plate, and let thaw for 4 to 5 hours at room temperature or overnight in the refrigerator.

NEW TIRAMISU

COFFEE-FLAVORED SPONGE CAKE

4 eggs, separated

⅔ cup (140 grams) sugar

¼ cup (60 grams) hot brewed espresso

1 cup (140 grams) unbleached all-purpose flour

Pinch of kosher salt

MASCARPONE MOUSSE

4 egg yolks

¼ cup (50 grams) sugar

¼ cup (70 grams) coffee liqueur such as Kahlúa or Tia Maria

Pinch of kosher salt

¾ cup (170 grams) mascarpone cheese

½ cup (120 grams) heavy cream

1 cup (240 grams) hot brewed espresso or double-strength coffee

1 ounce (28 grams) unsweetened chocolate

SERVES 10

During my time at Boston's Mistral restaurant, chef Jamie Mammano asked me to put this oh-so-1980s dessert on the menu. Tiramisu is typically made with store-bought ladyfingers, mascarpone cheese, brandy or Marsala, and cocoa powder. I wanted to make an updated version with my own touch. I tweaked a favorite sponge cake recipe and included some coffee in the cake; I made a mascarpone mousse and added Kahlúa for more coffee flavor; and I decided on grated chocolate rather than cocoa powder. Jamie and our customers were thrilled with the result. So, yes, tiramisu has had its heyday. And you may think you've already eaten enough to last you a lifetime. But I think you'll agree this version makes the old favorite worth revisiting.

➡ Position a rack in the center of the oven, and heat the oven to 350 degrees F. Line a 14-by-11-inch baking sheet or 15-by-10-inch jelly-roll pan with parchment paper.

➡ To make the sponge cake, using a stand mixer fitted with the whip attachment (or a handheld mixer), beat together 4 of the egg yolks, ⅓ cup (70 grams) of the sugar, and the ¼ cup (60 grams) hot espresso on high speed for at least 6 minutes (10 to 12 minutes if using a handheld mixer), or until thick and voluminous. Transfer to a large bowl and set aside.

➡ Clean the mixer bowl and the whip attachment (they must be spotlessly clean) and fit the mixer with the whip attachment. Place the egg whites in the bowl and beat on medium speed for 1 to 2 minutes, or until they hold soft peaks. The whites will start to froth and turn into bubbles, and eventually the yellowy viscous part will disappear. Keep whipping until you can see the tines of your whip leaving a slight trail in the whites. To test for the soft-peak stage, stop the mixer and lift the whip out of the whites; the whites should peak and then droop.

➡ On medium speed, slowly add the remaining ⅓ cup (70 grams) sugar and whip for 1 to 2 minutes, or until the whites are glossy and shiny and hold a peak when you slowly lift the whip straight up and out of the whites.

➡ Using a rubber spatula, gently fold about one-third of the whipped whites into the yolk mixture to lighten it. Then gently fold in the remaining egg whites. Sift the flour and salt over the top of the mixture and fold in gently. Spread the batter evenly in the prepared pan.

➡ Bake for 12 to 14 minutes, or until the top springs back when pressed in the center with fingertips and the cake doesn't stick to your fingers. Let cool in the pan on a wire rack for 5 minutes. Run a paring knife around the edge of the cake to loosen it from the pan sides, and invert the cake onto the rack. Gently peel off the parchment and allow the cake to cool completely.

➡ To make the mousse: Fill a large bowl with ice cubes and a little water. In a medium heatproof bowl, whisk together the remaining 4 egg yolks, the ¼ cup sugar, liqueur, and salt. Set the bowl over (not touching) simmering water in a saucepan and whisk for 6 to 7 minutes, or until the mixture thickens, the whisk leaves ribbons trailing off it, and you can see the bottom of the bowl when you scrape it with the whisk. Remove the bowl from the heat and nest it in the ice bath. Let cool completely, whisking occasionally.

➡ Meanwhile, in a medium bowl, whisk together the mascarpone and cream until the mixture holds peaks. When the yolk mixture is cool, gently fold in the cream mixture until combined. Keep the mixture cool.

➡ Cut the sponge cake crosswise into thirds (3 rectangles each about 4½ by 11 or 5 by 10 inches). Lay one rectangle on the bottom of a rectangular dish or pan (I use a Pyrex baking dish). Brush the top liberally with about ⅓ cup of the hot espresso. Spread slightly less than half of the mascarpone mixture over the rectangle. Grate about one-third of the chocolate on top of the mascarpone. Top with a second cake rectangle and brush with half of the remaining espresso. Spread all but ½ to ⅔ cup of the remaining mascarpone mixture over the top, and grate half of the remaining chocolate on top. Top with the third cake rectangle, brush on the last of the espresso, and spread the remaining mascarpone mixture in a very thin layer on top. Finally, grate the remaining chocolate on top. Cover and refrigerate for at least 3 hours or up to overnight before serving.

➡ The tiramisu can be stored in an airtight container in the refrigerator for up to 3 days.

HAZELNUT-ALMOND DACQUOISE

½ cup (70 grams) blanched whole hazelnuts, plus ¾ cup (75 grams) sliced almonds, toasted

½ cup (80 grams) blanched whole almonds, plus ¼ cup (35 grams) blanched whole hazelnuts, toasted

1⅓ cups (186 grams) confectioners' sugar

⅛ teaspoon kosher salt

6 egg whites

⅓ cup (70 grams) granulated sugar

BITTERSWEET CHOCOLATE GANACHE

1 pound (454 grams) semisweet or bittersweet chocolate, chopped

2 cups (480 grams) heavy cream

ESPRESSO BUTTERCREAM

¾ cup (150 grams) granulated sugar

¼ cup (60 grams) water

2 eggs

1 egg yolk

1½ cups (3 sticks/340 grams) unsalted butter, at room temperature, cut into 2-inch chunks

1 tablespoon instant espresso powder, 2 tablespoons instant coffee powder, or ¼ cup (60 grams) cooled brewed espresso

¼ teaspoon kosher salt

MAKES ONE 10-INCH-LONG RECTANGULAR CAKE (SERVES 10 TO 12)

Most of the offerings at Flour are decidedly American: chocolate chip cookies, banana bread, puddings, and muffins. But when I wrote the opening menu, I knew I wanted to include this very French cake. I still have the notebook I used to doodle in when I was coming up with ideas for Flour, and a detailed sketch of this cake is one of the first items in the book. I really like how dramatic it looks and how well all of the flavors and textures go together. *Dacquoise* refers to both the baked meringue layers within the cake and the composed cake itself. First, you make a light meringue and quickly and gently fold in hazelnut and almond flours. Then you pipe three long rectangles of the meringue onto a baking sheet and bake them in a slow oven overnight, so they dry out and get crispy. A creamy espresso buttercream that tastes like soft coffee ice cream and a chocolate ganache filling are sandwiched between the layers. The cake is not difficult to make, but all of its components make it important to read the recipe from start to finish so you can organize your prep schedule. Each component can be made in advance, which makes the final assembly of the cake easier.

⇒ Position a rack in the center of the oven, and heat the oven to 225 degrees F. Line an 18-by-13-inch baking sheet (if you don't have a sheet that large, line two smaller sheets) with parchment paper. Draw three 10-by-3-inch rectangles at least 3 inches apart on one side of the parchment paper, then turn over the parchment and liberally coat the other side of the paper with nonstick cooking spray or butter.

⇒ In a food processor, pulse the ½ cup hazelnuts until ground to a fine powder. (Stop grinding once they are powdery; if you continue, they will become a paste.) Transfer to a medium bowl. Repeat with the ½ cup almonds, and add the ground almonds to the hazelnuts. Sift the confectioners' sugar into the bowl holding the ground nuts. Add the salt and stir with a rubber spatula until all of the ingredients are well mixed.

➡ Using a stand mixer fitted with the whip attachment (or a handheld mixer), beat the egg whites on medium speed for 3 to 4 minutes, or until they hold soft peaks. (This will take 6 to 7 minutes with a handheld mixer.) The whites will start to froth and turn into bubbles, and eventually the yellowy viscous part will disappear. Keep whipping until you can see the tines of your whip leaving a slight trail in the whites. To test for the soft-peak stage, stop the mixer and lift the whip out of the whites; the whites should peak and then droop.

➡ On medium speed, add the granulated sugar to the whites in three equal additions, mixing for 30 seconds after each addition. When all of the sugar has been incorporated, increase the speed to high and beat for about 15 seconds longer. The meringue should be slightly glossy and white and somewhat stiff. Scrape the meringue into a large bowl.

➡ Sprinkle the nut-sugar mixture on top of the meringue. Working quickly and gently, use a rubber spatula to fold the nuts into the meringue, scraping the sides of the bowl to catch any loose nuts. The final consistency will be soupy, gloupy, and puddingy.

➡ Fit a pastry bag with a ½-inch round plain tip and fill the bag with the meringue (see page 15). Following the guidelines you drew on the underside of the parchment paper, pipe three rectangles of meringue, "fill in" the rectangles to form your individual layers. Space the rectangles about 3 inches apart (they will expand in the oven).

➡ Bake for about 3 hours, or until the *dacquoise* rectangles are firm to the touch. Turn off the oven and leave the rectangles in the closed oven for at least 6 hours or up to 12 hours.

➡ To make the chocolate ganache: Place the chocolate in a medium heatproof bowl. In a small saucepan, scald the cream over medium-high heat (bubbles start to form around the edge of the pan, but the cream is not boiling). Pour the hot cream over the chocolate and let sit for about 1 minute, then slowly whisk the chocolate and cream together until the chocolate is completely melted and the mixture is smooth. You should have about 4 cups. Let cool, cover, and store at room temperature for up to overnight. (The ganache can be made up to 1 week in advance and stored in an airtight container in the refrigerator. Remove it from the refrigerator 1 day before using.)

➡ To make the buttercream: In a small saucepan, stir together the granulated sugar and water. Place the pan over high heat, bring to a boil, and cook, without stirring, for 3 to 4 minutes, or until the syrup registers 238 degrees F on a candy thermometer (the soft-ball stage; see Cooking Sugar, page 13). Meanwhile, fit the stand mixer with the whip attachment (or use a handheld mixer) and beat together the eggs and egg yolk on medium speed for 3 to 4 minutes, or until pale and light.

➡ When the syrup is ready, remove from the heat. On low speed, slowly add the syrup into the eggs, drizzling it down the side of the bowl to keep it from hitting the whip and spattering. Turn up the speed to medium and whip for 6 to 8 minutes, or until the mixture turns light and fluffy, is pale, and is cool to the touch. Turn down the speed to low and add the butter, a few chunks at a time. Increase the speed to medium and continue to whip for 4 to 5 minutes. The mixture will break and look curdled at first, but don't worry. It will soon become smooth and silky.

(continued)

Add the espresso powder and salt and whip until completely combined. You should have about 3 cups. Use within 30 minutes, or cover and leave at room temperature for up to 8 hours, and then beat vigorously with a wooden spoon until smooth before using. (Or, transfer to an airtight container and store in the refrigerator for up to 5 days, then bring to room temperature and beat with the stand mixer fitted with the paddle attachment for a few minutes until smooth before using.)

When the *dacquoise* rectangles are ready, carefully peel them from the parchment paper. Using a small paring knife or a small, serrated knife, trim the edges so they are even and the rectangles are all about the same size. The rectangles are fairly delicate at this point, and if you are not careful, they could shatter. The best way to avoid this is to shave off a little piece at a time until the rectangles are roughly uniform. If a rectangle shatters as you are trimming it, don't fret. That rectangle can be the middle layer. If two or all three rectangles shatter, again don't fret. You can piece them together as you assemble the cake. The cake will not be quite as neat, but the final product will taste the same.

Cut a piece of cardboard the size of the *dacquoise* rectangles and place one rectangle on the cardboard. Fit a pastry bag with the 1/2-inch round plain tip and fill with about half of the ganache. Pipe a layer of ganache about 1/2 inch thick on top of the *dacquoise*. Gently press a second *dacquoise* rectangle directly on top of the ganache layer and press lightly to adhere the *dacquoise* to the ganache. Fill the pastry bag with about two-thirds of the espresso buttercream and pipe a layer of buttercream about 1/2 inch thick on top of the second *dacquoise* layer.

Top the buttercream with the last *dacquoise* rectangle, placing it upside down so the flat side is on top. Press lightly to adhere this last rectangle to the buttercream. Use a small offset spatula to spread the remaining buttercream into the gaps between the layers and to spread a very thin layer all over the *dacquoise*. Do your best to make the exterior of the cake as smooth as you can—you will need to use a fair amount of buttercream to fill in all the gaps.

Place the cake in the refrigerator for at least 1 hour to chill all of the layers. (At this point, the cake can be well wrapped in plastic wrap and stored in the refrigerator for up to 2 days or in the freezer for up to 2 weeks. If frozen, thaw overnight in the refrigerator before serving.)

When ready to serve, spoon the remaining ganache into a small heatproof bowl, place over (not touching) simmering water in a saucepan, and heat just until melted. (Or, place in a microwave-safe bowl and microwave on low power for 30 to 45 seconds, or just until melted and warmed enough to pour freely—not warmer than that.) Place a wire rack on a baking sheet (to catch the drips), and place the cake on the rack. Pour the melted ganache evenly over the entire *dacquoise*, so it covers the top and drips down the sides. Use a small offset spatula to level off the ganache on the top of the cake. Then, with the spatula, spread the ganache that drips down the sides so that it covers the sides evenly. Some of the ganache may mix into the buttercream, which is okay, because the sides will be covered with sliced almonds. Now, press the sliced almonds into the sides of the cake, covering them completely. (It helps to tilt the cake with one hand and press the almonds with your other hand.) Place the cake on a cake plate, and press the toasted hazelnuts along the top edge for decoration.

The cake can be stored in an airtight container in the refrigerator for up to 2 days.

Baker's Bite

To skin hazelnuts, toast them in the oven (see page 34) and then place the toasted nuts in a large waffle kitchen towel and rub them around so the skins slide off.

DEEP, DARK, SPICY GINGERBREAD WITH COFFEE GLAZE

1 cup (2 sticks/228 grams) unsalted butter, at room temperature

¾ cup (165 grams) packed light brown sugar

3 tablespoons grated fresh ginger

2 eggs

3½ cups (490 grams) unbleached all-purpose flour

1 tablespoon baking powder

½ teaspoon kosher salt

2 teaspoons ground ginger

1 teaspoon freshly ground black pepper

½ teaspoon ground cinnamon

¼ teaspoon ground cloves

1½ cups (480 grams) unsulfured light or dark molasses

1 cup (240 grams) boiling water

1 teaspoon baking soda

COFFEE GLAZE

1 cup (140 grams) confectioners' sugar

2 to 3 tablespoons double-strength brewed coffee

MAKES ONE 9-BY-13-INCH CAKE (SERVES 10 TO 12)

When I was pastry chef at Rialto restaurant, I was ecstatic when I was asked to make gingerbread. I enjoyed creating elegant desserts for our seasonal menu, but I missed making homey cakes. It was my first Christmas season at the restaurant and Christopher, one of the owners (and now my husband), wanted to give away little gingerbread cakes to our regular customers as holiday gifts. This gave me an excuse to develop my ideal recipe: soft, tender cake with lusty, bold flavors and a rich, sweet topping. I baked dozens of them in mini Bundt pans and drizzled them with large spoonfuls of coffee glaze while they were still warm, so they soaked up some of the glaze. We packaged them up in red and green cellophane, tied them with fancy ribbons, and stacked them at the dessert station (which was in the middle of the restaurant). When VIPs, regular customers, or friends of one of the owners came in, they were presented with a package. I loved watching their eyes light up as they received this unexpected bit of holiday cheer. I'm not shy with the spices in this cake. It has a good bit of fresh ginger along with an unusually large amount of black pepper. They make all the difference in this cake.

⇒ Position a rack in the center of the oven, and heat the oven to 350 degrees F. Butter and flour a 9-by-13-inch baking pan.

⇒ Using a stand mixer fitted with the paddle attachment (or a handheld mixer), cream together the butter and brown sugar for 2 to 3 minutes, or until light and fluffy. (This step will take 5 to 6 minutes if using a handheld mixer.) Stop the mixer a few times and use a rubber spatula to scrape the sides and bottom of the bowl and the paddle to release any clinging butter or sugar. In a small bowl, whisk together the grated ginger and eggs until blended. On low speed, slowly add the egg mixture to the butter mixture and mix just until combined. Scrape the sides and bottom of the bowl again and then beat on medium speed for 20 to 30 seconds, or until the mixture is homogeneous.

➡ In a medium bowl, sift together the flour, baking powder, salt, ground ginger, pepper, cinnamon, and cloves. In another medium bowl, whisk together the molasses, boiling water, and baking soda. It will foam up! On the lowest speed, add about one-third of the flour mixture to the egg-butter mixture and mix until incorporated. Immediately pour in about half of the molasses mixture and continue to mix on the lowest speed until combined. Stop the mixer and scrape the sides and bottom of the bowl well. Again on the lowest speed, add about half of the remaining flour mixture and mix until incorporated. Add the rest of the molasses mixture and mix until incorporated. Stop the mixer and scrape the sides and bottom of the bowl. Add the remaining flour mixture and mix on low speed for about 1 minute, or until the batter is homogeneous. Scrape the batter into the prepared pan.

➡ Bake for 50 to 60 minutes, or until the top of the cake springs back when lightly pressed in the middle with a fingertip. Let cool in the pan on a wire rack.

➡ To make the glaze: In a small bowl, whisk together the confectioners' sugar and enough of the coffee to make a smooth, thick, spreadable glaze.

➡ While the cake is still warm, spread the glaze evenly over the top. Let the glaze set for at least 1 hour before serving.

➡ The cake can be stored in an airtight container at room temperature for up to 3 days.

pies + tarts

DOUBLE TWO-APPLE PIE

1 recipe Pâte Brisée I (page 92)

4 large Granny Smith apples, peeled, cored, and sliced ¼ to ½ inch thick

3 medium Macintosh or Rome apples, peeled, cored, and sliced ¼ to ½ inch thick

¾ cup (165 grams) packed light brown sugar

¼ cup (35 grams) unbleached all-purpose flour

¼ teaspoon kosher salt

Pinch of ground cinnamon

1 egg, lightly beaten

2 tablespoons sanding sugar, pearl sugar, or granulated sugar

ONE 9-INCH PIE
(SERVES 8)

As a kid, I was nuts about McDonald's fried apple pies. The nifty cardboard holder; the golden brown cookielike crust; the chunks of appley, cinnamony, gooey sweetness— they were the perfect dessert to me. I still get a pang of desire when I see someone biting onto one. It was years before I realized there was any other sort of apple pie. I thought they were always half-moons! For this pie, why two apples? Many recipes recommend Rome or Macintosh or other such baking apples for pies. But I find that these cook up too soft and suffer from a one-dimensional sweetness. Using only tart, crisp apples (think Granny Smith) for the filling is no solution, because these stay firm and tend to dry out a bit in the oven. So I combine the two and get the best of both worlds: the juiciness of the softer apple and the brightness of the firmer apple. It's a mouthwatering combination. Macerating the apples before baking softens them, which means you can really pile the apples into the crust—almost twice as many as you can if you don't macerate. That means that you get a baked pie with apples all the way up to the lattice crust, rather than a lofty crust with a huge air pocket between it and the fruit.

⇒ Remove the dough from the refrigerator. On a well-floured work surface, roll out three-fourths of the dough into a circle about 12 inches in diameter and ⅛ inch thick. (Reserve the remaining dough for the lattice top.) Roll the dough circle around the pin and then unfurl it on top of a 9-inch aluminum pie pan or glass pie dish. Press the dough gently into the bottom and sides of the pan, leaving a ¼-inch lip around the edge of the pan (to allow for shrinkage in the oven). Refrigerate the pie shell for at least 30 minutes. (The pie shell can be tightly wrapped in plastic wrap and refrigerated for up to 1 day or frozen for up to 2 weeks. Bake directly from the refrigerator or freezer.)

⇒ Position a rack in the center of the oven, and heat the oven to 350 degrees F.

⇒ Line the pie shell with parchment paper, fill with pie weights, and blind bake (see page 13) for about 30 minutes, or until the entire shell is light brown.

(continued)

➡ Meanwhile, in a medium bowl, combine the apples, brown sugar, flour, salt, and cinnamon and toss to coat the apples evenly. Let sit at room temperature for about 30 minutes. This softens the apples so you can pack more of them into the pie.

➡ When the pie shell is ready, remove it from the oven and leave the oven set at 350 degrees F. Remove the weights and parchment, and pile the apples into the shell, pressing down lightly to compact them.

➡ On a well-floured work surface, roll out the remaining dough into a rectangle about 10 inches long by 6 inches wide and ¼ inch thick. Using a fluted pastry wheel or pizza wheel, cut length-wise into eight strips each about ¾ inch wide. Brush the strips with the beaten egg. Drape four of the dough strips on top of the apples, arranging them all in one direction and spacing them about 2 inches apart. Drape the remaining four dough strips at a 45-degree angle to the first four strips, again spacing them about 2 inches apart. Let the lattice strips drape over the edge of the pie shell (you will trim these after the pie bakes). If any of the strips break, press them back together. Or, if you need additional strips, you can trim the over-hanging dough and use it to create more strips. Sprinkle the strips with the sanding sugar.

➡ Bake for 1 hour and 10 minutes to 1½ hours, or until the lattice strips are golden brown all the way through. Make sure all of the strips are nicely golden brown without any pale spots, or they will be chewy. The apples should be soft and easy to pierce with a small knife. Let cool on a wire rack for at least 1 hour before serving. Use a small knife to trim any lattice overhang, so the strips are flush with the pie edge. Serve warm or at room temperature.

➡ The pie can be stored in an airtight container at room temperature for up to 2 days.

SOUTHERN PECAN PIE

Pâte Brisée II (page 216)

¾ cup (150 grams) sugar

½ cup (120 grams) water

1 cup (320 grams) light corn syrup

2 tablespoons (¼ stick) unsalted butter

3 eggs

1 teaspoon fresh lemon juice

1 teaspoon vanilla extract

¼ teaspoon kosher salt

2½ cups (250 grams) pecan halves

MAKES ONE 9-INCH PIE (SERVES 8)

Nothing in my family's background would lead anyone to suspect that my dad is a pecan pie addict. We don't eat typical American sweets. Our idea of snack food is preserved salty plums, and our usual dessert is some sort of red bean–filled pastry. But somehow Dad picked up the pecan pie–loving gene. I've made various versions of a traditional Karo syrup pecan pie recipe for him for years to satisfy his craving. Lightly caramelizing the sugar helps keep the pie from being too achingly sweet; a bit of lemon juice also helps balance out the sweetness. I don't skimp on the pecans, which means this pie has a lot more nuts than most pecan pies do. What makes it Southern? It has no extraneous ingredients—no chocolate or other flavors. It is a straight-up, old-fashioned (and in Dad's opinion, perfect) pecan pie.

➡ Remove the dough from the refrigerator. On a well-floured work surface, roll out the dough into a circle about 12 inches in diameter and ⅛ inch thick. Roll the dough circle around the pin and then unfurl it on top of a 9-inch aluminum pie pan or glass pie dish. Press the dough gently into the bottom and sides of the pan. Evenly pleat the overhanging dough with your fingers to create a decorative edge, or use scissors to trim the overhang, leaving a ¼-inch lip (to allow for shrinkage in the oven). Refrigerate the pie shell for at least 30 minutes. (The pie shell can be tightly wrapped in plastic wrap and refrigerated for up to 1 day or frozen for up to 2 weeks. Bake directly from the refrigerator or freezer.)

➡ Position a rack in the center of the oven, and heat the oven to 350 degrees F.

➡ Line the pie shell with parchment paper, fill with pie weights, and blind bake (see page 13) for about 30 minutes, or until the entire shell is light brown.

➡ Meanwhile, in a medium saucepan, combine the sugar and water and stir gently with a small rubber spatula until the sugar is dissolved. Be sure the sides of the pan do not have any sugar crystals on them; if they do, use a pastry brush dipped in water to wash down any clinging sugar. (This helps prevent crystallization of the sugar as you are caramelizing it.) Place over high heat and bring to a boil. Do not jostle the pan as it is coming to a boil, or the syrup may start to crystallize. Once the syrup starts to color to a pale brown, you can gently swirl the pan to even out the caramelization. It will take 3 to 4 minutes for the sugar to start caramelizing and another 30 seconds or so to even out.

➡ Once the sugar is golden brown, turn down the heat to medium and carefully pour in the corn syrup. It will sputter a bit and get clumpy. Continue to whisk for 1 to 2 minutes, or until all of the clumps of sugar have melted. Remove from the heat and whisk in the butter until melted and combined.

➡ In a medium heatproof bowl, whisk together the eggs, lemon juice, vanilla, and salt. Slowly pour the hot sugar mixture into the egg mixture, a little at a time, whisking constantly. When all of the sugar mixture has been incorporated, add the pecans and stir to coat well.

➡ When the pie shell is ready, remove from the oven and leave the oven set at 350 degrees F. Remove the weights and parchment, and pour the pecan mixture into the shell.

➡ Bake for 35 to 40 minutes, or until the pecan mixture has puffed up and doesn't move when you jiggle the pan. Let cool completely on a wire rack before serving.

➡ The pie can be stored in an airtight container at room temperature for up to 4 days.

RICH CHOCOLATE CREAM PIE

Pâte Sucrée 9-inch pie shell
(page 210)

6 ounces (168 grams) bittersweet
chocolate (62 to 70 percent cacao)
chopped

¾ cup (180 grams) half-and-half

2½ cups (600 grams) heavy cream

4 egg yolks

⅓ cup (70 grams) granulated
sugar

¼ teaspoon vanilla extract

¼ teaspoon kosher salt

3 tablespoons confectioners' sugar

1 tablespoon cornstarch

3- to 4-inch slab milk chocolate,
at warm room temperature, for
decorating

**MAKES ONE 9-INCH PIE
(SERVES 8)**

"What ever happened to pie?" is a common refrain in the Chang-Myers household. My husband grew up near diners and pie bakeries and is frustrated by the lack of pie available these days, at least near us in Boston. He's right. I went in search of a birthday pie for him when we first started dating, and I came up empty. That's a shame, because making a pie, as you'll see, is generally simple and straightforward. You do need a pie pan (glass, ceramic, or even a disposable—actually, recyclable—aluminum one will do), and for this pie, you need to allow time for the chocolate custard to set. But all in all, this recipe is an incredible dessert that is remarkably easy to make: an extra-thick version of Flour's chocolate pudding is poured into a crisp, buttery, cookielike crust; topped with clouds of whipped cream; and garnished with a blizzard of milk chocolate curls. It's quite a sight and certain to please friends, family, and husbands pleading for pie.

➡ Bake the pie shell as directed. Remove from the oven, sprinkle with 1 ounce (25 grams) of the bittersweet chocolate, and return to the oven for about 30 seconds. Remove from the oven and, using a pastry brush, carefully paint the bottom and sides of the shell with the melted chocolate. This will protect the shell from becoming soggy when you pour in the chocolate filling. Set the pie shell aside.

➡ In a medium saucepan, combine the half-and-half and 1 cup (240 grams) of the cream and scald over medium-high heat (bubbles start to form around the edge of the pan, but the liquid is not boiling). Meanwhile, place the remaining 5 ounces (140 grams) of the bittersweet chocolate in a medium heatproof bowl. Place over (not touching) barely simmering water in a saucepan and heat, stirring occasionally, until completely melted and smooth. Remove from the heat. Pour the hot cream mixture over the melted chocolate and whisk until thoroughly combined.

➡ Place the egg yolks in a medium bowl, and slowly whisk in the granulated sugar. Slowly pour the hot cream-chocolate mixture into the egg-sugar mixture, a little at a time, whisking constantly. When all of the cream-chocolate mixture has been incorporated, return the contents of the bowl to the saucepan, and return the saucepan to medium-low heat. Cook, stirring continuously with a wooden spoon and making sure to scrape the bottom of the pan often to prevent scorching, for 6 to 7 minutes, or until the mixture thickens and coats the spoon thickly. To test, draw your finger along the back of the spoon; the custard should hold the trail for a couple of seconds before it fills. (First, the mixture will be liquid and loose, and then it will start to get a little thicker at the bottom of the pan. As it continues to thicken, it will start to let off a little steam. When you see wisps of steam steadily rising from the pan, you know the filling is almost done.)

➡ When the custard is ready, immediately strain it through a fine-mesh sieve into a heatproof pitcher or bowl, and stir in the vanilla and salt. Pour the filling into the chocolate-lined pie shell and refrigerate, uncovered, for about 8 hours, or until set, or up to overnight.

➡ Fit the stand mixer with the whip attachment (or use a handheld mixer) and whip together the remaining 1½ cups (360 grams) cream, the confectioners' sugar, and cornstarch until stiff peaks form.

➡ Pile the whipped cream on top of the chocolate filling, spreading it to the edges of the pie. Using the back of a small knife or a vegetable peeler, shave curls from the milk chocolate slab. (Make sure the chocolate is slightly warm, or you will get splinters instead of curls.) Decorate the pie with the curls.

➡ The pie can be stored in an airtight container in the refrigerator for up to 2 days.

PÂTE SUCRÉE

½ cup (1 stick/114 grams) unsalted butter, at room temperature, cut into 8 pieces

¼ cup (50 grams) sugar

½ teaspoon kosher salt

1 cup (140 grams) unbleached all-purpose flour

1 egg yolk

**MAKES ONE FULLY BAKED
9-INCH PIE SHELL OR
10-INCH TART SHELL**

⟹ Using a stand mixer fitted with the paddle attachment, cream together the butter, sugar, and salt on medium speed for 2 to 3 minutes, or until pale and light. Scrape the sides and bottom of the bowl with a rubber spatula. Add the flour and beat on low speed for about 30 seconds, or until the flour mixes with the butter-sugar mixture. The mixture will look like wet sand. Add the egg yolk and continue to mix on low speed for about 30 seconds, or until the dough comes together.

⟹ Wrap the dough tightly in plastic wrap and refrigerate for about 1 hour. (At this point, the dough can be stored in the refrigerator for up to 5 days or in the freezer for up to 2 weeks. If frozen, thaw it in the refrigerator overnight before using.)

⟹ If making a pie shell, have ready a 9-inch pie pan dish. If making a tart shell, line a baking sheet with parchment paper and place a 10-inch tart ring on top. Remove the dough from the refrigerator and let soften at room temperature for about 30 minutes. Using a rolling pin, bang and flatten the dough into a disk about ½ inch thick. Flour the work surface, and sprinkle the dough disk with a little flour. Roll out the dough into a circle 10 to 11 inches in diameter and about ¼ inch thick for a 9-inch pie shell, or about 12 inches in diameter and just under ¼ inch thick for a 10-inch tart shell. Make sure the work surface is well floured so the dough doesn't stick to it, and make sure the disk itself is floured well enough to keep the rolling pin from sticking to it. Roll from the center of the disk outward, and gently rotate the disk a quarter turn after each roll to ensure the disk is evenly stretched into a nice circle. Don't worry if the dough breaks a bit, especially toward the edges. You can easily patch any tears once you have lined the pan.

⟹ Roll the dough circle around the pin and then unfurl it on top of the 9-inch pie pan or the 10-inch tart ring. Press the dough well into the bottom and sides of the pan or ring, and use any scraps or odd pieces to patch up any tears or missing bits. Make sure the entire interior is well covered with dough, and then press one last time all the way around to ensure any holes have been patched. Trim the edge of the dough so it is even with the rim of the pan or ring.

⟹ Refrigerate the pastry shell for at least 30 minutes. The gluten needs a little time to relax so the pastry doesn't shrink in the oven. (The pastry shell can be tightly wrapped in plastic wrap and refrigerated for up to 1 day or frozen for up to 2 weeks. Bake directly from the refrigerator or freezer.)

⟹ Position a rack in the center of the oven, and heat the oven to 350 degrees F.

⟹ Bake for 30 to 35 minutes, or until golden brown. Let cool to room temperature on a wire rack. If you are making a tart shell, remove the tart ring. Proceed as directed in individual recipes.

TOASTED COCONUT CREAM PIE
WITH LIME WHIPPED CREAM

1¼ cups (300 grams) heavy cream

1 teaspoon finely grated lime zest

1 can (14 ounces/400 grams) coconut milk

½ cup (120 grams) milk

⅔ cup (140 grams) granulated sugar

⅓ cup (40 grams) cake flour

1 egg

4 egg yolks

¼ teaspoon vanilla extract

½ teaspoon kosher salt

1 cup (120 grams) sweetened shredded coconut, lightly toasted

Pâte Sucrée 9-inch pie shell (facing page)

3 tablespoons confectioners' sugar

1 tablespoon cornstarch

MAKES ONE 9-INCH PIE (SERVES 8)

Flour is not a pie bakery (much to the dismay of my husband, who is a pie addict), but every year during the holidays we pull out all the stops and make pies in almost every flavor. This one is a late addition to our holiday roster that was prompted by the dessert menu at Myers+Chang, our pan-Asian restaurant. Coconut and lime are common Southeast Asian flavors, so I combined them in a made-to-order tart that has become the most popular dessert at the restaurant. I adapted the tart for this pie, and it became one of the most popular holiday pies at Flour. As with the tart, the components of the pie can be made in advance and then easily combined the day you want to eat it. That makes a great pie even better.

⇒ In a small saucepan, combine the cream and lime zest over medium-high heat and bring just to a boil. Remove from the heat, pour into a small airtight container, let cool, and refrigerate overnight.

⇒ In a medium saucepan, combine the coconut milk and milk and scald over medium-high heat (bubbles start to form around the edge of the pan, but the liquid is not boiling). While the milks are heating, in a small bowl, whisk together the granulated sugar and flour. (Mixing the flour with the sugar will prevent the flour from clumping when you add it to the eggs.) In a medium heat-proof bowl, whisk together the egg and egg yolks until blended, then slowly whisk in the sugar-flour mixture. The mixture will be thick and pasty.

⇒ Slowly pour the hot milk mixture into the egg-sugar mixture, a little at a time, whisking constantly. When all of the milk mixture has been incorporated, return the contents of the bowl to the saucepan, and return the saucepan to medium heat. Cook, whisking vigorously and continuously, for 4 to 5 minutes, or until the mixture thickens and comes to a boil. Make sure you get the whisk into the corners of the saucepan and that you are scraping the bottom often. First, the mixture will be thin and

(continued)

frothy; as it gets hotter and the eggs start to cook, it will get thicker and start to steam. Eventually, it will start to boil, but because you will be whisking continuously (don't forget to do that!) and because the mixture is so thick, it will be hard for you to know when it is boiling. Once it is thick, stop whisking for a few seconds and watch the surface to see if it starts to blub up. If it goes blub blub, you will know that it has come to a boil. When that happens, whisk even more vigorously for 30 seconds, then immediately take the custard off the stove and pour it through a fine-mesh sieve into a heatproof pitcher. Whisk in the vanilla, salt, and ¾ cup (90 grams) of the toasted coconut. Pour into the baked pie shell and refrigerate, uncovered, for about 4 hours, or until the filling is set.

⇒ Fit a stand mixer with the whip attachment (or use a handheld mixer) and whip together the lime zest–cream mixture, the confectioners' sugar, and the cornstarch until stiff peaks form.

⇒ Pile the whipped cream on top of the coconut filling, spreading it to the edges of the pie. Decorate the pie with the remaining ¼ cup (30 grams) toasted coconut.

⇒ The pie can be stored in an airtight container in the refrigerator for up to 2 days.

SUPER-PUMPKINY PUMPKIN PIE

Pâte Brisée II (page 216)

One 16 ounce (454 gram) can pumpkin puree

⅔ cup (150 grams) packed light brown sugar

1 teaspoon ground ginger

1 teaspoon ground cinnamon

½ teaspoon freshly grated nutmeg

Pinch of ground cloves

½ teaspoon kosher salt

½ cup plus 2 tablespoons (200 grams) sweetened condensed milk

⅔ cup (170 grams) evaporated milk

3 eggs

1 egg yolk

¾ cup (180 grams) heavy cream

½ teaspoon vanilla extract

MAKES ONE 9-INCH PIE (SERVES 8)

I'm embarrassed to admit that the first time I made (and ate) pumpkin pie was about two months after I opened Flour, in November 2000. We had created our first Thanksgiving menu and pumpkin pie was front and center. Of course, I was not oblivious to the idea of pumpkin pie; I knew what it was, and I was fully aware that it was a staple of an all-important food holiday. But I had never actually eaten a slice. I had only imagined what a pumpkin pie *should* be: deeply pumpkiny, with hints of cinnamon, ginger, and other holiday spices; creamy, though not as creamy as a custard; incredibly flaky crust; and not overly sweet, or the sweetness would interfere with the delicate flavor of the pumpkin. Pumpkin on its own tends to be somewhat watery and not that highly flavored, so I decided to cook it down until most of the water had evaporated, leaving a rich, dark puree that was all flavor. Creating layers of creaminess in the pie appealed to me, which I did by adding both sweetened condensed milk and evaporated milk along with the traditional heavy cream. A light hand with the spices ensured just enough of the requisite clove-nutmeg-cinnamon background flavor, but not so much that the subtle pumpkin flavor was masked. Every Thanksgiving we sell hundreds of these. *USA Today* even named us one of the top ten places in America to eat pumpkin pie!

➡ Remove the dough from the refrigerator. On a well-floured work surface, roll out the dough into a circle about 12 inches in diameter and ⅛ inch thick. Roll the dough circle around the pin and then unfurl it on top of a 9-inch aluminum pie pan or glass pie dish. Press the dough gently into the bottom and sides of the pan. Evenly pleat the overhanging dough with your fingers to create a decorative edge, or use scissors to trim the overhang, leaving a ¼-inch lip (to allow for shrinkage in the oven). Refrigerate the pie shell for at least 30 minutes. (The pie shell can be tightly wrapped in plastic wrap and refrigerated for up to 1 day or frozen for up to 2 weeks. Bake directly from the refrigerator or freezer.)

⇒ Position a rack in the center of the oven, and heat the oven to 350 degrees F.

⇒ Line the pie shell with parchment paper, fill with pie weights, and blind bake (see page 13) for 35 to 45 minutes, or until the entire shell is light brown all the way through.

⇒ Meanwhile, scrape the pumpkin puree into a medium saucepan and stir in the brown sugar. Place over medium-low heat and cook, stirring occasionally with a wooden spoon, for 40 to 45 minutes, or until the pumpkin has reduced to a somewhat thick paste and darkened. Remove from the heat and whisk in the ginger, cinnamon, nutmeg, cloves, and salt. Then whisk in the sweetened condensed milk and evaporated milk.

⇒ In a large bowl, whisk together the eggs and egg yolk until blended. Slowly whisk in the cream and vanilla, then gradually whisk in the pumpkin mixture and continue whisking until thoroughly mixed.

⇒ When the pie shell is ready, remove from the oven and leave the oven set at 350 degrees F. Remove the weights and parchment, and pour the pumpkin custard into the shell.

⇒ Bake for 55 to 60 minutes, or until the custard is just set. The edges of the custard will puff up a little and the center should still have a little wiggle in it. Let cool on a wire rack for at least 2 hours. Serve at room temperature or chilled.

⇒ The pie can be stored in an airtight container in the refrigerator for up to 3 days.

PÂTE BRISÉE II

1 cup (140 grams) unbleached all-purpose flour

2 teaspoons sugar

½ teaspoon kosher salt

½ cup plus 1 tablespoon (1 stick plus 1 tablespoon/128 grams) cold unsalted butter, cut into 8 pieces

1 egg yolk

2 tablespoons cold milk

MAKES ABOUT 10 OUNCES DOUGH, ENOUGH FOR ONE 9-INCH SINGLE-CRUST PIE, 10-INCH *CROSTATA*, OR 9-INCH QUICHE

→ Using a stand mixer fitted with the paddle attachment (or a handheld mixer), mix together the flour, sugar, and salt. Scatter the butter over the top and mix on low speed for about 45 seconds, or until the flour is no longer bright white and holds together when you clump it and pecan-size lumps of butter are visible throughout.

→ In a small bowl, whisk together the egg yolk and milk until blended. Add to the flour-butter mixture all at once. Mix on low speed for about 30 seconds, or until the dough barely comes together. It will look really shaggy and more like a mess than a dough.

→ Dump the dough out onto an unfloured work surface and gather it together into a tight mound. Using your palm and starting on one side of the mound, smear the dough bit by bit, starting at the top of the mound and then sliding your palm down the side and along the work surface (at Flour we call this "going down the mountain"), until most of the butter chunks are smeared into the dough and the dough comes together. Do this once or twice on each part of the dough, moving through the mound until the whole mess has been smeared into a cohesive dough with streaks of butter.

→ Gather up the dough, wrap tightly in plastic wrap, and press down to flatten into a disk about 1 inch thick. Refrigerate for at least 4 hours before using. The dough will keep in the refrigerator for up to 4 days or in the freezer for up to 1 month.

BLUEBERRY-LEMON PIE

Pâte Brisée I (page 92)

8 cups (1.2 kilograms) blueberries

3 tablespoons cornstarch

¾ cup (150 grams) granulated sugar

¼ teaspoon kosher salt

1 tablespoon finely grated lemon zest (about 1 lemon; or use zest of 2 lemons if you really like lemon)

1 egg, lightly beaten

2 tablespoons sanding sugar, pearl sugar, or granulated sugar

MAKES ONE 9-INCH PIE
(SERVES 8)

Blueberry pie holds a special place in my heart, because it is my husband's all-time favorite dessert. I make it for him for any special occasion: his birthday, our wedding anniversary, Valentine's Day, Christmas, Thanksgiving. You name the occasion and I'm making a blueberry pie for him to celebrate. Over the years, I've come up with several tricks to make this the blueberriest, fruitiest, most delicious pie ever. The point of any fruit pie is to highlight the fruit. But blueberries are so full of juice that it is hard to bake a pie that doesn't become blueberry soup, unless you thicken the berries some way. Traditional thickeners (flour, tapioca, cornstarch) can diminish the flavor of the berries. How to get around this? I create a thickener that is made with the fruit itself! I cook some of the blueberries down with just a little bit of thickener (cornstarch) and sugar until I get a gooey mess, and then I fold in lots more blueberries. I end up using 8 cups of berries—a lot of fruit for any pie. It's blueberry heaven. If you are patient enough to let this pie cool completely, then you'll find that the blueberries hold their shape when you cut into the pie . . . for about five seconds . . . and then they start to ooze just a bit of juice, which is perfect. Or, if you're like Christopher and you can't wait that long, you'll eat the pie warm with blueberries and blueberry juice flowing everywhere. Either way you can't go wrong.

➡ Remove the dough from the refrigerator. On a well-floured work surface, roll out two-thirds of the dough into a circle about 12 inches in diameter and ⅛ inch thick. (Reserve the remaining dough for the top.) Roll the dough circle around the pin and then unfurl it on top of a 9-inch aluminum pie pan or glass pie dish. Press the dough gently into the bottom and sides of the pan, leaving a ¼-inch lip around the edge of the pan (to allow for shrinkage in the oven). Refrigerate the pie shell for at least 30 minutes. (The pie shell can be tightly wrapped in plastic wrap and refrigerated for up to 1 day or frozen for up to 2 weeks. Bake directly from the refrigerator or freezer.)

(continued)

➡ Position a rack in the center of the oven, and heat the oven to 350 degrees F.

➡ Line the pie shell with parchment paper, fill with pie weights, and blind bake (see page 13) for about 30 minutes, or until the entire shell is light brown.

➡ Meanwhile, in a medium saucepan, combine 2 cups (300 grams) of the blueberries, the cornstarch, granulated sugar, and salt. Place over medium heat and cook, stirring occasionally, for 5 to 6 minutes, or until the berries, sugar, and cornstarch melt into a gooey mass. Remove the pan from the heat and stir in the remaining berries, and then stir in the lemon zest.

➡ When the pie shell is ready, remove from the oven and leave the oven set at 350 degrees F. Remove the weights and parchment, and pile the blueberries in the shell. Roll out the remaining dough into a circle about 10 inches in diameter and ⅛ inch thick. Roll the dough circle around the pin and then unfurl it over the filled pie shell, with the edge of the round overhanging the entire edge of the pan by ¼ to ½ inch (you will trim off this excess once the pie is baked). Brush the top crust evenly with the beaten egg, then sprinkle generously with the sanding sugar. Poke a hole in the center with the tip of a sharp knife. Place the pie on a baking sheet to catch any overflowing fruit juices.

➡ Bake for about 1½ hours, or until the entire top crust is golden brown. Let cool on a wire rack for 3 to 4 hours, or until room temperature, before serving. The longer you let it sit, the more "together" the blueberries will be. If you cut into it when it is still warm, the blueberries will be especially juicy and the filling especially runny. Use a small knife to trim any overhang of the top crust, so it is flush with the pie edge.

➡ The pie can be stored in an airtight container at room temperature for up to 2 days.

LEMON MARSHMALLOW MERINGUE PIE

1¼ cups (250 grams) sugar

6 tablespoons (54 grams) cornstarch

¼ teaspoon kosher salt

1¼ cups (300 grams) water

2 tablespoons heavy cream

6 egg yolks

1¼ cups (300 grams) fresh lemon juice (about 10 lemons)

2 tablespoons (¼ stick/28 grams) unsalted butter, at room temperature

1 teaspoon vanilla extract

Pâte Sucrée 9-inch pie shell (page 210)

MARSHMALLOW MERINGUE

2 teaspoons cornstarch

¾ cup (180 grams) water

1⅓ cups (270 grams) sugar

1 tablespoon light corn syrup

4 egg whites

1 teaspoon vanilla extract

Pinch of kosher salt

MAKES ONE 9-INCH PIE
(SERVES 8 TO 10)

I took this pie to the home of one of my closest friends on a recent visit. Her five-year-old son, Matthew, took one bite and immediately asked if I could move into the family attic and make pie every day. I was flattered by the invitation ("There's even a shower for you up there!" he insisted) and thrilled that the pie elicited such a heartfelt response. The lemon part of the pie is lemony enough to make your lips pucker, only to be tempered by mounds of fluffy, soft, sweet meringue. This pie is not hard to make, but you need to be aware of a few things. First, both the pie shell and the lemon mixture can be prepared in advance. The lemon mixture must be warm when you pile the meringue on top, however, so if you make it ahead of time, you will need to rewarm it gently over low heat until it is pourable and then pour it into the pie shell. Making the meringue involves cooking sugar to the firm-ball stage, so you will need either a candy thermometer or a bowl of ice water to test the sugar.

⟹ Position a rack in the center of the oven, and heat the oven to 375 degrees F.

⟹ In a medium saucepan, whisk together the sugar, cornstarch, salt, water, and cream. Place over medium-high heat and cook for 1 to 2 minutes, or until the mixture thickens and becomes translucent.

⟹ Meanwhile, in a medium bowl, whisk together the egg yolks and lemon juice. When the sugar mixture is ready, slowly pour it into the egg yolk mixture, a little at a time, whisking constantly. When all of the sugar mixture has been incorporated, return the contents of the bowl to the saucepan, and return the saucepan to medium heat. Cook over medium heat, stirring constantly with a wooden spoon, for 3 to 4 minutes, or until the mixture thickens. Remove from the heat and whisk in the butter and vanilla. Pour into the baked pie shell. (Or, let cool, transfer to an airtight container, and refrigerate for up to 3 days, then rewarm over low heat before filling the pie shell.)

→ To make the meringue: In a small saucepan, whisk together the cornstarch and ¼ cup (60 grams) of the water. Place over medium-high heat and cook, whisking constantly, for about 2 minutes, or until thick and translucent. It will turn into a jelly-like blob. Remove from the heat and set aside.

→ In a separate small saucepan, combine the sugar, corn syrup, and the remaining ½ cup (120 grams) water and stir gently to combine. Place over high heat, bring to a boil, and cook, without stirring, for 3 to 5 minutes, or until the syrup registers 248 degrees F on a candy thermometer (the firm-ball stage; see Cooking Sugar, page 13).

→ While the sugar is cooking, place the egg whites in the bowl of a stand mixer fitted with the whip attachment (or use a hand-held mixer). When the sugar reaches 248 degrees F, turn on the mixer to high speed and slowly add the sugar syrup into the egg whites, drizzling it down the side of the bowl to keep it from hitting the whip and spattering. When all of the syrup has been added, continue whipping on high speed for 2 to 3 minutes, or until the mixture turns white and billowy. Turn down the speed to medium, add the cornstarch mixture, vanilla, and salt, and whip until fully incorporated. Continue whipping for 3 to 4 minutes, or until barely warm to the touch. (The meringue does not hold, and the filling must be warm when the meringue is piled on top of it, so you must work quickly.)

→ Heap the marshmallow meringue on top of the pie in billowing piles, making sure to cover the entire top of the pie all the way to the edge of the crust. Use the back of a spoon to tap the top of the meringue lightly and quickly to create tall peaks.

→ Bake for 15 minutes, or until the meringue is lightly browned all over. Let cool on a wire rack for about 1 hour, then refrigerate for at least 4 hours before serving.

→ The pie can be stored in an airtight container in the refrigerator for up to 3 days.

Baker's Bite

To make the characteristic peaks in the meringue topping, tap the back of a spoon or a rubber spatula firmly on top of the meringue and quickly lift straight up after each tap. The meringue will stick to the spoon and lift up into tall points, making for a dramatic-looking pie.

APRICOT-ALMOND TART

PÂTE SUCRÉE

1 cup (2 sticks/228 grams) unsalted butter, at room temperature

½ cup (100 grams) granulated sugar

1 teaspoon kosher salt

2 cups (280 grams) unbleached all-purpose flour

2 egg yolks

1 cup Frangipane (page 239)

1 jar (12 ounces/340 grams) apricot jam or preserves (not jelly), about 1 cup

10 fresh apricots, pitted and chopped into 1-inch pieces, or one 15 ounce (425 gram) can apricots, well drained and chopped into 1-inch pieces (about 2½ cups)

½ cup (50 grams) sliced almonds

1 egg, lightly beaten

2 tablespoons sanding sugar, pearl sugar, or granulated sugar

MAKES ONE 10-INCH TART (SERVES 8 TO 10)

If you crack open the pit of an apricot (or of a plum or a peach), you'll find inside a soft, oval kernel that smells faintly of almonds. The apricot and the almond are actually related, with both belonging to the genus *Prunus*. Stone fruits and almonds are a natural pairing, and this piece of botanical trivia helps to explain why they work so well together in baking. This tart puts both flavors front and center. Sweet tart dough is spread with a layer of *frangipane* (almond cream) and then topped with apricot preserves. Chopped apricots and sliced almonds are strewn on top, and then more tart dough is used for a gorgeous lattice finish. By all means, use fresh apricots if you have them. I've also used both fresh and canned peaches (rinse well if in heavy syrup) for the apricots.

➡ Line a baking sheet with parchment paper, and place a 10-inch tart ring on top.

➡ To make the pâte sucrée: Using a stand mixer fitted with the paddle attachment (or a hand-held mixer), cream together the butter, granulated sugar, and salt on medium-low speed for 2 to 3 minutes, or until pale and light. Scrape down the sides and bottom of the bowl with a rubber spatula. Add the flour and beat on low speed for about 30 seconds, or until the flour mixes with the butter-sugar mixture. The mixture will look like wet sand. Add the egg yolks and continue to mix on low speed for about 30 seconds, or until the dough comes together.

➡ Wrap the dough tightly in plastic wrap and refrigerate for about 1 hour. (At this point, the dough can be stored in the refrigerator for up to 5 days or the freezer for up to 2 weeks. If frozen, thaw in the refrigerator overnight before using.)

➡ Remove the dough from the refrigerator. Using a bench scraper or a chef's knife, divide into two-thirds and one-third. Return the smaller portion to the refrigerator. Let the larger portion soften at room temperature for about 15 minutes. Using a rolling pin, bang and flatten the dough into a disk about ½ inch thick. Flour the work surface, then sprinkle the dough disk with a little flour. Roll out the dough into a circle about 12 inches in diameter and ¼ inch thick. Make sure the surface you are rolling on is well floured so the dough does not stick to it, and make sure the disk itself is floured well enough to keep the rolling pin from sticking to it. Roll from the center of the disk outward, and gently rotate the disk a quarter turn after each roll to ensure the disk is evenly stretched into a nice circle. Don't worry if the dough breaks a bit, especially toward the edges. You can easily patch any tears once you have lined the tart ring.

⇒ Roll the dough circle around the rolling pin and then unfurl it on top of the tart ring. Press the dough well into the bottom and sides of the ring, and use any scraps or odd pieces to patch up any tears or missing bits. Make sure that the entire interior is evenly covered with dough, and press one last time all the way around to ensure any holes have been patched. Trim the edge of the dough so it is even with the rim of the tart ring.

⇒ Refrigerate the tart shell for at least 30 minutes. The gluten needs a little time to relax so the pastry doesn't shrink in the oven. (The pastry shell can be tightly wrapped in plastic wrap and refrigerated for up to 1 day or frozen for up to 2 weeks. Bake directly from the refrigerator or freezer.)

⇒ Position a rack in the center of the oven, and heat the oven to 350 degrees F.

⇒ Remove the tart shell from the refrigerator. Using a small offset spatula or the back of a spoon, spread the frangipane evenly over the bottom of the tart shell. Bake for 15 minutes, or until the frangipane just begins to set. Remove from the oven. Leave the oven set at 350 degrees F.

⇒ Scrape the apricot jam into a small bowl, and beat it briefly with a fork to loosen it up. Carefully spread the apricot jam evenly on top of the frangipane. The heat of the tart shell will help soften the jam to ease spreading. Scatter the chopped apricots evenly on top of the jam, and press them in gently. Sprinkle the almonds on top of the apricots, and pat them down as well.

⇒ Remove the remaining dough from the refrigerator and let it sit at room temperature for 15 minutes to soften. Generously flour the work surface and roll out the dough into a rectangle about 10 inches long by 5 inches wide and ¼ inch thick. Using a fluted pastry wheel or pizza wheel, cut lengthwise into ten strips each about ½ inch wide. Brush the strips with the beaten egg. Drape five of the dough strips on top of the almonds, arranging them all in one direction and spacing them about 1¼ inches apart. Drape the remaining five dough strips at a 45-degree angle to the first five strips, again spacing them about 1¼ inches apart. If any of the strips break, piece them back together. Some of the strips will be too long, and you can trim the overhang and press the pieces together to make more strips, if you want to fit in more strips along the edges of the tart. Trim the lattice strips so they are flush with the edge of the tart shell. Sprinkle the strips with the sanding sugar.

⇒ Bake for 45 to 50 minutes, until the lattice strips are golden brown all the way through. Make sure all of the strips are nicely golden brown without any pale spots, or they will be chewy. Let cool on the pan on a wire rack for 2 to 3 hours, or until room temperature, before serving.

⇒ The tart can be stored in an airtight container at room temperature for up to 2 days.

HOMEMADE-NUTELLA TART

1 cup (140 grams) whole natural hazelnuts

2 cups (480 grams) heavy cream

1 pound (454 grams) milk chocolate, chopped

2 ounces (56 grams) semisweet chocolate, chopped

½ teaspoon kosher salt

½ teaspoon vanilla extract

Pâte Sucrée 10-inch tart shell (page 210)

MAKES ONE 10-INCH TART
(SERVES 8 TO 10)

My first experience with Nutella was in Switzerland. I was a tenth-grader spending the summer abroad in a foreign-exchange student program, at the urging of my high school French teacher. Every morning for breakfast, my host mother offered up coffee (ick) and fresh baguettes (mmm) with butter, fruit jam, and Nutella. I spent the first few nervous days tentatively helping myself to the *beurre* and *confiture* and avoiding the brown stuff. My French was okay, but I wasn't sure I understood the answer to my query, "Qu'est-ce que c'est?" (What is it?) Maman kept saying "Chocolat!" and I thought I must be misunderstanding, because I couldn't imagine that anyone really ate chocolate for breakfast. Turns out they do, and for good reason. I'd never had anything so rich and decadent in the morning, or anytime for that matter, as that chocolate-hazelnut spread. I indulged in this European treat daily for the rest of the summer. When I opened Flour, I re-created this taste memory by coming up with a homemade version of Nutella and serving it in a tart. The Flour hazelnut spread is much chunkier than the original. While some of the hazelnuts are finely ground to infuse the cream and then strained out, we liked the crunch and taste of chopped nuts in the mix, too. Filling a tart with homemade Nutella makes a crazy good company dessert that never fails to elicit praise from guests. Or, you can eat this concoction like we do at Flour: paired with banana slices between thick slices of brioche and grilled on a panini press. Straight up on a baguette remains my personal favorite way.

⇒ Position a rack in the center of the oven, and heat the oven to 350 degrees F.

⇒ Spread the hazelnuts on a baking sheet and toast in the oven for 10 to 12 minutes, or until dark brown and fragrant. Transfer to a plate to cool.

➡ Set aside 16 to 20 whole hazelnuts for the gar-nish. In a food processor, pulse about half of the remaining hazelnuts until finely ground. Roughly crush the other half of the nuts, either by hand (place in a heavy-duty plastic bag and roll a rolling pin over the bag) or by pulsing in the food proces-sor. Set aside.

➡ In a small saucepan, combine the cream and the finely ground nuts and scald over medium-high heat (bubbles start to form around the edge of the pan, but the cream is not boiling).

➡ Remove from the heat and let sit for about 1 hour to infuse the cream. Strain the cream through a fine-mesh sieve into a bowl or pitcher.

➡ Place the milk chocolate and semisweet choc-olate in a medium heatproof bowl. Place over (not touching) barely simmering water in a saucepan and heat, stirring occasionally, until completely melted and smooth. Remove from the heat.

➡ Whisk the cream into the chocolate until fully combined. Add the crushed hazelnuts, salt, and vanilla and whisk until combined.

➡ Slide a cardboard circle or flat plate under the baked tart shell, and carefully pour the chocolate-hazelnut mixture into the shell. It should fill to the rim of the shell. Carefully place the tart in the refrigerator for 3 to 4 hours, or until the filling has set.

➡ Remove the tart from the refrigerator, and gar-nish the edges with the reserved whole hazelnuts, pressing them gently into the filling.

➡ The tart can be stored in an airtight container in the refrigerator for up to 2 days. For the best serving temperature, remove the tart from the refrigerator about 2 hours in advance, so the filling can soften up a bit.

BITTERSWEET CHOCOLATE TRUFFLE TART

8 ounces (228 grams) bittersweet chocolate (at least 70 percent cacao), finely chopped

¾ cup (180 grams) heavy cream

½ cup (120 grams) milk

2 egg yolks

2 tablespoons (¼ stick/28 grams) unsalted butter, at room temperature

¼ teaspoon kosher salt

Pâte Sucrée 10-inch tart shell (page 210)

¼ cup (30 grams) Dutch-processed cocoa powder

MAKES ONE 10-INCH TART (SERVES 8 TO 10)

Before I went to work at Payard Patisserie, I went to New York to meet François Payard and to take his two-day in-depth pastry seminar. The weekend was a great success: Not only did I get to learn from a third-generation French pastry chef who is one of the best pastry chefs in the United States, but I also landed a job at the patisserie he was about to open. This simple chocolate truffle tart was by far my favorite of the desserts I learned that weekend. I've added a touch more chocolate to the original and showered the entire thing with a dusting of cocoa powder. It's rich, silky, creamy, decadent—and it's as straightforward to make as it is delicious. François taught me many things over the years. This tart is a perfect example of his lesson that the least-complicated pastries are often the best.

➡ Position a rack in the center of the oven, and heat the oven to 350 degrees F.

➡ Place the chocolate in a medium heatproof bowl. In a small saucepan, combine the cream and milk and scald over medium-high heat (bubbles start to form around the edge of the pan, but the liquid is not boiling). Pour the hot cream mixture over the chocolate and let sit for about 1 minute, then whisk gently until the chocolate is completely melted and the mixture is smooth. Slowly whisk in the egg yolks one at a time. Add the butter and salt and whisk until the butter is thoroughly incorporated.

➡ It is easier to move the tart around when it is on a baking sheet, so put the baked tart shell on a baking sheet and pour the chocolate truffle mixture into it. It should fill to the rim of the shell.

➡ Bake for about 15 minutes, or until the edges of the chocolate truffle mixture start to set and the middle is still a little jiggly, like Jell-O. Let cool on a wire rack for at least 2 hours, or until the truffle filling has set, or up to 6 hours. Using a fine-mesh sieve, dust the top of the tart with the cocoa powder just before serving.

➡ The tart can be stored in an airtight container in the refrigerator for up to 1 day. Remove the tart from the refrigerator 5 to 6 hours before serving so it comes fully to room temperature, then dust with the cocoa powder just before serving.

OOEY, GOOEY CARAMEL-NUT TART

2 cups (400 grams) sugar

½ cup (120 grams) water

2 cups (480 grams) heavy cream

1 teaspoon finely grated orange zest

½ cup (70 grams) whole natural hazelnuts, toasted

¾ cup (75 grams) pecans, toasted and chopped

½ cup (50 grams) walnuts, toasted and chopped

¾ cup (75 grams) sliced almonds, toasted

¾ cup (75 grams) pistachios, toasted

½ cup (80 grams) dried cranberries

½ teaspoon vanilla extract

¼ teaspoon kosher salt

Pâte Sucrée 10-inch tart shell (page 210)

MAKES ONE 10-INCH TART (SERVES 8 TO 10)

I created this tart for the first holiday dessert menu I wrote at Rialto. I wanted to put pecan pie on the menu, but I knew that it would have to be gussied up to be served in a four-star restaurant. So I translated "pie" into "tart" and added an assortment of nuts in addition to the pecans to jazz it up. Rather than the traditional supersweet corn syrup filling, this tart is bound together by a rich, dark caramel scented with hints of orange and vanilla. A scattering of dried cranberries adds a lovely color contrast and brightens up the whole tart. It is perfect for a holiday party, but it's so good that you shouldn't save it just for special occasions.

➡ Position a rack in the center of the oven, and heat the oven to 350 degrees F.

➡ Place the sugar in the bottom of a medium saucepan and slowly pour in the water. Stir gently to moisten the sugar. If any sugar crystals are clinging to the sides of the pan, brush them down with a pastry brush dipped in water. Place the pan over high heat and leave it undisturbed until the mixture comes to a rolling boil. (You want to avoid crystallization of the syrup, which can happen if the pan is disturbed before the sugar starts to color.) Then continue to boil rapidly without moving the pan until the sugar syrup starts to caramelize. This will take 6 to 8 minutes: the sugar syrup will boil furiously; then as it thickens, it will boil more languidly; and then you will see some of the syrup starting to color and darken around the edge of the pan.

➡ When you start to see color in the pan, gently swirl it in a circular motion so the sugar caramelizes evenly. The syrup will start to turn golden brown, and then as you swirl the pan, the syrup will continue to get a bit darker and then darker still. To check the true color of the caramel, tilt the pan so you can see the syrup covering the bottom. This is the actual color of the caramel, and you want to keep cooking the caramel until this layer is a deep amber-brown. It takes just seconds for caramel to go from great to burnt, so be sure to tilt and check constantly.

→ As soon as the caramel is ready, slowly add the cream and then reduce the heat to low. Be careful, because the steam that rises when the cream hits the caramel is extremely hot. Let the caramel and cream sputter for a few seconds until the mixture settles down, and then whisk to mix in the cream. Turn up the heat to medium and whisk together the caramel and cream (the mixture will have hardened a bit) for 2 to 3 minutes, or until they come together. Whisk in the orange zest and remove the pan from the heat.

→ Add the hazelnuts, pecans, walnuts, almonds, pistachios, cranberries, vanilla, and salt to the caramel mixture and stir to combine.

→ It is easier to move the tart around when it is on a baking sheet, so put the baked tart shell on a baking sheet and pour the caramel-nut mixture into it. It should fill to the rim of the shell.

→ Bake for about 15 minutes, or until the caramel filling starts to bubble. Let cool on a wire rack for at least 1 hour, or until the filling has set, or up to 4 hours.

→ The tart can be stored in an airtight container in the refrigerator for up to 2 days. Remove the tart from the refrigerator 3 to 4 hours before serving so it comes fully to room temperature.

MILKY WAY TART

MILK CHOCOLATE MOUSSE

5 ounces (140 grams) milk chocolate, chopped

2 cups (480 grams) heavy cream

2 teaspoons instant coffee powder

⅛ teaspoon kosher salt

CARAMEL FILLING

¾ cup (150 grams) sugar

⅓ cup (80 grams) water

¾ cup (180 grams) heavy cream

2 tablespoons (¼ stick/28 grams) unsalted butter

¼ teaspoon kosher salt

2 teaspoons vanilla extract

Pâte Sucrée 10-inch tart shell (page 210)

3- to 4-inch slab milk chocolate, at warm room temperature, for decorating

MAKES ONE 10-INCH TART (SERVES 8 TO 10)

I got the idea for this tart many years ago from Maury Rubin's *Book of Tarts*, and it has become a favorite of Flour customers. In the book, Rubin offers myriad creative, unconventional fillings for tarts, including the idea of re-creating the popular Milky Way candy bar in tart form. For the Flour version, I make a buttery caramel (which is a pretty amazing ice cream or dessert sauce in its own right) and layer it on the bottom of a sweet tart shell. Then I pile on a mound of light, fluffy milk chocolate mousse that has a hint of coffee flavor to give it extra depth and to keep it from being too sweet. More caramel is drizzled on top, and a shower of milk chocolate curls finishes it off. To me, the finished tart tastes far better than any candy bar!

→ To make the mousse: Place the chocolate in a small heatproof bowl. In a medium saucepan, combine the cream and instant coffee powder and scald over medium-high heat (bubbles start to form around the edge of the pan, but the cream is not boiling). Pour the hot cream mixture over the chocolate and let sit for about 1 minute, then whisk gently until the chocolate is completely melted and the mixture is smooth. Strain through a fine-mesh sieve into a small container, stir in the salt, cover tightly, and refrigerate for at least 8 hours, or until it is absolutely completely chilled, or up to 3 days. A few hours is *not* enough here. Because the cream has been heated, it will not whip properly unless it is very cold.

→ To make the caramel filling: Place the sugar in the bottom of a medium saucepan and slowly pour in the water. Stir gently to moisten the sugar. If any sugar crystals are clinging to the sides of the pan, brush them down with a pastry brush dipped in water. Place the pan over high heat and leave it undisturbed until the mixture comes to a rolling boil. (You want to avoid crystallization of the syrup, which can happen if the pan is disturbed before the sugar starts to color.) Then continue to boil rapidly without moving the pan until the sugar syrup starts to caramelize. This will take 3 to 4 minutes: the sugar syrup will boil furiously; then as it thickens, it will boil more languidly; and then you will see some of the syrup starting to color and darken around the edge of the pan.

(continued)

➡ When you start to see color in the pan, gently swirl it in a circular motion so the sugar caramelizes evenly. The syrup will start to turn golden brown, and then as you swirl the pan, the syrup will continue to get a bit darker and then darker still. To check the true color of the caramel, tilt the pan so you can see the syrup covering the bottom. This is the actual color of the caramel, and you want to keep cooking the caramel until this layer is a deep amber-brown. It takes just seconds for caramel to go from great to burnt, so be sure to tilt and check constantly.

➡ As soon as the caramel is ready, slowly add the cream and then reduce the heat to low. Be careful, because the steam that rises when the cream hits the caramel is extremely hot. Let the caramel and cream sputter for a few seconds until the mixture settles down, and then whisk to mix in the cream. Turn up the heat to medium and whisk together the caramel and cream (the mixture will have hardened a bit) for 2 to 3 minutes, or until they come together. Whisk in the butter, salt, and vanilla.

➡ Remove from the heat, pour into an airtight, heatproof container, and refrigerate for at least 4 hours or up to 1 week.

➡ Place the tart shell on a flat plate. Spread about three-fourths of the caramel filling evenly in the bottom of the tart shell. Using a stand mixer fitted with the whip attachment (or a handheld mixer or a whisk), whip the mousse on medium speed until it holds soft peaks. Mound the mousse in the shell, and spread it evenly over the caramel filling. Drizzle the remaining caramel filling in a crisscross pattern on top of the mousse. Using the back of a small knife or a vegetable peeler, shave curls from the milk chocolate slab. (Make sure the chocolate is slightly warm, or you will get splinters instead of curls.) Decorate the tart with the curls.

➡ Chill for at least 30 minutes before serving.

➡ The tart can be stored in an airtight container in the refrigerator for up to 8 hours.

APPLE AND QUINCE TARTE TATIN

CARAMEL

1½ cups (300 grams) sugar

¾ cup (180 grams) water

6 tablespoons (¾ stick/86 grams) unsalted butter

Pinch of kosher salt

6 quinces, peeled, quartered, and cored

2 cups (400 grams) sugar

6 cups (1.4 kilograms) water

1 cinnamon stick

½ recipe Quick Puff Pastry (page 235)

6 Granny Smith or other tart apples, peeled, quartered, and cored

Ice cream or heavy cream for serving

MAKES ONE 9-INCH TART (SERVES 10)

The delightful, oft-told story about *tarte Tatin* is that the Tatin sisters, who ran the Hôtel Tatin in France's Loire Valley in the late 1800s, accidentally created this tart one day when one of the sisters got flummoxed and forgot the bottom crust of her signature apple tart. She hastily rolled out a piece of puff pastry, draped it on top, and crossed her fingers as she put the whole thing in the oven. When it came out, the sugar and butter from the bottom of the pan had combined with the juices of the cooked apples to create a luscious, dark caramel sauce. The sisters inverted the tart and served it to their hotel guests, and a classic was born. Would that every time I was flustered I came up with a national treasure! Many recipes call for caramelizing sugar and butter in an ovenproof skillet, which then serves as the baking vessel for the tart. In this recipe, I make the caramel separately and pour it into a cake pan, which is better for holding lots of fruit. Plus, you can make the caramel in advance and use it whenever you are ready to bake the tart.

⮕ Generously butter a 9-inch cake pan or coat it with nonstick cooking spray.

⮕ To make the caramel: Place the sugar in the bottom of a small saucepan and slowly pour in the water. Stir gently to moisten the sugar. If any sugar crystals are clinging to the sides of the pan, brush them down with a pastry brush dipped in water. Place the saucepan over high heat and leave it undisturbed until the mixture comes to a rolling boil. (You want to avoid crystallization of the syrup, which can happen if the pan is disturbed before the sugar starts to color.) Then continue to boil rapidly without moving the pan until the sugar syrup starts to caramelize. This will take 3 to 4 minutes: the sugar syrup will boil furiously; then as it thickens, it will boil more languidly; and then you will see some of the syrup starting to color and darken around the edge of the pan.

⮕ When you see color in the pan, gently swirl it in a circular motion so the sugar caramelizes evenly. Turn down the heat to medium and keep swirling the pan gently until the caramel is a dark amber-brown. Once the sugar has started to caramelize, watch it carefully and have the butter ready to go. It may smoke

(continued)

a little bit, which is fine. It takes just seconds for caramel to go from great to burnt, so be sure to tilt and check constantly. At the same time, you want to make sure it turns a nice, deep amber-brown, because if you don't, it won't have the characteristically bittersweet edge you want for your caramel.

⇒ As soon as the caramel is ready, immediately add the butter. Be careful, because it will sputter and spatter when it hits the caramel. Whisk the butter into the caramel until it is completely incorporated. It will seize up at first and get foamy; eventually the hard caramel will melt and combine with the butter. Whisk in the salt and immediately pour the mixture into the prepared pan. Swirl the pan until it is evenly coated with the caramel. Use the same day, or cover the pan tightly and store at cool room temperature for up to 1 week.

⇒ In a medium saucepan, combine the quinces, sugar, water, and cinnamon and bring to a boil over high heat, stirring to dissolve the sugar. Reduce the heat to low and simmer, uncovered, for 2 to 2½ hours, or until the quinces are cooked. They should be tender enough to pierce easily with a knife. The quinces will slowly undergo a transformation from pale to semitranslucent to rosy.

⇒ Remove the pan from the heat and let the quinces cool in the syrup until they are cool enough to handle. (The quinces can be prepared up to 1 week in advance and stored in their syrup in an airtight container in the refrigerator.)

⇒ On a well-floured work surface, roll out the puff pastry dough into a circle 10 to 11 inches in diameter and about ¼ inch thick. Don't be afraid to be rough with the dough: flip it upside down, turn it side to side, and pound it with the rolling pin to flatten it as you roll it into a nice circle. Transfer the dough circle to a baking sheet and place in the refrigerator to rest for at least 20 minutes or up to 1 day.

⇒ Position a rack in the center of the oven, and heat the oven to 350 degrees F.

⇒ Arrange the apple quarters, rounded-side down, in the caramel in the cake pan, using as many as will fit snugly in the bottom and covering the entire bottom of the pan. Drain the quince quarters, discard the cinnamon, and place a layer of quince on top of the apples, again filling the pan as tightly as you can with the fruit. You want every single inch of the pan to be covered with apples and quinces. The fruit cooks down and reduces somewhat in the oven, so don't be shy about packing the fruit quarters tightly. Place the rest of the apples and quinces into the pan, arranging the fruit so that it is fairly level on top.

⇒ Remove the dough circle from the refrigerator, and trim it so it is about 10 inches in diameter. Drape the dough directly on top of the apples and quinces, and tuck the edge of the dough into the rim of the pan, fitting it snugly around the fruit.

⇒ Bake for 1 hour to 1 hour and 10 minutes, or until the puff pastry is golden brown through and through. Let cool in the pan on a wire rack for about 20 minutes.

⇒ Tilt the cake pan a little, and if you see a lot of juice, drain some of it out. Place a large serving plate upside down on top of the cake pan, then holding the pan and the plate tightly together, carefully and quickly invert them onto a firm surface. Carefully lift off the cake pan. Sometimes the fruit pieces get jostled loose and fall off the pastry, so replace them as needed. Serve warm with a scoop of ice cream alongside or with a drizzle of cream on top.

⇒ The tart can be stored in an airtight container at room temperature for up to 2 days.

Baker's Bite

This tarte Tatin features both apples and quinces. Quinces are hard, knobby, pear-looking fruits that perfume the whole room with their pineappley smell as they sit on the counter. Don't be tempted to eat them raw, however, as they are much too hard and astringent. You must first poach them in a light sugar syrup for a couple of hours. Initially, you'll notice nothing special as they cook. But after a while, jiggle the pan, and as you watch the syrup flow over them, you will witness an awesome transformation: they go from almost white to golden yellow to, finally, a deep rose. (Sometimes the rose color develops only after they have finished poaching and have sat for a few more hours off the heat.) Their taste reminds me of lychees, one of my favorite childhood fruits, and it goes marvelously with the caramelized apples.

QUICK PUFF PASTRY

2⅓ cups (330 grams) unbleached all-purpose flour

½ cup (60 grams) cake flour

1¼ teaspoons kosher salt

1 pound (4 sticks/454 grams) cold unsalted butter, cut into ½-inch cubes

½ cup (120 grams) ice water

MAKES ABOUT 2 POUNDS DOUGH, ENOUGH FOR 2 *TARTES TATIN*

➡ Using a stand mixer fitted with the paddle attachment (or a handheld mixer), mix together the all-purpose flour, cake flour, and salt on low speed until combined. Scatter the butter over the top. On the lowest speed, pulse the mixer on and off for 45 seconds to 1 minute, or until the butter is broken down into pieces the size of a lima bean. Pour in the ice water and mix on the lowest speed for 10 to 15 seconds, or until everything comes together in a shaggy, rough-looking dough.

➡ Dump out the dough onto a generously floured work surface and pat it into about an 8-inch square. Using a rolling pin, roll out the dough from left to right as well as you can into a rectangle 15 to 18 inches wide, 8 inches from top to bottom, and about ½ inch thick. Flour the dough as needed to prevent the rolling pin from sticking. Don't worry if it seems really messy and not at all smooth. Just do your best to roll the square into a rectangle.

➡ Using a bench scraper or a knife, lightly score the rectangle into thirds vertically. Each third should be 5 to 6 inches wide and 8 inches from top to bottom. Brush any loose flour off the dough. As best you can, lift the right third of the dough and flip it over onto the middle third. Then take the left third of the dough and, again as best you can, flip that third on top of the middle and right third. You should now have a messy pile of dough about 6 inches wide, 8 inches from top to bottom, and about 2 inches thick. Rotate the dough pile clockwise 90 degrees; it will now be 8 inches wide and about 6 inches from top to bottom. This process—folding the dough in thirds and then rotating it 90 degrees—is called "turning the dough." The dough should still look rough and bits of butter will be visible throughout.

(continued)

➡ Using the rolling pin, roll out the folded dough again into a rectangle about 18 inches wide and about 8 inches from top to bottom. This time the dough should be a little more cohesive, and you should find it a little easier to roll. Make sure your work surface and dough are well floured. Do your best to roll the dough into as even a rectangle with sharp corners as you can. (See Baker's Bite, page 97), for tips on rolling out a laminated dough like this one.)

➡ Again, give the dough a turn by dividing it into thirds, flipping the right third onto the middle third, the left third on top (like folding a letter), and then turning the entire pile of dough 90 degrees. Dust off any loose flour between folds.

➡ Repeat this process twice more, for a total of four turns. By the time you get to the fourth turn, the dough should be completely cohesive and almost smooth. Small chunks of butter may still be visible, but the dough should no longer be shaggy or difficult to work with.

➡ Place the dough on a baking sheet and cover it completely with plastic wrap, tucking the plastic under the dough as if you are tucking it into bed. Refrigerate for at least 1 hour and no more than 2 hours.

➡ Remove the dough from the refrigerator, and place it on a work surface, with a long side of the rectangle facing you. Turn the dough (fold it in thirds, then rotate it 90 degrees) twice more. Give the dough two more turns. Flip the dough over occasionally during the rolling process to make sure the top and bottom layers are getting equal attention from the rolling pin.

➡ The puff pastry dough is now finished, but it needs to rest before you can use it. Wrap the dough in plastic wrap and let rest in the refrigerator for at least 1 hour. The dough can be stored in the refrigerator for up to 2 days or frozen, well wrapped in plastic wrap, for up to 1 month. If frozen, thaw it overnight in the refrigerator.

ROASTED PEAR AND CRANBERRY CROSTATA

9 Bosc pears, peeled, halved, and cored

1-inch knob fresh ginger, thinly sliced

½ cup (100 grams) granulated sugar

¼ cup (½ stick/56 grams) unsalted butter, cut into 4 pieces

Pâte Brisée II (page 216)

Frangipane (recipe follows)

1 cup (100 grams) fresh or frozen cranberries

1 egg, lightly beaten

2 tablespoons sanding sugar, pearl sugar, or granulated sugar

MAKES ONE 9-INCH *CROSTATA* (SERVES 8 TO 10)

We've offered this scrumptious open-faced rustic tart for years at Flour, and I started making it long before that. It's my go-to holiday dessert to take to dinner parties and such, and it never fails to stop conversation as everyone takes a first bite and exhales with a collective "mmmmmm." It's a sheet of flaky *pâte brisée* rolled out into a large circle, a generous layer of frangipane (almond cream) spread in the middle, and pears (roasted with butter, sugar, and fresh ginger) and fresh cranberries placed on top. It's finished with an egg wash and lots of sanding sugar, and when it emerges from the oven, it is guaranteed to impress everyone with its gorgeous appearance and delicious taste.

➡ Position a rack in the center of the oven, and heat the oven to 400 degrees F. Line a baking sheet with parchment paper.

➡ In a 9-by-13-inch baking pan, toss together the pears, ginger, granulated sugar, and butter. Roast, stirring occasionally, for 1 to 1½ hours, or until the pears are soft when pierced with a knife tip and golden. Let cool completely. (The pears can be roasted up to 5 days in advance and stored in an airtight container in the refrigerator.)

➡ Remove the dough from the refrigerator. On a well-floured work surface, roll out the dough into a circle about 12 inches in diameter and ¼ inch thick. Place the dough circle on the prepared baking sheet.

➡ Using the back of a spoon or a small rubber spatula, spread the frangipane in the middle of the dough round in a circle about 9 inches in diameter, leaving a 3-inch border uncovered.

➡ Place about 8 pear halves, cut-side down, in a circle in a single layer on top of the frangipane, lining them up with the edge of the frangipane and with the stem ends pointing toward the middle. Place 1 or 2 pear halves in the center to cover the frangipane circle completely. Sprinkle ¾ cup (75 grams) of the cranberries evenly on top of the pears. Top the first layer of pears with a second layer of pears, using about 7 halves and reserving 1 pear half, arranging them in a smaller concentric circle. Sprinkle the remaining ¼ cup (25 grams) of cranberries evenly on top of the second layer of pears.

(continued)

⇒ Place the reserved pear half on a cutting board. Using a paring knife, and starting at the squat bottom end, cut four or five lengthwise slices, stopping just short of the stem end. Fan the slices, and place the pear half in the center of the second layer of pear halves. Starting at one side of the *crostata*, fold the 3-inch border of dough up and over the fruit, forming six to eight loose pleats around the perimeter and pressing the pleats firmly together onto the fruit. The center of the *crostata* will remain exposed in a 3- to 4-inch circle, showing off the fanned pear. Refrigerate the assembled *crostata* for at least 1 hour before baking. (At this point, the *crostata* can be covered with plastic wrap and stored in the refrigerator for up to 1 day before baking.)

⇒ Position a rack in the center of the oven, and heat the oven to 350 degrees F.

⇒ Brush the pleated pastry with the beaten egg, then sprinkle evenly with the sanding sugar. Bake for about 1 hour and 20 minutes, or until the pleats are golden brown. Make sure all of the folds are evenly browned, so there are no chewy underbaked bits of dough in the finished *crostata*. Let cool on the pan on a wire rack for at least 2 hours. Serve warm or at room temperature.

⇒ The *crostata* can be stored in an airtight container at room temperature for up to 2 days.

FRANGIPANE

⅓ cup (50 grams) blanched whole almonds, or ½ cup (50 grams) almond flour

¼ cup (½ stick/56 grams) unsalted butter, at room temperature

¼ cup (50 grams) sugar

1 egg

2 teaspoons unbleached all-purpose flour

⅛ teaspoon vanilla extract

Pinch of kosher salt

MAKES ABOUT 1 CUP

⇒ If using whole almonds, grind them in a food processor as finely as possible without turning them into a paste. Set aside.

⇒ Using a stand mixer fitted with the paddle attachment (or a hand-held mixer or wooden spoon), cream together the butter and sugar on medium speed for 1 to 2 minutes, or until light. Add the ground almonds or almond flour and beat on medium speed for 1 minute, or until thoroughly incorporated. Stop the mixer and scrape the bottom and sides of the bowl.

⇒ On low speed, beat in the egg. Add the all-purpose flour, vanilla, and salt and mix until combined. You should have about 1 cup. Use immediately, or store in an airtight container in the refrigerator for up to 1 week, then let sit for a few hours at room temperature before using. Or, freeze in an airtight container for up to 3 weeks, then thaw it in the refrigerator before using.

COUNTRY HAM, CHEDDAR, AND TOMATO QUICHE

Pâte Brisée II (page 216)

6 egg yolks

3 tablespoons unbleached all-purpose flour

1 cup (240 grams) heavy cream

1 cup (240 grams) half-and-half

½ teaspoon kosher salt

¼ teaspoon freshly ground black pepper

½ teaspoon freshly grated nutmeg

4 ounces (114 grams) smoked country ham, cut into 1-inch pieces

3 ounces (86 grams) sharp Cheddar cheese, cut into ½-inch cubes

1 ripe tomato, cored and chopped

MAKES ONE 9-INCH QUICHE (SERVES 6 TO 8)

Real men may not eat quiche, but that might be because they haven't tried this one. We routinely sell out of quiche, and I can assure you our customers are not all female! This quiche starts with the flakiest, butteriest, most tender crust and is filled with a rich custard base flavored with (surprise!) nutmeg. The spice lends an elusive nutty background note that goes supremely well with our quiche fillings. Here I offer you a few of our favorites.

➡ Remove the dough from the refrigerator. On a well-floured work surface, roll out the dough into a circle about 12 inches in diameter and ⅛ inch thick. Roll the dough circle around the pin and then unfurl it on top of a 9-inch aluminum pie pan or glass pie dish. Press the dough gently into the bottom and sides of the pan. Evenly pleat the overhanging dough with your fingers to create a decorative edge, or use scissors to trim the overhang, leaving a ¼-inch lip (to allow for shrinkage in the oven). Refrigerate the quiche shell for at least 30 minutes. (The shell can be tightly wrapped in plastic wrap and refrigerated for up to 1 day or frozen for up to 2 weeks. Bake directly from the refrigerator or freezer.)

➡ Position a rack in the center of the oven, and heat the oven to 350 degrees F.

➡ Line the shell with parchment paper, fill with pie weights, and blind bake (see page 13) for 35 to 45 minutes, or until the entire shell is light brown all the way through.

➡ Meanwhile, in a small bowl, whisk together the egg yolks and flour until well mixed. Whisk in the heavy cream and half-and-half, and season with the salt, pepper, and nutmeg.

➡ When the shell is ready, remove from the oven and scatter the ham pieces evenly over the bottom. Scatter the cheese evenly on top of the ham, and then the tomato evenly on top of the cheese. Slowly pour the custard base into the shell, being careful not to dislodge the ham, cheese, and tomato.

➡ Bake for about 1 hour, or until the custard is set. Let cool on a wire rack for at least 45 minutes, then serve warm or at room temperature.

➡ The quiche can be tightly covered with plastic wrap and stored in the refrigerator for up to 2 days. Reheat in a 350-degree F oven for 10 to 15 minutes, or until warmed through, before serving.

Same recipe, different flavors

SMOKED SALMON, HERBED CREAM CHEESE, AND RED ONION: Omit the ham, Cheddar, and tomato. Chop 4 ounces (114 grams) smoked salmon into 1-inch pieces and scatter on the bottom of the baked shell. Beat 4 ounces (114 grams; about ½ cup) cream cheese and 1 tablespoon fresh dill in a small bowl with a wooden spoon until soft. Spoon small bits of the herbed cream cheese evenly over the salmon. Cut ¼ red onion into thin slices and scatter over the top. Proceed as directed.

SPINACH, ZUCCHINI, AND FETA: Omit the ham, Cheddar, and tomato. In a large skillet, heat 1 tablespoon canola oil over high heat until hot. Add 10 ounces (280 grams) spinach to the skillet. Cook for 2 to 3 minutes, or until lightly wilted. Season with ½ teaspoon kosher salt and ½ teaspoon freshly ground black pepper and remove from the heat. Cut 1 medium zucchini into ½-inch dice. Rinse and dry the skillet, return to high heat, and heat 1 tablespoon canola oil. Add the zucchini and sauté for 2 to 3 minutes, or until browned. Break up 4 ounces (114 grams) feta cheese into small pieces. Squeeze the spinach dry, roughly chop it, and scatter it over the bottom of the baked shell. Scatter the zucchini and feta over the top. Proceed as directed.

CARAMELIZED ONION AND BACON: Omit the ham, Cheddar, and tomato. In a small skillet, heat 2 tablespoons canola oil over medium heat. Add 1 thinly sliced small yellow onion, and cook, stirring occasionally, for about 30 minutes, or until softened. Reduce the heat to low and continue cooking for another 30 to 40 minutes, or until the onion is caramelized. Remove from the heat. When the onion is cool enough to handle, chop roughly and season with ½ teaspoon kosher salt, ½ teaspoon freshly ground black pepper, and 1 teaspoon finely chopped fresh thyme. Scatter the onion evenly over the bottom of the baked shell. Top with 2 or 3 slices bacon, cooked and chopped. Proceed as directed.

other sweets

BUTTERSCOTCH PUDDING

2 cups (480 grams) whole milk

2 cups (480 grams) half-and-half

½ vanilla bean, split lengthwise

1 cup plus 2 tablespoons
(248 grams) packed dark
brown sugar

2 tablespoons cornstarch

8 egg yolks

½ cup plus 2 tablespoons
(1¼ sticks/140 grams) unsalted
butter, softened, cut into 8 to
10 pieces

½ teaspoon vanilla extract

1 teaspoon kosher salt

SERVES 6

You might think that butterscotch pudding is easily made with butterscotch chips, and you would be right. But using artificially flavored chips is so unnecessary when true butterscotch flavor is easily attained with two key ingredients: butter and brown sugar. You're more likely to have these two ingredients in your pantry than a bag of butterscotch chips anyway. Real butterscotch pudding is a revelation, with none of the processed overtones of bagged chips or boxed mixes. This pudding strikes a lovely balance among all the main flavorings: butter and vanilla for richness, brown sugar for deep molasses flavor, and salt to contrast with the rich sweetness. I love it as is; for a fancier presentation, try adorning it with whipped cream or candied pecans.

⇒ In a medium saucepan, combine the milk and half-and-half. Use the tip of a knife to scrape the seeds from the vanilla bean directly into the pan and then add the pod. Place the pan over medium-high heat and scald the mixture (bubbles start to form around the edge of the pan, but the liquid is not boiling).

⇒ Meanwhile, in a small bowl, stir together the brown sugar and cornstarch. Place the egg yolks in a medium bowl, and slowly whisk in the sugar-cornstarch mixture. Slowly pour the hot milk mixture into the egg yolk mixture, a little at a time, whisking constantly. When all of the milk mixture has been incorporated, return the contents of the bowl to the saucepan, and return the saucepan to medium-low heat. Cook, whisking vigorously and making sure to scrape the bottom of the pan often to prevent scorching, for 6 to 7 minutes, or until the custard starts to thicken. The mixture will be thin and liquid at first, then it will start to steam, and finally it will start to get thicker. As you whisk the mixture, you will start to feel it getting thicker at the bottom. Remove the pudding from the heat as soon as it thickens and the whisk leaves a trail in the pudding as you whisk.

(continued)

⇒ Immediately strain the pudding through a fine-mesh sieve into a medium bowl. Whisk in the butter, vanilla extract, and salt until thoroughly incorporated, and divide among dessert bowls or ramekins. If you don't want a skin, press plastic wrap directly onto the surface of each serving; if you don't mind the skin, leave uncovered. Refrigerate for at least 6 hours before serving, or up to overnight.

⇒ The pudding can be stored, tightly covered, in the refrigerator for up to 4 days.

BEST EVER
CHOCOLATE PUDDING

1½ cups (360 grams) half-and-half

1¾ cups (420 grams) heavy cream

9 ounces (255 grams) bittersweet chocolate (70 to 77 percent cacao), chopped

7 egg yolks

¾ cup (150 grams) vanilla sugar (see page 29)

½ teaspoon vanilla extract

¼ teaspoon kosher salt

Unsweetened whipped cream and chocolate shavings for serving (optional)

**MAKES 4½ CUPS
(SERVES 4 TO 6)**

I grew up thinking pudding came out of a box. Buy the little box at the grocery store, mix it with cold milk at home, and within minutes you have pudding. I didn't even know you could make pudding from scratch until I was well into my culinary career. Lucky for me (and you), I learned to make pudding, specifically chocolate pudding, from my first pastry chef mentor, Rick Katz. Rick is a purist and doesn't like to use any superfluous ingredients or extraneous flavorings. In that vein, he taught me to forgo the traditional thickener for pudding, cornstarch, and simply increase the amount of chocolate to a level that the chocolate itself thickens the pudding—and, man, you can tell. This is like eating smooth, silky, thick fudge. There's a touch of vanilla to round out the flavor and a big pinch of salt to heighten the experience. It makes a fantastic dessert as is, or it is the main component in the best chocolate cream pie you'll ever eat (see page 208).

➡ In a medium saucepan, combine the half-and-half and heavy cream and scald over medium-high heat (bubbles start to form around the edge of the pan, but the liquid is not boiling). Place the chocolate in a medium heatproof bowl. Place over (not touching) barely simmering water in a saucepan and heat, stirring occasionally, until completely melted and smooth. Remove from the heat. Pour the hot cream mixture over the melted chocolate and whisk until thoroughly combined.

➡ Place the egg yolks in a medium bowl, and slowly whisk in the vanilla sugar. Slowly pour the hot cream-chocolate mixture into the egg-sugar mixture, a little at a time, whisking constantly. When all of the cream-chocolate mixture has been incorporated, return the contents of the bowl to the saucepan, and return the saucepan to medium-low heat. Cook, stirring continuously with a wooden spoon and making sure to scrape the bottom of the pan often to prevent scorching, for 5 to 6 minutes, or until the mixture thickens and coats the spoon thickly. To test, draw your finger along the back of the spoon; the custard should hold the trail for a couple of seconds before it fills. (First the mixture will be liquid and loose, and then it will start to get a little thicker at the bottom of the pan. As it continues to thicken, it will start to let off a little steam. When you see wisps of steam steadily rising from the pan, you will know the pudding is almost done.)

➡ When the pudding is ready, immediately strain it through a fine-mesh sieve into a bowl, and stir in the vanilla extract and salt. Press a piece of plastic wrap directly on top of the pudding to prevent a skin from forming and refrigerate for at least 3 hours, or until cold. The pudding can be stored in an airtight container in the refrigerator for up to 4 days.

➡ Just before serving, stir up the pudding to smooth it out. Spoon into dessert bowls and garnish with whipped cream and chocolate shavings (if using).

CLASSIC CRÈME BRÛLÉE

1½ cups (360 grams) heavy cream

1½ cups (360 grams) half-and-half

1 vanilla bean, split lengthwise

8 egg yolks

¾ cup (150 grams) sugar, plus ⅓ to ½ cup (70 to 100 grams) for the top

¼ teaspoon kosher salt

SERVES 8

Many people think making crème brûlée at home is beyond their reach, but they are mistaken. My theory is that crème brûlée appears on so many restaurant dessert menus not only because it's so darn delicious, but also because it's really simple to make. I've yet to work in a restaurant or bakery that didn't offer crème brûlée in some form or another. Because it's such an iconic dessert, pastry chefs like to add their own signature element by flavoring it, layering it within a dessert, or otherwise tinkering with it. I'll admit that I've flavored it with everything from ginger to milk chocolate to coffee. But for me the hands-down best way to enjoy crème brûlée is in its most elementary form: flavored only with vanilla bean. I inherited this recipe when I was pastry chef at Mistral, and I've done little to change it, other than adding a bit of salt to help highlight the vanilla flavor. It is absolutely worth splurging on a vanilla bean for this dessert. I don't even want to suggest the alternative of vanilla extract, because it just wouldn't be the same! (Fine. If you must, use about 2 teaspoons and stir it into the strained custard.) If you don't have a kitchen torch, I have included instructions for how to caramelize the custards in a broiler.

➡ Position a rack in the center of the oven, and heat the oven to 325 degrees F. Place eight 4-ounce ramekins in a large roasting pan with at least 3-inch-high sides.

➡ In a medium saucepan, combine the cream and half-and-half. Use the tip of a knife to scrape the seeds from the vanilla bean directly into the pan and then add the pod. Place the pan over medium-high heat and scald the mixture (bubbles start to form around the edge of the pan, but the liquid is not boiling).

➡ Meanwhile, in a medium bowl, whisk the egg yolks until blended, and then slowly whisk in the ¾ cup (150 grams) sugar until combined. Slowly pour the hot cream mixture into the egg-sugar mixture, a little at a time, whisking constantly. Strain the mixture through a fine-mesh sieve into a pitcher or liquid measuring cup. Stir in the salt.

➡ Pour the custard into the ramekins, dividing it evenly. Carefully move the pan with the ramekins to the oven. Pour hot water into the roasting pan to reach the same level as the custard in the ramekins. (This is a bain-marie, described on page 21.) Cover the pan with aluminum foil or a baking sheet.

➡ Bake for 25 to 30 minutes, or until the custard is just set. Start testing the custards at around 20 minutes: Lift the foil and wiggle the pan. If the custards are sloshy and liquidy, they need more time. If they are jiggly like Jell-O, remove them from the oven. If they don't really wiggle at all, they are probably a bit overdone, which is not tragic, but the custards won't be as silky and creamy as they could be. Carefully remove the roasting pan from the oven; let the custards cool in the water bath until they are cool enough to handle, then remove them. Place the ramekins in an airtight container and refrigerate for at least 1 day before serving, or up to 4 days.

➡ Sprinkle about 2 teaspoons sugar on top of each custard, and spread the sugar evenly with your finger. Light a kitchen torch and wave it back and forth over the surface of each custard, with the flame about 1 inch from the sugar, burning the sugar until it melts and then starts to caramelize. Move the torch around slowly and don't linger on any one spot or hold the torch too close the sugar, or it might burn. Torch the custards until the tops are dark golden brown.

(If you don't have a kitchen torch, preheat the broiler. Place the ramekins in a roasting pan and fill it with ice water. Sprinkle about 2 teaspoons sugar on top of each custard, and spread the sugar evenly with your finger. Carefully place the pan with the custards under the broiler, ideally with the heat source 2 to 3 inches from the surface of the custards. Don't walk away. Close the oven door and watch the custards through the oven window as the sugar melts and then starts to caramelize. When the tops are dark golden brown, immediately remove the custards from the oven.)

➡ Let the sugar cool and form a crunchy shell for at least 5 minutes before serving. The caramelized custards can also be returned to the refrigerator for a few hours before serving.

VANILLA CRÈME CARAMEL

1¼ cups (250 grams) sugar

¼ cup (60 grams) water

2 cups (480 grams) heavy cream

1 cup (240 grams) milk

½ vanilla bean, split lengthwise

3 egg yolks

2 eggs

¼ teaspoon kosher salt

SERVES 6 TO 8

When I interviewed for the pastry chef position at Rialto, part of my interview process involved preparing a few desserts for the chef and general manager. One I presented was crème caramel. It's an unassuming dessert with just a few key ingredients, but when made properly it never fails to impress. I learned how to make a killer crème caramel, from Rick Katz at Bentonwood Bakery. The tricks he taught me then were nothing Earth-shattering; as with most baking, the key is doing a lot of little things correctly. To make a great crème caramel, you first need to make a great caramel, one that is burnt enough to be bittersweet and not just sugary sweet. Then you need to bake the custards slowly at a low temperature. Don't go over 300 degrees F and you'll be rewarded with smooth, dreamy custards. Test them frequently as they are nearing completion. You want the centers of the custards to jiggle like Jell-O. Finally, the salt in this recipe is a must. It brings out the full flavor of the vanilla and highlights the sharpness of the dark caramel. I'd like to think it was my interviewing prowess and irresistible charm that landed me the pastry chef gig at Rialto, but it was probably this crème caramel.

→ Position a rack in the center of the oven, and heat the oven to 300 degrees F. Place eight 4-ounce ramekins or six 6-ounce ramekins in a large roasting pan with at least 3-inch-high sides.

→ Put ¾ cup (150 grams) of the sugar in the bottom of a small saucepan and slowly pour in the water. Stir gently to moisten the sugar. If any sugar crystals are clinging to the sides of the pan, brush them down with a pastry brush dipped in water. Place the saucepan over high heat and leave it undisturbed until the mixture comes to a rolling boil. (You want to avoid crystallization of the syrup, which can happen if the pan is jostled before the sugar starts to color.) Then continue to boil rapidly without moving the pan until the sugar syrup starts to caramelize. This will take 3 to 4 minutes: the sugar will boil furiously; then as it thickens, it will boil more languidly; and then you will see some of the syrup starting to color and darken around the edge of the pan.

→ As soon as you see color in the pan, gently swirl it in a circular motion so the sugar caramelizes evenly. Turn down the heat to medium and keep swirling the pan gently until the caramel is a dark amber-brown. Once the sugar has started to caramelize, watch it carefully. It takes just seconds for caramel to go from great to burnt, so be sure to tilt and check constantly. At the same time, you want to make sure it turns a nice, deep amber-brown, because if you don't, it won't have the characteristically bittersweet edge you want for your caramel.

➡ When the caramel is ready, immediately and carefully pour it into the bottom of the ramekins, dividing it evenly. Set the ramekins aside.

➡ In a medium saucepan, combine the cream and milk. Use the tip of a knife to scrape the seeds from the vanilla bean directly into the pan, then add the pod. Place the pan over medium-high heat and scald the mixture (bubbles start to form around the edge of the pan, but the liquid is not boiling).

➡ Meanwhile, in a medium bowl, whisk together the egg yolks and eggs, and then slowly whisk in the remaining ½ cup (100 grams) sugar until combined. Slowly pour the hot cream mixture into the egg-sugar mixture, a little at a time, whisking constantly. Strain the mixture through a fine-mesh sieve into a pitcher or liquid measuring cup. Stir in the salt.

➡ Pour the custard into the caramel-lined ramekins, dividing it evenly. Carefully move the pan with the ramekins to the oven. Pour hot water into the roasting pan to reach the same level as the custard in the ramekins. (This is a bain-marie, described on page 21.) Cover the pan with aluminum foil or a baking sheet.

➡ Bake for 25 to 30 minutes, or until the custard is just set. Start testing the custards at around 20 minutes: Lift the foil and wiggle the pan. If the custards are sloshy and liquidy, they need more time. If they are jiggly like Jell-O, remove them from the oven. If they don't really wiggle at all, they are probably a bit overdone, which is not tragic, but the custards won't be as silky and creamy as they could be. Carefully remove the roasting pan from the oven, and let the custards cool in the water bath until they are cool enough to handle, then remove them. Place the ramekins in an airtight container and refrigerate for at least 1 day before serving, or up to 5 days.

➡ To serve, run a thin knife along the inside edge of each ramekin and invert the custard onto a dessert plate, scraping any liquid caramel from the ramekin onto the custard.

Same recipe, different flavors

ESPRESSO CRÈME CARAMEL: Omit the vanilla bean. Crush ½ cup (50 grams) espresso beans into coarse pieces, add them to the cream mixture, and heat to a simmer. Remove from the heat and let infuse for 5 minutes. Strain through a fine-mesh sieve, return to the pan, and bring back to a simmer, then proceed as directed.

GINGER CRÈME CARAMEL: Omit the vanilla bean. Peel and finely chop a 3-inch piece of fresh ginger, add it to the cream mixture, and heat to a simmer. Remove from the heat and let infuse for 15 to 20 minutes. Strain through a fine-mesh sieve, return to the pan, and bring back to a simmer, then proceed as directed.

PLUM CLAFOUTIS

¼ cup (½ stick/56 grams) unsalted
butter, melted

6 medium plums, pitted and
cut into eighths (about 5 cups/
850 grams)

½ cup (100 grams) granulated
sugar

4 eggs

⅓ cup (48 grams) unbleached
all-purpose flour

½ teaspoon kosher salt

1 cup (240 grams) milk

1 tablespoon vanilla extract

½ teaspoon almond extract

Confectioners' sugar for dusting

SERVES 8

Clafoutis (clah-foo-TEE) has to be one of the most fun pastry words to say, right up there with *croquembouche* (crow-kem-BOOSH) and *pithivier* (pee-tee-vee-YAY). Those French pastry chefs certainly know how to name their pastries. A *clafoutis* is composed of a pancake-like batter poured over fruit (traditionally, unpitted cherries, though most people these days make it with pitted fruit) and baked until custardy and poufy. My dear friend and fellow chef Denise Drower Swidey, who was the first employee I hired when I was pastry chef at Rialto, presented this *clafoutis* to me as a wedding gift. She said she was nervous about giving it to me, but she shouldn't have been. Christopher and I devoured the whole thing that evening in lieu of dinner. Eating it reminded me how much I appreciate the simplicity of rustic French country desserts. The tartness of the plums melds beautifully with the creamy texture of the batter, and the plum juice caramelizes on top to make an irresistible treat.

→ Position a rack in the center of the oven, and heat the oven to 400 degrees F.

→ Pour the melted butter into a 9-by-13-inch baking dish, and swirl the dish to coat the bottom and sides with the butter.

→ In a medium bowl, toss the plums with ¼ cup (50 grams) of the sugar and then pour into the baking dish, spreading evenly.

→ In a medium bowl, whisk the eggs until blended. In a separate bowl, whisk together the remaining ¼ cup (50 grams) sugar, the flour, and salt. Whisk the sugar-flour mixture into the eggs. Then whisk the milk and the vanilla and almond extracts into the egg mixture. Pour the batter over the plums.

→ Bake for 40 to 45 minutes, or until the *clafoutis* is golden brown and puffy. Let cool on a wire rack for about 30 minutes. Dust generously with confectioners' sugar and serve warm.

→ The *clafoutis* tastes best on the day it is baked, but it may also be enjoyed the next day for a decadent breakfast or midday snack. Store, covered, at room temperature.

CHOCOLATE BANANA
BREAD PUDDING

6 to 7 cups ½-inch-cubed day-old white bread (the weight depends on type of bread)

6 ounces (170 grams) milk chocolate, chopped

2 ounces (56 grams) semisweet or bittersweet chocolate, chopped into pebble-sized pieces

6 cups (1.4 kilograms) half-and-half

2 eggs

6 egg yolks

½ cup (100 grams) sugar

¼ teaspoon kosher salt

3 ripe bananas, peeled and cut into slices ⅛ to ¼ inch thick

SERVES 10 TO 12

We started making Berry Bread Pudding (page 256) at Flour as a way to use up all of the bread ends we generated from the house-made bread for our popular sandwiches. But one type of bread pudding wasn't always enough: on some days, we still found ourselves with a pretty large tub of bread ends. So we came up with a second bread pudding version that has proven to be as popular as the first. I used to make a divine milk chocolate crème brûlée when I was pastry chef at Rialto. After baking each batch, I'd usually consume an entire custard warm out of the oven, proclaiming that the dessert was definitely best served warm. After the custards had cooled down, I would try one cold (all in the name of testing, of course) and change my mind. They were terrific when chilled: thick and fudgy and creamy. That milk chocolaty custard was the starting point for this bread pudding. I toss some cubed bread and sliced bananas with a custard base, and then I bake it up into a fantastic pudding that is equally delicious warm or cold. If you want to pull out all the stops, drizzle it with chocolate sauce.

➡ Spread the bread cubes evenly over the bottom of a deep 9-by-13-inch baking dish or roasting pan. Place the milk chocolate and semisweet chocolate in a medium heatproof bowl. In a medium saucepan, scald the half-and-half over medium-high heat (bubbles start to form around the edge of the pan, but the cream is not boiling). Pour the hot cream over the chocolate and let sit for 1 minute, then gently whisk together the chocolate and cream until the chocolate is completely melted and the mixture is smooth.

➡ In a medium bowl, whisk together the eggs and egg yolks until blended, and then slowly whisk in the sugar and salt until combined. Slowly add the hot chocolate-cream mixture to the egg-sugar mixture, a little at a time, whisking constantly. Strain the mixture through a fine-mesh sieve, then pour it over the bread. Mix the custard and bread well to make sure all of the bread cubes are soaking evenly. Cover the baking dish with plastic wrap and refrigerate for at least 8 hours or up to 24 hours.

➡ When you are ready to bake, position a rack in the center of the oven, and heat the oven to 300 degrees F.

➡ Stir the banana slices into the bread pudding. Bake for 1 hour and 10 minutes to 1 hour and 20 minutes, or until just barely set. To test for doneness, insert a knife in the middle of the pudding and bend it back a bit to see if the custard mix has set up. If liquid fills the hole made with the knife, the pudding needs more time. When the pudding is ready, remove from the oven and let rest for at least 2 hours. Serve warm, or cover and refrigerate and serve chilled.

➡ The bread pudding can be stored, tightly covered, in the refrigerator for up to 4 days.

BERRY BREAD PUDDING

10 cups ½-inch-cubed day-old bread (the weight depends on type of bread)

3 eggs

7 egg yolks

1⅔ cups (340 grams) vanilla sugar (see page 29)

6 cups (1.4 kilograms) half-and-half

1 cup (150 grams) blueberries

1 cup (130 grams) raspberries

SERVES 12 TO 15

We almost always have leftover bread at the bakery: some goes to staff members, some gets dropped off at a local shelter, some gets made into bread crumbs, and, of course, some gets turned into bread pudding. It's always amazing to me how popular this treat is—a humble bread pudding made extra delicious with fresh berries and vanilla sugar.

➡ Spread the bread cubes evenly over the bottom of a deep 9-by-13-inch baking dish or roasting pan. In a medium bowl, whisk together the eggs and egg yolks until blended, and then slowly whisk in 1 cup (200 grams) of the vanilla sugar. Whisk in the half-and-half. Pour the mixture over the bread and mix to make sure that all of the bread pieces are soaking. Cover the baking dish with plastic wrap and refrigerate for at least 8 hours or up to 24 hours.

➡ When you are ready to bake, position a rack in the center of the oven, and heat the oven to 300 degrees F.

➡ Sprinkle the top of the soaked bread cubes evenly with the blueberries and raspberries. Then sprinkle the remaining ⅔ cup (140 grams) vanilla sugar over the berries.

➡ Bake for 1 to 1½ hours, or until just barely set. To test for doneness, insert a knife in the middle of the pudding and bend it back a bit to see if the custard mix has set up. If liquid fills the hole made with the knife, the pudding needs more time. When the pudding is ready, remove from the oven and let rest for at least 2 hours. Serve warm, or cover and refrigerate and serve chilled.

➡ The bread pudding can be stored, tightly covered, in the refrigerator for up to 4 days.

COFFEE ICE CREAM
WITH COCOA NIB BRITTLE

COCOA NIB BRITTLE

1 cup (200 grams) sugar

¼ cup (60 grams) water

¼ cup (30 grams) cocoa nibs

2 tablespoons (¼ stick/28 grams) unsalted butter

Pinch of kosher salt

1⅓ cups (320 grams) heavy cream

2 cups (480 grams) milk

½ vanilla bean, split lengthwise

⅓ cup (35 grams) ground French or other dark roast coffee

8 egg yolks

1 cup (200 grams) sugar

¼ teaspoon kosher salt

MAKES ABOUT 1¼ QUARTS

I like to think that my ice cream obsession indirectly stems from the fact that my parents' first date was at an ice cream parlor. While I was conceived many years after that occasion, the ice cream that brought my mom and dad together somehow made its way to the *I-gotta-have-it* part of my brain. I could eat ice cream morning, noon, and night, and every year on my birthday, I do exactly that. If I had to pick a favorite ice cream flavor, it would be coffee. I love how the bitter coffee flavor is smoothed over by a minimum of sugar. I don't normally like mix-ins in my ice cream, but the cocoa nib brittle here takes the dessert over the top. It is slightly bitter, slightly buttery, slightly crunchy, and completely irresistible.

⇒ To make the brittle: Line a baking sheet with parchment paper. Coat the parchment liberally with nonstick cooking spray or butter it lightly.

⇒ Place the sugar in the bottom of a medium saucepan and slowly pour in the water. Stir gently to moisten the sugar. If any sugar crystals are clinging to the sides of the pan, brush them down with a pastry brush dipped in water. Place the saucepan over high heat and leave it undisturbed until the mixture comes to a boil. (You want to avoid crystallization of the syrup, which can happen if the pan is jostled.) Then continue to boil rapidly without moving the pan until the sugar syrup starts to color and turn light brown. This will take 3 to 5 minutes.

⇒ When you see color in the pan, gently swirl it in a circular motion so the sugar caramelizes evenly. Add the cocoa nibs and swirl them around in the caramel until the caramel turns medium amber-brown. (The caramel may foam a bit when you add the nibs. This is normal, and once you swirl the pan for a few seconds, the foaming will subside.)

⇒ When the caramel is medium amber-brown, immediately remove the pan from the heat and carefully whisk in the butter and salt. Quickly pour the brittle mixture onto the prepared baking sheet, and tilt the sheet back and forth to spread the brittle in a thin, even layer. Be careful; the brittle is very hot! Let cool for 30 to 40 minutes, or until the brittle is cool to the touch.

(continued)

➡ Place about two-thirds of the cooled brittle into a plastic bag or between two sheets of parchment or waxed paper, and press a rolling pin up and down on the bag. Set aside the smashed bits of brittle to mix into your ice cream, and reserve the remaining brittle to use as garnish for the ice cream. (The brittle can be made up to 1 week in advance and stored in an airtight container at room temperature.)

➡ In a medium saucepan, combine the cream and milk. Use the tip of a knife to scrape the seeds from the vanilla bean directly into the pan and add the pod, as well. Then add the ground coffee. Scald the cream mixture over medium-high heat (bubbles start to form around the edge of the pan, but the liquid is not boiling). Remove from the heat and let the coffee and vanilla steep in the cream for about 1 hour.

➡ In a medium bowl, whisk the egg yolks until blended, and then slowly whisk in the sugar until combined. Return the cream mixture to medium-high heat and scald again. Slowly pour the hot cream mixture into the egg yolk mixture, a little at a time, whisking constantly. When all of the hot cream mixture has been incorporated, return the contents of the bowl to the saucepan, and return the saucepan to medium heat. Cook, stirring continuously with a wooden spoon, for 6 to 8 minutes, or until the mixture thickens and coats the back of the spoon. The mixture will seem watery at first, then it will start to steam, and then it will start to develop a little body and get thicker. Remove from the heat and immediately strain through a fine-mesh sieve into an airtight container. Whisk in the salt. Cover and refrigerate for at least 2 hours, or until cold, or up to overnight.

➡ Churn in an ice-cream maker according to the manufacturer's directions.

➡ When the ice cream is finished churning, mix in the crushed brittle by hand and freeze for at least 2 hours to allow the ice cream to ripen. During the ripening process, the ice cream becomes harder and smoother and the flavors more fully develop. The ice cream keeps in an airtight container in the freezer for up to 1 week. When serving, garnish with the reserved brittle.

HONEY-CINNAMON ICE CREAM

2 cups (480 grams) milk

2 cups (480 grams) heavy cream

1 cinnamon stick, 2 inches long

8 egg yolks

¾ cup (255 grams) honey

2 tablespoons sugar

½ teaspoon ground cinnamon

¼ teaspoon kosher salt

MAKES ABOUT 1¼ QUARTS

The first time my parents came to Rialto, site of my first pastry chef gig, my mom laughed out loud when she saw the dessert menu. Every dessert featured ice cream, and one dessert had two. My dad and I are both complete ice creamaholics, and once I was in a position to make my own ice creams, they showed up everywhere I could put them! I made fruit ice creams, nut ice creams, spiced ice creams. You name the ingredient and I made it into ice cream. This was one of my favorites. Originally it was a honey-vanilla ice cream, but this variation popped up one day when my vanilla supplier missed a shipment. Needing to make a quick ice-cream base for that evening's service and stuck without vanilla beans, I turned to the spice larder and selected a few cinnamon sticks, and a new flavor was born. I like the way the warm cinnamon flavor melds with the natural earthiness and roundness of the honey. Honey is a sweetener that lends itself to extra-creamy ice creams, which you'll notice immediately when you taste this one after churning.

⇒ In a medium saucepan, combine the milk and cream. Break the cinnamon stick into several pieces and toss them into the pan. Scald the milk mixture over medium-high heat (bubbles start to form around the edge of the pan, but the liquid is not boiling). Remove from the heat and let the cinnamon steep in the milk mixture for about 1 hour.

⇒ In a medium bowl, whisk the egg yolks until blended, and then slowly whisk in the honey, sugar, and ground cinnamon until combined. Return the milk mixture to medium-high heat and scald again. Slowly add the hot milk mixture to the egg yolk mixture, a little at a time, whisking constantly. When all of the hot milk mixture has been incorporated, return the contents of the bowl to the saucepan, and return the saucepan to medium heat. Cook, stirring continuously with a wooden spoon, for 6 to 8 minutes, or until the mixture thickens and coats the back of the spoon. The mixture will seem watery at first, then it will start to steam, and then it will start to develop a little body and get thicker. Remove from the heat and immediately strain through a fine-mesh sieve into an airtight container. Whisk in the salt. Cover and refrigerate for at least 2 hours, or until cold, or up to overnight.

➡ Churn in an ice-cream maker according to the manufacturer's directions.

➡ When the ice cream has finished churning, freeze it for at least 2 hours to allow it to ripen. During the ripening process, the ice cream becomes harder and smoother and the flavors more fully develop. The ice cream can be stored in an airtight container in the freezer for up to 1 week.

LEMON SHERBET AND PROSECCO SORBET
WITH STRAWBERRIES

LEMON SHERBET

1 cup (240 grams) fresh lemon juice (6 to 7 lemons)

2 teaspoons finely grated lemon zest (about ⅔ lemon)

1¼ cups (250 grams) sugar

½ cup (120 grams) water

Pinch of kosher salt

1½ cups (360 grams) half-and-half

PROSECCO SORBET

⅔ cup (140 grams) sugar

1 cup (240 grams) water

1 cup (240 grams) Prosecco

3 tablespoons fresh lemon juice (about 1½ lemons)

Pinch of kosher salt

1 pint (300 grams) strawberries, stemmed and chopped into small pieces

¼ cup (50 grams) sugar

1 teaspoon finely grated lemon zest

About 2½ cups (600 grams) Prosecco (remainder of bottle from the sorbet recipe)

SERVES 8

This is the most refreshing, light, and fizzy ice cream float ever. I came up with this dessert by accident for my first springtime menu at Rialto. Strawberries were just coming into season, and the farmers were dropping off casefuls at the restaurant. The wine cellar was fully stocked with Prosecco, in anticipation of the warmer weather. And I had just churned a quick lemon sherbet to use up an abundance of lemon juice I found in the refrigerator. Combining these ingredients just seemed to make sense, and with a little reworking, I turned that combo into this dessert. I churned the Prosecco into an icy sorbet, and I let the strawberries macerate with a little sugar and lemon to bring out their juices. Then I filled tall glasses with tiny scoops of the Prosecco sorbet and the creamy, tart lemon sherbet, alternating them with spoonfuls of strawberries, and finished it off with a generous pour of Prosecco. It's springtime in a glass!

➡ To make the lemon sherbet: In a small saucepan, combine the lemon juice, lemon zest, and sugar and bring to a boil over medium-high heat, stirring to dissolve the sugar. Remove from the heat, strain through a fine-mesh sieve into an airtight container, and stir in the water and salt. Let cool, cover, and refrigerate for at least 3 hours, or until cold, or up to 1 week.

➡ When you are ready to churn the sherbet, whisk the half-and-half into the lemon base until combined. Churn in an ice-cream maker according to the manufacturer's directions. You should have about 3½ cups. Transfer to an airtight container and place in the freezer until serving.

➡ To make the Prosecco sorbet: In a small saucepan, combine the sugar and water and bring to a boil over medium-high heat, stirring to dissolve the sugar. Remove from the heat, let cool, transfer to an airtight container, cover, and refrigerate for at least 3 hours, or until cold, or up to 3 weeks.

➡ When you are ready to churn the sorbet, stir the Prosecco, lemon juice, and salt into the sugar syrup. Churn in an ice-cream maker according to the manufacturer's directions. You should have about 2 cups. Transfer to an airtight container and place in the freezer until serving.

➡ In a medium bowl, combine the strawberries, sugar, and lemon zest and stir gently to coat the berries evenly. Let macerate for 15 to 20 minutes.

➡ To serve, using half the lemon sherbet, scoop small scoops and divide evenly among 8 tall flutes. Spoon the macerating strawberries on top of the sherbet, dividing them evenly. Layer scoops of the Prosecco sorbet on top of the strawberries, then scoop the remaining lemon sherbet on top of the Prosecco layer. Pour the Prosecco over the tops, filling each flute to the rim. Serve immediately with long spoons.

BITTERSWEET
CHOCOLATE SORBET

1 cup (200 grams) sugar

3½ cups (840 grams) water

¾ cup (90 grams) Dutch-processed cocoa powder

4 ounces (114 grams) bittersweet chocolate (62 to 70 percent cacao), finely chopped

1 teaspoon vanilla extract

½ teaspoon kosher salt

MAKES ABOUT 1 QUART

When I was pastry chef at the consistently packed Mistral restaurant in Boston, I quickly learned how to make desserts that not only appealed to a broad audience but also offered twists on presentation or technique that kept me and my pastry cooks challenged. We always had an ice cream and sorbet sampler on the menu, and it was regularly one of the most popular desserts. We played around with fruit and herb infusions such as lemon-thyme sorbet, and we re-created soda fountain classics, like malted milk ice cream. We changed flavors as often as we could to stay in tune with the season (and because it was a lot of fun). One sorbet we made was requested over and over, and we decided we could never take it off the menu. By the time I left Mistral, it had become its own dessert: Three Scoops of Dark Chocolate Sorbet. I wanted a sorbet that tasted like a frozen deep, dark chocolate bar, and we did it with this recipe.

One trick I use is to caramelize the sugar before combining it with the sorbet base. Because there is no cream or milk in this recipe, it is a challenge to create a smooth, creamy texture. Caramelizing the sugar means you can use more sugar than you would normally (since straight sugar is pure sweet and the sweetness of caramelized sugar is offset by its characteristic bitterness). The extra sugar-disguised-as-caramel helps to lower the freezing point of the sorbet base, which means it won't freeze solid. The result is a creamier, softer, not-icy treat.

⇒ Put the sugar in the bottom of a medium saucepan. Add ½ cup (120 grams) of the water and gently swirl the pan to moisten the sugar. Place the pan over high heat and leave it undisturbed until the contents come to a rolling boil. Then continue to boil rapidly without moving the pan until the sugar syrup starts to caramelize. This will take 3 to 4 minutes: the sugar syrup will boil furiously, then as it thickens it will boil more languidly, and then you will see some of the syrup start to color and darken around the edge of the pan.

⇒ When you see color in the pan, gently swirl it in a circular motion so the sugar caramelizes evenly, and then keep swirling gently until the caramel is a medium golden brown. Turn down the heat to low and slowly and carefully add the remaining 3 cups (720 grams) water. Be careful, because it will sputter and spatter when it hits the caramel. The caramel will harden at the bottom of the pan; turn up the heat to high, bring the mixture back to a boil, and whisk for a few minutes until the caramel fully dissolves. Then whisk in the cocoa powder until fully dissolved.

⇒ Place the chocolate in a medium heatproof bowl. Pour the hot caramelized liquid over the chocolate and let sit for 1 minute, then whisk gently until the chocolate is completely melted and the mixture is smooth. Strain the mixture through a fine-mesh sieve into an airtight container, and whisk in the vanilla and salt. Cover and refrigerate for at least 2 hours, or until cold, or up to 1 week.

⇒ Churn in an ice-cream maker according to the manufacturer's directions. Sorbet can be stored in an airtight container in the freezer for up to 1 week.

DOUBLE-CHOCOLATE AND ORANGE SEMIFREDDO

4 ounces (114 grams) bittersweet chocolate (62 to 70 percent cacao)

6 egg yolks

1 cup (200 grams) sugar

½ cup (120 grams) water

⅓ cup (40 grams) Dutch-processed cocoa powder

¼ teaspoon kosher salt

2 cups (480 grams) heavy cream

2 tablespoons finely grated orange zest (about 1 orange)

SERVES 8

Semifreddo, which means "half cold" in Italian, is a creamy frozen dessert that lies somewhere between soft-serve ice cream and regular hard ice cream. It has the same ingredients as ice cream, but does not rely on an ice-cream maker to churn in air and freeze it. Instead, you beat air into the ingredients beforehand and place the confection directly into the freezer—no churning necessary. It then freezes into a soft dessert that you can scoop or slice. The first time I made *semifreddo*, I was pastry chef at Rialto. I plated it simply, with a drizzle of chocolate sauce, a mound of whipped cream, and some orange segments. The classic pairing of chocolate and orange was an instant hit; the elegance of the *semifreddo* (both in name and in appearance) belied what I knew to be true: this dessert is just a fancier way of serving a big bowl of chocolate ice cream! Rather than folding in chocolate chips, you drizzle melted chocolate into the *semifreddo* before you freeze it. That way you get fine splinters of chocolate that add a bit of crunch when you bite down and then instantly dissolve in your mouth.

⇒ Line a 9-by-5-inch loaf pan with plastic wrap.

⇒ Place the chocolate in a small heatproof bowl. Place over (not touching) barely simmering water in a saucepan and heat, stirring occasionally, until completely melted and smooth. Remove from the heat and let cool.

⇒ Using a stand mixer fitted with the whip attachment (or a handheld mixer), whip the egg yolks on medium speed for 3 to 4 minutes, or until pale and somewhat frothy.

⇒ Meanwhile, in a small saucepan, combine the sugar and water and stir gently to combine. Place over high heat, bring to a boil, and cook, without stirring, for 3 to 4 minutes, or until the syrup registers 238 degrees F on a candy thermometer (the soft-ball stage; see Cooking Sugar, page 13).

➡ When the syrup is ready, remove from the heat. With the mixer on medium speed, drizzle the syrup into the egg yolks, pouring it down the side of the bowl to keep it from hitting the whip and spattering. Add the cocoa powder and salt and continue whipping for 5 to 6 minutes, or until the mixture thickens, is fluffy, and is cool to the touch.

➡ In a separate bowl, using the mixer or by hand, whip the heavy cream until it holds stiff peaks. Fold the orange zest into the whipped cream. Fold a little of the whipped cream into the cooled sugar-cocoa mixture to loosen it a bit. Then gently fold the remaining whipped cream into the cooled sugar-cocoa mixture until completely combined.

➡ Spoon about one-fourth of the *semifreddo* mixture into the prepared pan, and smooth into an even layer. Use a spoon to drizzle about one-third of the melted chocolate on top. Carefully spoon about one-third of the remaining *semifreddo* on top of the melted chocolate. Drizzle with about half of the remaining melted chocolate. Carefully spoon about half of the remaining *semifreddo* on top of the chocolate, and drizzle with the remaining chocolate. Top with the remaining *semifreddo*. Be careful that you don't mix the melted chocolate into the *semifreddo*. If it does mix, it won't freeze into little, crispy bits. Wrap the entire pan in plastic wrap and place in the freezer for at least 8 hours or up to 1 week.

➡ To serve, remove the *semifreddo* from the freezer, invert the pan to unmold it, peel off the plastic, cut into 8 slices, and place on dessert plates.

HAZELNUT-VANILLA ICE MILK

4 cups (960 grams) whole milk

¼ cup (50 grams) nonfat dry milk

¾ cup (150 grams) sugar

½ vanilla bean, split lengthwise

1½ cups (210 grams) blanched whole hazelnuts, toasted dark brown and finely ground

¼ teaspoon kosher salt

MAKES ABOUT 1 QUART

I don't see ice milk very often these days, which is a shame because it's just as delicious and irresistible to me as ice cream. Without the heavy cream and yolks, it's not quite as creamy and unctuous, but I crave it just as much. It's milky and cold and because it has less fat, the flavors chosen for the ice milk come through more clearly. This recipe uses hazelnuts, but you could easily substitute almonds or even peanuts if you prefer. Toasting the nuts to a deep golden brown brings out their rich flavor, and then steeping the ground nuts in the milk for at least an hour ensures that their flavor permeates the ice milk. Adding a little dry milk powder helps with the texture, delivering a bit of richness to a relatively ascetic dessert.

➡ In a medium saucepan, combine the whole milk, dry milk, and sugar and bring to a boil over high heat, stirring to dissolve the sugar. Remove from the heat. Use the tip of a knife to scrape the seeds from the vanilla bean directly into the pan and add the pod, as well. Then add the ground hazelnuts and salt. Let sit at room temperature for at least 1 hour or up to 2 hours. Strain through a fine-mesh sieve into an airtight container and refrigerate for at least 2 hours, or until cold, or up to 4 days.

➡ Churn in an ice-cream maker according to the manufacturer's directions.

GINGER TUILE CUPS
WITH CHAMPAGNE SABAYON AND FRESH BERRIES

GINGER TUILE CUPS

¾ cup (150 grams) sugar

3 egg whites

½ cup (1 stick/228 grams) unsalted butter, melted and cooled

½ cup (70 grams) unbleached all-purpose flour

1 teaspoon ground ginger

CHAMPAGNE SABAYON

12 egg yolks

¾ cup (150 grams) sugar

¾ cup (180 grams) Champagne or other sparkling white wine

¼ teaspoon kosher salt

2 cups (480 grams) heavy cream

1 pint (300 grams) blueberries

1 pint (300 grams) strawberries, stemmed and quartered

1 pint (260 grams) raspberries

1 pint (300 grams) blackberries

Small handful of fresh mint leaves, torn into pieces (optional)

SERVES 10

Traditionally, these thin, crisp cookies are shaped to resemble the curved roof tiles commonly found on European country houses (*tuile*, pronounced "tweel," is French for "tile"). I first learned to make them at Payard Patisserie, where we sprinkled them with sliced almonds and used them to garnish sorbets and ice creams. I appreciated their buttery taste and I appreciated their versatility even more. The cookies are pliable when they first come out of the oven, lending themselves to numerous shapes and variations. Depending on chef Payard's mood, we would roll the hot dough to make cigarette cookies; we would cut long, thin strips of hot dough and gather them up into jumbled pastalike bundles; or we would cut the hot dough into perfect rectangles and layer them with Bavarian cream for a nontraditional napoleon. When I got to Mistral, the kitchen was using *tuile* batter to make wavy, elegant "bowls" for holding mousses and other creamy desserts. My favorite variation was this ginger-infused tuile cup with Champagne-flavored sabayon and fresh berries. Feel free to substitute another seasonal fruit for the berries. For example, in winter, when berries are absent from the market, assorted citrus fruits (grapefruit, blood orange, orange, tangerine) make a delightful version.

➡ To make the *tuile* cups: In a medium bowl, whisk together the sugar and egg whites until combined. Whisk in the butter, then the flour, and then the ginger. Pour the batter into an airtight container and refrigerate for at least 4 hours or up to 1 week.

➡ Position a rack in the center of the oven, and heat the oven to 325 degrees F. Line a very flat baking sheet with parchment paper, and liberally coat the parchment with nonstick spray, or line the baking sheet with a silicone baking mat.

➡ Spoon about 1 tablespoon of the batter onto the baking sheet, and use the back of the spoon or an offset spatula to spread it carefully into a circle 6 to 7 inches in diameter. The first few times you make these cookies, you should probably stick to baking them one at a time. But once you get the hang of it, try baking two or three at a time.

(continued)

➡ Bake for 12 to 14 minutes, or until the *tuile* is golden brown all over.

➡ As soon as the *tuile* is done baking, remove it from the oven and immediately start to slide a small, thin metal spatula underneath the *tuile* to loosen it from the sheet. The *tuile* will go through several stages before it gets to its final cooled and crispy state. Directly out of the oven, it is too hot and delicate to handle. After about 10 seconds, it firms up enough to hold its shape, so you can handle it and shape it. It stays pliable for about 10 seconds more, and this is your window of opportunity to work with the cookie. Once you have worked the spatula under the whole *tuile*, pick it up and very quickly drape it over an inverted drinking glass, shaping it into a cup and molding wavy pleats with your hands as it cools. If you wait too long, the *tuile* will start to harden and cool, and if you attempt to shape it, it will shatter. You can place the cookie back in the oven for a few seconds to rewarm it until it is once again pliable, but with each reheating the cookie cools down even faster, so I recommend only two reheatings. Use a new, cool baking sheet and new parchment (or more spray) for each batch. Or, if you have only one baking sheet, cool it under running cold water before reusing. If you try to spoon the batter onto a hot sheet, it will immediately start to melt and become unspreadable. Repeat with the remaining batter, ending up with 10 cups total. Let the cups cool for 30 minutes. (The cups can be stored in an airtight container at room temperature for up to 1 day.)

➡ To make the sabayon: Fill a large bowl with ice cubes and a little water. In a large heatproof bowl (select a size that you can easily nest in the ice bath later), whisk together the egg yolks, sugar, Champagne, and salt until thoroughly combined. Place the bowl over (not touching) simmering water in a saucepan and whisk continuously (your arm may get a little tired) for 10 to 12 minutes, or until the mixture is thick, light, and lemon colored. The mixture is ready when the whisk leaves ribbons trailing off it and you can see the bottom of the bowl when you scrape it with the whisk. Remove the bowl from the heat and nest it in the ice bath. Let cool, whisking occasionally, for 5 to 8 minutes, or until completely cooled.

➡ In a medium bowl, using a handheld mixer or a whisk, whip the cream until it holds soft peaks. Using a rubber spatula, fold the whipped cream into the egg yolk mixture just until combined. You should have about 6 cups. (The sabayon can be stored in an airtight container in the refrigerator for up to 2 days. Stir well before serving.)

➡ To serve, place each *tuile* cup on an individual dessert plate. Spoon a heaping ½ cup of the sabayon into each cup. Divide the berries evenly among the cups. Top with the mint, if desired.

Baker's Bite

You might want to wear sturdy rubber gloves when handling the hot tuiles. The point at which the cookies can be shaped seems to coincide with the point at which they are still a bit too hot to touch.

Same recipe, different flavors

To change the flavor of the *tuiles*, substitute 1 teaspoon vanilla extract, ½ teaspoon ground cinnamon, or ½ teaspoon almond extract for the ginger.

CARAMELIZED APPLE-RAISIN CHARLOTTES
WITH VANILLA CARAMEL SAUCE

VANILLA CARAMEL SAUCE

1 cup (200 grams) sugar

½ cup (120 grams) water

1 cup (240 grams) heavy cream

¼ teaspoon kosher salt

Seeds scraped from ½ vanilla bean, split lengthwise

1 cup (200 grams) sugar

½ cup (120 grams) water

½ cup (1 stick/114 grams) unsalted butter, plus 2 tablespoons (¼ stick), melted

8 Granny Smith or other firm, tart apples (about 3 pounds), peeled, cored, and roughly chopped (about 9 cups chopped)

½ teaspoon ground cinnamon

¼ teaspoon kosher salt

½ cup (80 grams) raisins

Seeds scraped from ½ vanilla bean, split lengthwise

1 loaf brioche, at least 9 inches long (recipe on page 73 or from your favorite bakery)

SERVES 8

This dessert is a perfect example of the whole being greater than the sum of its parts. Line ramekins with slices of buttery brioche, fill them with a caramelized apple and raisin compote scented with vanilla, bake them together, and serve with a vanilla bean–caramel sauce. Once you have the components of this dessert ready, it goes together easily; it is perfect for a dinner party or holiday gathering.

⇒ To make the caramel sauce: In a medium saucepan, combine the sugar and water and stir gently with a small rubber spatula until the sugar is dissolved. Be sure the sides of the pan do not have any sugar crystals on them; if they do, use a pastry brush dipped in water to wash down any clinging sugar. (This helps prevent crystallization of the sugar as you are caramelizing it.) Place over high heat and bring to a boil. Do not jostle the pan as it is coming to a boil, or the syrup may start to crystallize. Once the syrup starts to color to a pale brown, you can gently swirl the pan to even out the caramelization. It will take 3 to 4 minutes for the sugar to start caramelizing and another 30 seconds or so to even out.

⇒ Once the sugar is deep golden brown, turn down the heat to low and slowly and carefully whisk in the cream, salt, and vanilla seeds. (Reserve the pod for another use. You can slip it into a container of sugar to make vanilla sugar; see page 29.) Be careful, as the caramel will sputter and spatter. Once the mixture has settled, whisk until the cream is completely incorporated into the caramel. Remove from the heat and let cool to room temperature. You should have about 2 cups. (The sauce can be stored in an airtight container in the refrigerator for up to 1 week.)

⇒ In a medium saucepan, combine the 1 cup (200 grams) sugar and ½ cup (120 grams) water and stir gently with a small rubber spatula until the sugar is dissolved. Place over high heat and bring to a boil. Then continue to boil as directed for the caramel sauce, swirling the pan only after you see color and continuing to boil until the caramel is a deep golden brown. Then turn down the heat to low and whisk in the ½ cup butter; be careful, as the caramel will sputter and steam. Add the apples, cinnamon, salt, raisins, and vanilla bean seeds (again reserving the pod for another use). Mix as well as you can with a wooden spoon. The caramel will harden at the bottom of the pan, but as you mix the butter and apples into it, it will gradually dissolve. Continue to cook over low heat, stirring occasionally, for about 1 hour, or until the apples start to break down and the mixture thickens and turns golden brown. There will still be pieces of chopped apple within the appley sauce. Remove from the heat and let cool. (The mixture can be stored in an airtight container in the refrigerator for up to 4 days or in the freezer for up to 2 weeks.)

➡ Position a rack in the center of the oven, and heat the oven to 350 degrees F. Generously butter and sugar eight 6-ounce ramekins.

➡ Trim the crusts off the brioche loaf, and cut into ¼-inch-thick slices (from a 9-inch loaf, you will get about 32 slices). Cut out 16 circles from the brioche slices, 8 that fit the bottoms of the ramekins and 8 that fit the tops. Cut the rest of the brioche slices into rectangles that fit the sides of the ramekins. The brioche shrinks down when it is in the oven, so cut your circles a bit larger and the rectangles a bit taller than you think they should be. For each ramekin, place the first circle of brioche in the bottom of the ramekin. Because it will be just a little bigger than the bottom of the ramekin, you will have to smoosh it in. Carefully line the sides of the ramekin with overlapping slices of the rectangular brioche. Make sure the rectangles fit snugly along the sides and that they go all the way up to the top of the ramekin.

➡ Fill the brioche-lined ramekins with the apple-raisin mixture, making sure to pack it in well. Top the filling with a second circle of brioche, and press down firmly. Lightly brush the top of the brioche circles with the melted butter. Place the ramekins on a baking sheet.

➡ Bake for 30 to 40 minutes, or until the brioche on the top and sides is toasty golden brown. (To check if the brioche on the sides is toasted, partially invert a ramekin and take a peek.) If the tops start browning too quickly before the charlottes are done, cover the charlottes with aluminum foil halfway through baking.

➡ When the charlottes are done, transfer to a wire rack and let cool until they can be handled. Invert the charlottes onto warmed dessert plates and drizzle with the caramel sauce. Serve immediately.

BALSAMIC STRAWBERRY SHORTCAKES

SHORTCAKES

2½ cups (350 grams) unbleached all-purpose flour

½ cup (100 grams) plus 1 tablespoon sugar

2 teaspoons baking powder

1 teaspoon kosher salt

¾ cup (1½ sticks/170 grams) cold unsalted butter, cut into 12 to 14 pieces

3 eggs

½ cup (120 grams) heavy cream

2 pints (600 grams) strawberries

2 teaspoons balsamic vinegar

2 teaspoons finely grated lemon zest (about ⅔ lemon)

6 tablespoons (75 grams) plus 1 tablespoon sugar

1¼ cups (300 grams) heavy cream

1 teaspoon vanilla extract

SERVES 8

The idea of combining strawberries with balsamic vinegar may sound unusual to you (it did to me when I first heard of it!), but the Italians have been doing it for centuries, taking advantage of how vinegar's sweet-tart acidity beautifully complements the natural sugars in strawberries. You don't need super-expensive balsamic vinegar, but a cheap one will likely be too harsh. Look for a good-quality aged vinegar let the strawberries macerate in it, and you'll see what I mean. These light, flaky shortcakes are perfect for soaking up the syrupy juices from the strawberries, and lightly whipped cream holds the whole dessert together.

⇒ To make the shortcakes: Position a rack in the center of the oven, and heat the oven to 350 degrees F.

⇒ Using a stand mixer fitted with the paddle attachment (or a hand-held mixer), mix together the flour, ½ cup (100 grams) sugar, baking powder, and salt on low speed for 10 to 15 seconds, or until combined. Scatter the butter over the top and beat on medium-low speed for about 30 seconds, or until the butter is broken down and the mixture gets sort of mealy. (Depending on the size of your mixer, the flour may fly out at first. If it does, use the on-off switch in a pulse fashion until the flour mixes with the butter a bit.)

⇒ In a small bowl, whisk together 2 of the eggs and the cream until thoroughly mixed. On low speed, pour in the egg mixture all at once and beat for 10 to 15 seconds, or until the dough comes together. (Alternatively, whisk together the dry ingredients in a medium bowl, scatter the butter over the top, and use a pastry cutter or fork to cut the butter into the flour mixture until the butter is broken down into small pea-sized pieces and the mixture is somewhat mealy. Slowly add the egg mixture, tossing and stirring with a fork until the dough comes together.)

➡ Dump the dough out onto a floured work surface and press it out into a circle about 8 inches in diameter and 1 inch thick. Using a 3-inch biscuit cutter, cut out circles, rerolling scraps as necessary to get 8 circles total. Place them on an ungreased baking sheet several inches apart.

➡ In a small bowl, whisk the remaining egg until blended. Brush the tops of the dough circles with the egg. Sprinkle evenly with the 1 tablespoon sugar.

➡ Bake for 35 to 40 minutes, or until light golden brown. Let cool on the pan on a wire rack for about 10 minutes, or until cool enough to handle. Transfer to the rack and let cool until warm. (The shortcakes are best enjoyed the same day you bake them, but they can be stored in an airtight container at room temperature for 2 to 3 days. If you keep them for longer than 1 day, refresh them in a 300-degree-F oven for 4 to 5 minutes. Or, you can freeze them, tightly wrapped in plastic wrap, for up to 1 week; reheat, directly from the freezer, in a 300-degree-F oven for 8 to 10 minutes.)

➡ While the shortcakes are in the oven, stem the strawberries, and cut each berry lengthwise into four or five slices. In a medium bowl, toss the strawberries with the vinegar, lemon zest, and the 6 tablespoons (75 grams) sugar, and let macerate for about 30 minutes.

➡ Using a handheld mixer or a whisk, whip the cream with the 1 tablespoon sugar and the vanilla just until it holds soft peaks.

➡ Split each shortcake in half horizontally. Set the bottom halves, cut-sides up, on individual serving plates. Divide the strawberries and their syrup evenly among the bottom halves, then top the strawberries with the whipped cream, again dividing evenly. Balance the top halves on the whipped cream and serve immediately.

PEDRO XIMINEZ
SHERRY PARFAIT
WITH TEA-SOAKED AUTUMN FRUITS

PARFAIT

6 egg yolks

1 cup (200 grams) sugar

½ cup (120 grams) water

½ teaspoon kosher salt

2 cups (480 grams) heavy cream

6 tablespoons (45 grams) Pedro Ximinez or another dark sweet sherry

FRUIT COMPOTE

6 cups (1.4 kilograms) water

¾ cup (60 grams) Darjeeling tea leaves

1 cup (200 grams) sugar

1 tablespoon fresh lemon juice (about 1 lemon)

2 Bosc pears, peeled, quartered, and cored

8 fresh figs, halved

¼ cup (40 grams) dried apricots, halved

½ cup (80 grams) golden raisins

¼ cup (40 grams) dried currants

¼ cup (40 grams) pitted prunes, halved

¼ cup (40 grams) dried cherries

¼ cup (40 grams) dried cranberries

SERVES 8

I made many, many desserts as pastry chef at Rialto, and this one was the favorite of the owners, Jody and Christopher. Christopher was hosting a Spanish wine dinner at the restaurant and asked me to come up with a dessert that included Pedro Ximenez sherry. Pedro Ximinez is a sweet amber sherry with a raisinlike flavor. (Vanilla ice cream drizzled with Pedro Ximinez is a classic dessert in Jerez, home of the finest Spanish sherry.) This dessert has a Gallic element, too: A traditional French parfait is a frozen, creamy confection that closely resembles ice cream. It softens the intensity of the sherry, so you can better taste its smooth flavor. If you can't find Pedro Ximinez, substitute another sweet sherry. Pair this parfait with autumnal fruits soaked in tea for an awesome grown-up sundae.

➡ To make the parfait: Line a 9-by-5-inch loaf pan with plastic wrap.

➡ Using a stand mixer fitted with the whip attachment (or a handheld mixer), whip the egg yolks for 3 to 4 minutes on medium speed, or until pale and somewhat frothy.

➡ Meanwhile, in a small saucepan, combine the sugar and water and stir gently to combine. Place over high heat, bring to a boil, and cook, without stirring, for 3 to 4 minutes, or until the syrup registers 238 degrees F on a candy thermometer (the soft-ball stage; see Cooking Sugar, page 13).

➡ When the syrup is ready, remove from the heat. With the mixer on medium speed, drizzle the hot syrup into the egg yolks, pouring it down the side of the bowl to keep it from hitting the whip and spattering. Add the salt and continue whipping for 5 to 6 minutes, or until the mixture thickens, is fluffy, and is cool to the touch.

➡ In a separate bowl, using the mixer, whip the cream until it holds soft peaks. Fold a little of the whipped cream into the cooled egg-sugar mixture to loosen it a bit. Then fold in the remaining whipped cream just until combined. Fold in the sherry until completely combined. Spoon the parfait mixture into the prepared pan, making sure to fill the corners. Cover the entire pan with plastic wrap. Place the pan in the freezer for at least 8 hours or for up to 1 week.

➡ To prepare the fruit compote: Tn a heavy, medium saucepan, bring the water to a boil over high heat. Remove from the heat, add the tea leaves, and let steep for 6 to 8 minutes. Strain through a fine-mesh sieve, return to the pan, and bring the tea back to a boil. Add the sugar and lemon juice, reduce the heat to low, and simmer, stirring, until the sugar is dissolved.

➡ Add the pears to the tea, adjust the tea so it is at a bare simmer, and cook the pears for about 10 minutes, or until just tender. Using a slotted spoon, transfer the pears to a medium bowl. Add the figs to the simmering tea and poach for about 2 minutes, or until tender. Transfer the figs to the bowl holding the pears. Add the apricots, raisins, currants, prunes, cherries, and cranberries to the tea and poach for about 10 minutes, or until all of the fruits are softened and plump. Using the slotted spoon, transfer the fruits to the bowl holding the already-poached fruits.

➡ Turn up the heat to medium-high and boil the tea for about 10 minutes, or until reduced by half. Remove from the heat and pour over the fruits. Place the bowl, uncovered, in the refrigerator for at least 1 hour, or until cold. (The compote can be transferred to an airtight container and stored in the refrigerator for up to 1 week.)

➡ To serve, remove the parfait from the freezer, invert the pan to unmold it, peel off the plastic, and cut into 8 slices. Place on dessert plates and top with the fruit compote.

BROWN SUGAR POPOVERS

2 cups (280 grams) unbleached
all-purpose flour

½ teaspoon kosher salt

¼ teaspoon ground cinnamon

2 tablespoons packed light brown
sugar, plus ½ cup (110 grams)

2 cups (480 grams) milk, at room
temperature

4 eggs

¼ cup (½ stick/56 grams) unsalted
butter, melted and cooled

MAKES 10 TO 12 POPOVERS

When I wrote my last dessert menu at Rialto, before heading to New York to work for the famed François Payard, I pulled out all the stops. It was spring, and it was a bitter-sweet time for me. I was thrilled that I would be working under one of the best pastry chefs in America, but I was sad to be leaving a wonderful job where I had enjoyed carte blanche to create fanciful desserts. I decided to put every-thing on the menu that I had not yet had a chance to feature. I'd never had a popover before but was tickled by the idea of an eggy, rich pastry that baked up hollow inside. Think of the possibilities! I could fill them with ice cream or custard or sabayon or fruit compote. I ended up filling them with a tangerine crème brûlée and berries. That creation was my swan song and I was darn proud of it. Here are popovers treated more simply: brushed with butter and tossed in brown sugar. Fill them if you like, or serve them as is for a no-frills dessert or a fantastic breakfast.

➡ Position a rack in the center of the oven, and heat the oven to 425 degrees F. Butter a popover pan or standard muffin tin, and place it in the oven for about 10 minutes, or until it is hot.

➡ In a small bowl, whisk together the flour, salt, cinnamon, and 2 tablespoons brown sugar. In a medium bowl, whisk together the milk (make sure it is at room temperature, or the butter will form lumps), eggs, and 2 tablespoons of the melted butter. Gradually whisk the flour mixture into the milk-egg mixture until thoroughly combined. The batter will be loose and liquidy and not completely smooth.

➡ Remove the pan from the oven and pour the batter into the cups, filling the cups to the rim. Bake for 20 minutes, then turn down the temperature to 325 degrees F and continue to bake for another 40 minutes, or until the popovers are completely browned and poufy. Don't open the oven door to look at the popovers until at least 40 minutes into baking. You want them to be golden brown all over and tall; if you open the oven door too soon, they will deflate once they are out of the oven. Let cool in the pan on a wire rack for about 10 minutes, or until cool enough to handle.

➡ Place the ½ cup (110 grams) brown sugar in a small bowl. Brush the remaining 2 tablespoons melted butter on the tops of the popovers, and then remove the popovers from the pan. One at a time, toss them in the brown sugar, coating each popover completely. Serve immediately if possible (they are best when eaten warm) or within 2 to 3 hours.

➡ If you must hold the popovers, remove them from the pan, let them cool completely, and store them plain in an airtight container at room temperature for up to 2 days. When ready to serve, refresh them in a 350-degree-F oven for 4 to 5 minutes and then brush with the butter and toss in the sugar.

Baker's Bite

What makes popovers hollow? The batter contains a lot of liquid, and you pour it into a hot pan. In the hot oven and in a hot pan, the liquid in the batter immediately starts to steam, which causes the popovers to puff up and fill with air. To make sure this reaction takes place as it should, heat the pan for 10 minutes before pouring the batter into it, and do not open the oven door (which would let heat escape) until the popovers are just about ready.

ÉCLAIRS OR CREAM PUFFS

PÂTE À CHOUX

½ cup (1 stick/114 grams) unsalted butter

1 tablespoon sugar

¼ teaspoon kosher salt

1 cup (240 grams) water

1 cup plus 1 tablespoon (150 grams) unbleached all-purpose flour

4 eggs

TROPEZ CREAM

1 cup (240 grams) milk

¼ vanilla bean, split lengthwise, or 1 teaspoon vanilla extract

½ cup (100 grams) sugar

3 tablespoons cake flour

Pinch of kosher salt

1 egg

1 egg yolk

½ cup (120 grams) heavy cream

GANACHE

4 ounces (114 grams) semisweet or bittersweet chocolate, chopped, or semisweet or bittersweet chocolate chips (about ⅔ cup)

½ cup (120 grams) heavy cream

MAKES ABOUT 12 ÉCLAIRS OR 24 CREAM PUFFS

When I was in middle school, the school bus used to drop me off at a tiny strip mall several miles from my house. My parents both worked, so I usually had an hour or so to occupy before they could pick me up. I spent most afternoons hanging out at the mall's little bakery, where I was introduced to my first éclair. It was the size of a hot dog, full of supersweet, thick vanilla custard and dripping with a chocolaty frosting. I loved it because it was so unlike anything I'd ever had before, but even back then I sensed that something better must exist in Éclair-Land. Many years later, when I was working at Payard Patisserie, I got closer to the ideal. I learned how to make a proper *pâte à choux* (so-named because the puffs, when baked, resemble little *choux*, or "cabbages"), traditional *crème pâtissière* (pastry cream), and classic chocolate fondant. The éclairs were small, elegant, and pretty as a picture.

Once I ventured out on my own, I decided to make my own version of the perfect éclair. I use the same dough, but the pastry cream is made with vanilla bean and lightened with a bit of whipped cream. I call it Tropez cream because it is often the filling for the traditional French pastry called St. Tropez, in which a brioche roll is soaked in sugar syrup and filled with the fluffy vanilla cream. And I opt for the pure, deep chocolate flavor of ganache to finish the eclairs. Made with just two ingredients, hot cream and chocolate, ganache is the little black dress of dessert finishings. I use it to fill, frost, cover, and glaze. And sometimes I simply eat it as is. Once you know how to make ganache—and see how easy it is—you can use it again and again to dress up a pastry or cake. Traditional éclairs are often glazed with fondant, which is beautiful but less tasty than ganache. I always go for taste over looks, and once you've tried these éclairs, you will too. We make smaller versions of the éclairs (a.k.a. cream puffs) for charity events in Boston and people go nuts for them.

(continued)

To make the *pâte à choux*: Position a rack in the center of the oven, and heat the oven to 400 degrees F. Butter two baking sheets, or line with parchment.

In a medium saucepan, heat the butter, sugar, salt, and water over medium heat until the butter is melted. Do not let the mixture come to a boil or some of the water will evaporate. Add the flour all at once and use a wooden spoon to stir the flour into the liquid until it is fully incorporated. The mixture will look like a stiff pancake batter. Keep stirring vigorously over medium heat until the mixture slowly starts to get stiffer and looks more like loose dough and less like stiff batter. It will lose its shine and become more matte as well. Stir continuously for 3 to 4 minutes, or until the dough starts to leave a film at the bottom of the pan.

Remove the pan from the heat and transfer the dough to the bowl of a stand mixer fitted with the paddle attachment. Mix the dough on medium-low speed for 1 minute. This will allow some of the steam to escape and the dough will cool slightly. (Or, beat the mixture in a bowl with a wooden spoon for 2 to 3 minutes.) Crack the four eggs into a small pitcher and whisk to break up the yolks. On medium-low speed (or beating vigorously by hand), gradually add the eggs to the dough. When all of the whisked eggs have been added, turn up the speed to medium and beat for about 20 seconds, or until the dough is glossy and shiny.

Fit a pastry bag with a 1-inch round tip and fill the bag with the dough (see page 15). For éclairs, pipe out strips about 5 inches long and 1 inch wide, or for cream puffs, pipe out balls about 1½ inches in diameter, onto the prepared baking sheets, spacing them a few inches apart.

Place the baking sheets in the oven. The heat of the oven will immediately start turning the liquid in the batter into steam, which will cause the pastries to inflate. After about 15 minutes, when the pastries have puffed up and are starting to turn golden brown, turn down the oven to 325 degrees F and continue to bake for another 30 minutes, or until the pastries are entirely brown. Let cool completely on the pans on wire racks. (The cooled pastries can be stored unfilled in an airtight container in the freezer for up to 2 weeks. Remove from the freezer and refresh, directly from the freezer, in a 325-degree-F oven for 6 to 8 minutes, or until thawed. Let cool completely before filling. You can also store them unfilled in an airtight container at room temperature for up to 2 days. Refresh in a 325-degree-F oven for 2 to 3 minutes, then let cool before filling.)

To make the Tropez cream: Put the milk in a medium saucepan. Use the tip of a knife to scrape the seeds from the vanilla bean directly into the pan and then add the pod. (If using vanilla extract, reserve to add later.) Place the pan over medium-high heat and scald the milk (bubbles start to form around the edge of the pan, but the milk is not boiling).

While the milk is heating, in a small bowl, stir together the sugar, cake flour, and salt. (Mixing the flour with the sugar will prevent the flour from clumping when you add it to the eggs.) In a medium bowl, whisk together the egg and egg yolk until blended, then slowly whisk in the flour mixture. The mixture will be thick and pasty.

➡ Remove the milk from the heat and slowly add it to the sugar-flour mixture, a little at a time, whisking constantly. When all of the milk has been incorporated, return the contents of the bowl to the saucepan and place over medium heat. Whisk continuously and vigorously for 4 to 6 minutes, or until the mixture thickens and comes to a boil. At first, the mixture will be very frothy and liquid; as it cooks longer, it will slowly start to thicken until the frothy bubbles disappear and it becomes more viscous. Once it thickens, stop whisking every few seconds to see if the mixture has come to a boil. If it has not, keep whisking vigorously. As soon as you see it bubbling, immediately go back to whisking for just 10 seconds, and then remove the pan from the heat. Boiling this mixture will thicken it and cook out the flour taste, but if you let it boil for longer than 10 seconds, it can become grainy.

➡ Pour the custard through a fine-mesh sieve into a heatproof, medium bowl. (If using vanilla extract, stir it in now.) Cover with plastic wrap, placing it directly on the surface of the custard. This will prevent a skin from forming. Refrigerate for at least 4 hours, or until cold. Or, transfer to an airtight container and refrigerate for up to 3 days.

➡ Just before you are ready to fill your éclairs or cream puffs, in a medium bowl, using a handheld mixer or a whisk, whip the heavy cream until it holds a peak and is thick and soft. Whisk the chilled custard to smooth it out, then, using a rubber spatula, fold the whipped cream into the chilled custard until thoroughly combined. You should have about 3 cups. Cover and refrigerate until using.

➡ To make the ganache: While the Tropez cream is chilling, place the chocolate in a small heatproof bowl. In a small saucepan, scald the ½ cup (120 grams) cream over medium-high heat (bubbles start to form around the edge of the pan, but the cream is not boiling). Pour the hot cream over the chocolate and let sit for 30 seconds, then slowly whisk together the chocolate and cream until the chocolate is completely melted and the mixture is smooth. Let cool to room temperature. (The ganache can be stored in an airtight container in the refrigerator for up to 1 week. Bring to room temperature before using.)

➡ If making éclairs, split the pastries in half lengthwise and fill with the Tropez cream. Turn the top half of each éclair upside down and dip it into the room-temperature ganache, coating the top. Set the top halves on the cream-filled bottoms and let sit for 6 to 8 minutes to allow the chocolate to set. Serve within 4 hours.

If making cream puffs, fit the pastry bag with a small round tip and fill the bag with the Tropez cream. Using the tip of a small knife, poke a hole in the bottom of each puff, and then pipe the cream into the puffs. One at a time, turn the puffs upside down and dip the tops into the room-temperature ganache. Let sit for 6 to 8 minutes to allow the chocolate to set. Serve within 4 hours.

MIXED-NUT BRITTLE

2 cups (400 grams) sugar

1 cup (240 grams) water

¼ cup (80 grams) light corn syrup

⅔ cup (100 grams) whole raw cashews, toasted golden brown

⅔ cup (100 grams) whole natural hazelnuts, toasted golden brown

⅔ cup (110 grams) whole natural almonds, toasted golden brown

3 tablespoons unsalted butter

1 teaspoon kosher salt

1 teaspoon vanilla extract

1½ teaspoons baking soda

MAKES ABOUT TWELVE 3- TO 4-INCH PIECES

At the beginning of each holiday season, we go through the same routine at Flour: Nicole (our head pastry chef) and I sit in the office and write up a menu for Thanksgiving and Christmas. We decide which new items we want to bring onto the menu, and which old recipes need to be retested. Certain holiday specials never leave the list, such as our pumpkin pie (see page 214) for Thanksgiving. New items are always a bit of a gamble, because we are never sure if they will appeal to our customers. I'm happy to say that we are often caught off guard by the popularity of new items! This brittle is a perfect example. We offered it one year on a whim after Nicole fancied up a traditional peanut brittle recipe with cashews, almonds, and hazelnuts. We made a big batch, devoured lots of it in the kitchen, and put the rest into cellophane bags tied with festive ribbons. Our inability to keep from snacking on the brittle during the testing phase should have been a tip-off. We sold out immediately, and the brittle has gained permanent status on our holiday menu.

➡ Line a baking sheet with parchment paper.

➡ In a medium saucepan, combine the sugar, water, and corn syrup and bring to a boil over high heat. Continue to boil the mixture on high heat, swirling the pan gently, for 8 to 10 minutes (or more, depending on your stove), or until the sugar syrup turns an even golden brown. Watch the sugar carefully as it is cooking, and turn down the heat to low right away when it is evenly golden brown.

→ Using a wooden spoon, quickly stir in the cashews, hazelnuts, almonds, butter, salt, and vanilla, mixing until the butter is completely melted. Working quickly, stir in the baking soda. The mixture will foam up a bit and turn an orange-brown. Stir vigorously for about 5 seconds more.

→ Immediately pour the mixture onto the prepared baking sheet, and spread it out as evenly as possible to about ½ inch thick, using the wooden spoon to level it. Let the brittle cool at room temperature for at least 1 hour before breaking it into 3- to 4-inch pieces.

→ The brittle tastes best once it has cooled completely, 3 to 4 hours later. It can be stored in an airtight container at room temperature for up to 1 week.

breads

BREAD SPONGE

¾ cup (180 grams) water

1¼ cups (175 grams) unbleached
all-purpose flour

¼ teaspoon active dry yeast or
0.06 ounce (1.7 grams) fresh
cake yeast

MAKES ABOUT 12 OUNCES
(340 GRAMS)

Most people don't realize what an entirely different beast bread baking is from cooking, or for that matter, from most other baking. Bread is alive. It's filled with yeast spores that eat and sleep and burp and hiccup and grow and die. I once explained to my husband, Christopher, that working with bread is fun because it is always changing, depending on the weather, its mood, the stars, or how it was treated the day before or that morning. He looked at me and said, "Are you sure you're talking about bread?!?"

One way to add a lot of flavor to your bread with little effort is to make it with a sponge (also known as a mother). A sponge contains natural yeast, which is much more flavorful than the packaged kind. Here is how a sponge works: natural yeast spores in the air gravitate to the mother, "eat" the flour in it, and then "burp" carbon dioxide and alcohol into the sponge, both of which add delicious flavor. In bread speak, this slurry of fermented water and flour, the foundation of countless flavorful breads, goes by many names. Mother is my favorite, but it is also known as a sponge, starter, *biga*, *poolish*, and *levain*, among others. Some sponges are sloshy, some are doughlike; some are started naturally, and some get some help from commercial yeast. At Flour, our mother came from the batch I used while at Rialto and we call it Mom.

If you are going to be using a sponge for more than one batch of bread, you will need to feed it regularly to keep it going. As I explained, a sponge is full of wild yeast spores that feed off the flour in the sponge. At a certain point, they will eat everything available, and if you don't feed the sponge more flour and water (add them in the same proportions used for the original sponge), the yeast spores will die. If you are not making a lot of bread, your sponge will get bigger and bigger as you keep feeding it, so you should throw away a little and then feed it a small amount, or your sponge will take over your fridge. At Flour, we use our sponge to make bread every day, so we feed our sponge every day. That task appears on our production list as "Feed Mom." When my mother was visiting one day, she noticed it on the list and got indignant. "I can feed myself, thank you," she promptly told me!

(continued)

You absolutely can make wonderful breads with only packaged yeast, but if you have the time and inclination, I recommend delving into the world of bread starters. You'll be rewarded with breads with a more complex flavor, a more interesting texture, and a better shelf life. (French baguettes, which are made with only commercial yeast, are not supposed to be sold after 3 hours!)

This isn't a bread book, so I am just barely scratching the surface in explaining all that goes on in the world of bread and offering only a handful of recipes in this chapter. Hopefully you will be interested enough in the list to make at least some of them, and then perhaps seek out other bread books that offer more detailed instructions and background. (*Amy's Bread* by Amy Scherber, *The Italian Baker* by Carol Field, and *Breads from the La Brea Bakery* by Nancy Silverton are three good volumes.) The starter I offer here is a quick and easy introduction to bread baking.

⇒ In a medium bowl, stir together the water, 1 cup (140 grams) of the flour, and the yeast until well mixed and sloshy. Place in a covered container and leave at room temperature for at least 4 hours or up to 8 hours.

⇒ Stir in the remaining ¼ cup (35 grams) flour, which will cause the sponge to stiffen up into a loose dough. Re-cover and leave in the refrigerator overnight.

⇒ Use as directed in individual recipes.

COUNTRY BREAD

1½ cups (360 grams) water, at body temperature (when you put your finger in it, it should feel neither cold nor hot)

2 cups (280 grams) unbleached all-purpose flour, plus 2 to 3 tablespoons for baking

2 cups (300 grams) bread flour

12 ounces (340 grams) Bread Sponge (page 287)

Pinch of active dry yeast

2 teaspoons kosher salt

1 teaspoon sugar

A big handful of medium-coarse yellow cornmeal for the baking sheet

MAKES TWO 8-INCH ROUND LOAVES

I call this rustic, chewy loaf "Country Bread" because it is what I imagine would be on a long, wooden farm table in the country, alongside a hunk of cheese, a mound of fresh butter, and a bowl of olives. It's not ethereal and light like a classic French baguette, nor is it hearty and sour like an artisanal sourdough loaf. Rather, it falls deliciously in between: soft and fragrant and a little holey, with a golden crust and an ever-so-slight sourdough taste that elevates it from plain-white-bread status. It is amazing as a dinner bread, grilled as a sandwich bread, or toasted with butter for breakfast. Since they are made with a starter, the loaves last for a few days on the counter, unlike yeast-only French baguettes, which lose their freshness after a few hours. These also freeze well.

➡ Using a stand mixer fitted with the dough hook attachment (or a large bowl and wooden spoon), mix together the water, 2 cups (280 grams) all-purpose flour, and bread flour on low speed for about 1 minute, or until the flour is mixed into the water and you have a shaggy, stiff dough. (To prevent the flour from flying out of the bowl, turn the mixer on and off several times until the flour is mixed into the liquid, and then keep it on low speed.) Cover the bowl with a piece of plastic wrap and let sit for about 10 minutes. (This is called an autolyse, and it allows the water to hydrate the flour, which makes for better mixing down the road.)

➡ On medium-low speed, add the sponge, yeast, salt, and sugar and mix for 3 to 4 minutes, or until they are incorporated into the dough. The dough should be somewhat sticky but still smooth and feel like an earlobe (strange as that may sound) when you grasp a bit between your fingers. If it is stiffer than this, mix in a few tablespoons water; if it is looser than this, mix in a few table-spoons all-purpose flour. You may need to stop the mixer a few times to pull off any dough that has gathered around the hook or on the sides of the bowl. (If you are using a wooden spoon to mix the dough, you must dump out the dough onto a floured work surface and knead for 5 to 6 minutes, or until smooth.)

(continued)

➡ Lightly oil a large bowl. Transfer the dough to the oiled bowl, and turn the dough to coat it with oil. Lightly cover the bowl with an oiled piece of plastic wrap or a lint-free damp cloth. Place the bowl in a draft-free, warm place (78 to 82 degrees F is ideal; an area near the stove or in the oven with only the pilot light on is good) for 2 to 3 hours. The dough will rise up a little bit (but not a lot) and it will feel a little loose and relaxed and somewhat sticky.

➡ Flour your hands and your work surface and turn the dough out of the bowl. Divide the dough in half with a knife or a bench scraper. Shape each half into a ball by tucking the edges of the dough underneath and then continuing to tuck the edges underneath until the dough naturally gathers into a ball with a taut surface. (At this point, you can cover the shaped loaves and store them in the refrigerator overnight. Remove them the next day and proceed as directed.)

➡ Sprinkle the cornmeal on a baking sheet to keep the loaves from sticking, and place the loaves on the sheet, spacing them at least 3 inches apart. Cover them loosely but completely with plastic wrap and let them sit at room temperature for 2 to 3 hours, or until they have loosened up and seem relaxed. They won't pouf up too much, but they will seem much softer, and you may see some bubbles forming just under the surface of the dough as it proofs.

➡ Position a rack in the center of the oven, and heat the oven to 500 degrees F. (It is important that the oven comes to temperature before you place the bread inside. The correct temperature ensures that your loaves will get enough oomph to rise and grow.)

➡ Sprinkle the tops of the loaves with the 2 to 3 tablespoons all-purpose flour. Slash the loaves with a knife (see page 17), and place the baking sheet in the oven. Place a rimmed baking sheet or shallow pan filled with about 2 cups water on the oven rack below the bread. The steam from the water will create a nice moist atmosphere for your bread to grow. Bake for 35 to 40 minutes, or until the loaves are dark golden brown on top and make a hollow sound when you thump them on the bottom.

➡ Transfer the loaves to wire racks and let cool for at least 1 hour before serving. Once the loaves have cooled completely, they can be stored in a paper bag (plastic seals out the air and keeps the bread from breathing, which turns it too soft) at room temperature for 2 to 3 days. You can also freeze this bread, well wrapped in plastic wrap, for up to 2 weeks.

MARVELOUS MULTIGRAIN SOURDOUGH

1½ cups (360 grams) water, at body temperature (when you put your finger in it, it should feel neither cold nor hot)

¾ cup (125 grams) whole-wheat flour

¾ cup (125 grams) buckwheat flour

3 cups (420 grams) unbleached all-purpose flour, plus 2 to 3 tablespoons for baking

About 12 ounces (340 grams) Bread Sponge (page 287)

⅓ cup (114 grams) honey

1 tablespoon kosher salt

⅓ cup (70 grams) millet

⅓ cup (40 grams) sunflower seeds

⅓ cup (50 grams) flaxseeds

Big handful of medium-coarse yellow cornmeal for the baking sheet

MAKES TWO 8-INCH ROUND LOAVES

I first learned about baking bread during my days as a pastry chef at Rialto. The bread baker was, to me, the Bread Whisperer. Glee (that was both her name and her temperament) taught me that if you accept that bread will change from day to day and don't expect precise measurements and exact times, you'll be friends with bread. She is absolutely right. In this recipe and other bread recipes in the book, I give you measurements that work for me, but depending on the heat and humidity in your kitchen, the amount of moisture in your flour, the brand of your yeast, and other factors, you may end up needing to add more of this or less of that. I describe what to look for at each step of the process, so use these visual and tactile cues to guide you. Glee taught me a great deal about bread and shared her recipes freely. If I had to pick one recipe that I am most grateful for, it would be this one. This is a slightly sweet, hearty, earthy multigrain loaf that makes unbelievable toast. I'm not kidding when I say that the reason we make and sell bread at Flour is that I wanted to be able to enjoy this particular bread each morning, which I do almost every day, and have since we opened.

⇒ Using a stand mixer fitted with the dough hook attachment (or a large bowl and wooden spoon), mix together the water, whole-wheat flour, buckwheat flour, and 3 cups (420 grams) all-purpose flour on low speed for about 1 minute, or until the flour is mixed into the water and you have a shaggy, stiff dough. (To prevent the flour from flying out of the bowl, turn the mixer on and off several times until the flour is mixed into the liquid, and then keep it on low speed.) Cover the bowl with a piece of plastic wrap and let sit for about 10 minutes. (This is called an autolyse, and it allows the water to hydrate the flour, which makes for better mixing down the road.)

⇒ On medium-low speed, add the sponge, honey, and salt and mix for 3 to 4 minutes, or until they are incorporated into the dough. The dough should be somewhat sticky but still smooth and feel like an earlobe (strange as that may sound) when you grasp a bit between your fingers. If it is stiffer than this, mix in a few tablespoons water; if it is looser than this, gradually mix in a few tablespoons all-purpose flour. You may need to stop the mixer a few times to pull off any dough that has gathered around the hook or on the sides of the bowl. Add the millet, sunflower seeds, and flax-seeds and mix for another 2 to 3 minutes, or until the seeds are evenly distributed throughout the dough. (If you are using a wooden spoon to mix the dough, you must dump out the dough onto a floured work surface and knead for 5 to 6 min-utes, or until smooth, then return the dough to the bowl.)

➡ Lightly cover the dough, still in the bowl, with an oiled piece of plastic wrap or a lint-free kitchen towel. Place the bowl in a draft-free, warm place (78 to 82 degrees F is ideal; an area near the stove or in the oven with only the pilot light on is good) for 3 to 4 hours. The dough will rise up a little bit (but not a lot) and it will feel a little loose and relaxed.

➡ Flour your hands and your work surface and turn the dough out of the bowl. Divide the dough in half with a knife or a bench scraper. Shape each half into a ball by tucking the edges of the dough underneath and then continuing to tuck the edges underneath until the dough naturally gathers into a ball with a taut surface. (At this point, you can cover the shaped loaves and store them in the refrigerator overnight. Remove them the next day and proceed as directed.)

➡ Sprinkle the cornmeal on a baking sheet to keep the loaves from sticking, and place the loaves on the sheet, spacing them at least 3 inches apart. Cover them loosely but completely with plastic wrap and let them sit at room temperature for 2 to 3 hours, or until they have loosened up and seem relaxed. They won't pouf up too much, but they will seem much softer.

➡ Position a rack in the center of the oven, and heat the oven to 500 degrees F. (It is important that the oven comes to temperature before you place the bread inside. The correct temperature ensures that your loaves will get enough oomph to rise and grow.)

➡ Sprinkle the tops of the loaves with the 2 to 3 tablespoons all-purpose flour. Slash the loaves with a knife (see page 17), and place the baking sheet in the oven. Place a rimmed baking sheet or shallow pan filled with about 2 cups water on the oven rack below the bread. The steam from the water will create a nice moist atmosphere for your bread to grow. Bake for about 30 minutes, or until the loaves are golden brown on top and make a hollow sound when you thump them on the bottom.

➡ Let the loaves cool on the baking sheet on a wire rack for 15 to 20 minutes, then transfer the loaves to the rack and let cool for at least 2 hours before serving. Once the loaves have cooled com-pletely, they can be stored in a paper bag (plastic seals out the air and keeps the bread from breath-ing, which turns it too soft) at room temperature for 2 to 3 days. You can also freeze this bread, well wrapped in plastic wrap, for up to 2 weeks.

Baker's Bite

Anything that can be shaped into a round loaf can be shaped into small, round rolls. This recipe, as well as Country Bread (page 289), Potato Bread (page 294), and Golden Raisin–Pecan Bread (page 296), will yield 16 to 18 peach-size rolls. Bake for 20 to 35 minutes, or until the rolls are golden brown on top and make a hollow sound when you thump them on the bottom.

POTATO BREAD

1¼ cups (300 grams) water, at body temperature (when you put your finger in it, it should feel neither cold nor hot)

2¼ cups (315 grams) unbleached all-purpose flour, plus 2 to 3 tablespoons for baking

2 cups (300 grams) bread flour

12 ounces (340 grams) Bread Sponge (page 287)

1 tablespoon kosher salt

1 tablespoon sugar

2 russet potatoes (about 1 pound/ 454 grams), completely baked through until soft and cooled to room temperature

¼ cup (50 grams) olive oil

½ teaspoon chopped fresh rosemary

Big handful of medium-coarse yellow cornmeal for the baking sheet

MAKES TWO 8-INCH ROUND LOAVES

Adding potatoes to bread dough brings an earthy taste and fluffy texture that is truly delicious. At Flour, we have one sandwich bread (the focaccia on page 298) that we make for all our sandwiches, but our chefs are always clamoring for new breads to try. One day, Nicole and I came up with this one. After tasting it and then snacking on it all day, there was hardly any left for making sandwiches. So we made another batch, and one of our chefs made a meatloaf sandwich with homemade ketchup on grilled slices of the bread. It was incredible! This bread is fabulous toasted for sandwiches or just spread with a little butter.

➡ Using a stand mixer fitted with the dough hook attachment (or a large bowl and a wooden spoon), mix together the water, 2¼ cups (315 grams) all-purpose flour, and bread flour on low speed for about 1 minute, or until the flour is mixed into the water and you have a shaggy, stiff dough. (To prevent the flour from flying out of the bowl, turn the mixer on and off several times until the flour is mixed into the liquid, and then keep it on low speed.) Cover the bowl with a piece of plastic wrap and let sit for about 10 minutes. (This is called an autolyse, and it allows the water to hydrate the flour, which makes for better mixing down the road.)

➡ On medium-low speed, add the sponge, salt, and sugar and mix for 1 to 2 minutes, or until they are incorporated into the dough. In a small bowl, break open the potatoes and take out the potato flesh with a spoon, throwing away the skins. Mash the potato flesh with a fork until fairly smooth (you can still have some small chunks), then add it along with the oil and the rosemary to the dough. Mix for another 2 to 3 minutes, or until they are evenly mixed into the dough. The dough should be somewhat sticky but still smooth and feel like an earlobe (strange as that may sound) when you grasp a bit between your fingers. If it is stiffer than this, mix in a few tablespoons water; if it is looser, mix in a few tablespoons all-purpose flour. You may need to stop the mixer a few times to pull off any dough that has gathered around the hook or on the sides of the bowl. (If you are using a wooden spoon to mix the dough, you must dump out the dough onto a floured work surface and knead for 5 to 6 minutes, or until smooth.)

➡ Lightly oil a large bowl. Transfer the dough to the oiled bowl, and turn the dough to coat it with oil. Lightly cover the bowl with an oiled piece of plastic wrap or a lint-free damp cloth. Place the bowl in a draft-free, warm place (78 to 82 degrees F is ideal; an area near the stove or in the oven with only the pilot light on is good) for 2 to 3 hours. The dough will rise up a little bit (but not a lot) and it will feel a little loose and relaxed and somewhat sticky.

➡ Flour your hands and your work surface and turn the dough out of the bowl. Divide the dough in half with a knife or a bench scraper. Shape each half into a ball by tucking the edges of the dough underneath and then continuing to tuck the edges underneath until the dough naturally gathers into a ball with a taut surface. (At this point, you can cover the shaped loaves and store them in the refrigerator overnight. Remove them the next day and proceed as directed.)

➡ Sprinkle the cornmeal on a baking sheet to keep the loaves from sticking, and place the loaves on the sheet, spacing them at least 3 inches apart. Cover them loosely and completely with plastic wrap and let them sit at room temperature for 2 to 3 hours, or until they have loosened up and seem relaxed. They won't pouf up too much, but they will seem much softer, and you may see some bubbles forming just under the surface of the dough as it proofs.

➡ Position a rack in the center of the oven, and heat the oven to 450 degrees F. (It is important that the oven comes to temperature before you place the bread inside. The correct heat ensures that your loaves will get enough oomph to rise and grow.)

➡ Sprinkle the tops of the loaves with the 2 to 3 tablespoons all-purpose flour. Slash the loaves with a knife (see page 17), and place the baking sheet in the oven. Place a rimmed baking sheet or shallow pan filled with about 2 cups water on the oven rack below the bread. The steam from the water will create a nice moist atmosphere for your bread to grow. Bake for 40 to 45 minutes, or until the loaves are dark golden brown on top and make a hollow sound when you thump them on the bottom.

➡ Transfer the loaves to wire racks and let cool for at least 1 hour before serving. Once the loaves have cooled completely, they can be stored in a paper bag (plastic seals out the air and keeps the bread from breathing, which turns it too soft) at room temperature for 2 to 3 days. You can also freeze this bread, well wrapped in plastic wrap, for up to 2 weeks.

GOLDEN RAISIN-PECAN BREAD

1¼ cups (300 grams) water, at body temperature (when you put your finger in it, it should feel neither cold nor hot)

2 cups (280 grams) unbleached all-purpose flour, plus 2 to 3 tablespoons for baking

1¾ cups (260 grams) bread flour

12 ounces (340 grams) Bread Sponge (page 287)

¼ cup (85 grams) honey

2 teaspoons kosher salt

1 cup (100 grams) pecan halves, toasted

¾ cup (120 grams) golden raisins

Big handful of medium-coarse yellow cornmeal for the baking sheet

MAKES TWO 8-INCH
ROUND LOAVES

I crave a little toast in the morning, and even more than that, I crave a little sweet. A toasted slice of this bread satisfies me on both counts. The dough, lightly sweetened with honey, is soft and sticky, allowing you to knead in lots and lots of golden raisins and toasted pecans. It gives off the most wonderful aroma as it bakes, and it is pretty hard to resist fresh out of the oven. If you can control yourself, this bread freezes beautifully, so you can always have home-made bread in the house.

⇒ Using a stand mixer fitted with the dough hook attachment (or a large bowl and a wooden spoon), mix together the water, 2 cups (280 grams) all-purpose flour, and bread flour on low speed for about 1 minute, or until the flour is mixed into the water and you have a shaggy, stiff dough. (To prevent the flour from flying out of the bowl, turn the mixer on and off several times until the flour is mixed into the liquid, and then keep it on low speed.) Cover the bowl with a piece of plastic wrap and let sit for about 10 minutes. (This is called an autolyse, and it allows the water to hydrate the flour, which makes for better mixing down the road.)

⇒ On medium-low speed, add the sponge, honey, and salt and mix for 3 to 4 minutes, or until the dough is smooth. The dough should be somewhat sticky but still smooth and feel like an ear-lobe (strange as that sounds) when you grasp a bit between your fingers. If it is stiffer than this, mix in a few tablespoons water; if it is looser than this, mix in a few tablespoons all-purpose flour. On low speed, add the pecans and raisins and mix for another 4 to 5 minutes, or until the nuts and raisins are evenly distributed throughout the dough. You may need to stop the mixer a few times to pull off any dough that has gathered around the hook or on the sides of the bowl. (If you are using a wooden spoon to mix the dough, you must dump out the dough onto a floured work surface and knead for 5 to 6 minutes, or until smooth.)

⇒ Lightly oil a large bowl. Transfer the dough to the oiled bowl, and turn the dough to coat it with oil. Cover the bowl with an oiled piece of plastic wrap or a lint-free damp cloth. Place the bowl in a draft-free, warm place (78 to 82 degrees F is ideal; an area near the stove or in the oven with only the pilot light on is good) for 2 to 3 hours. The dough will rise up a little bit (but not a lot) and it will feel a little loose and relaxed and somewhat sticky.

➡ Flour your hands and your work surface and turn the dough out of the bowl. Divide the dough in half with a knife or a bench scraper. Shape each half into a ball by tucking the edges of the dough underneath and then continuing to tuck the edges underneath until the dough naturally gathers into a ball with a taut surface. (At this point, you can cover the shaped loaves and store them in the refrigerator overnight. Remove them the next day and proceed as directed.)

➡ Sprinkle a generous amount of cornmeal on a baking sheet to keep the loaves from sticking, and place the loaves on the sheet, spacing them at least 3 inches apart. Cover them loosely but completely with plastic wrap and let them sit at room temperature for 2 to 3 hours, or until the loaves have loosened up and seem relaxed. They won't pouf up too much, but they will seem much softer.

➡ Position a rack in the center of the oven, and heat the oven to 500 degrees F. (It is important that the oven comes to temperature before you place the bread inside. The correct heat ensures that your loaves will get enough oomph to rise and grow.)

➡ Sprinkle the tops of the loaves with the 2 to 3 tablespoons all-purpose flour. Slash the loaves with a knife (see page 17), and place the baking sheet in the oven. Place a rimmed baking sheet or shallow pan filled with about 2 cups water on the oven rack below the bread. The steam from the water will create a nice moist atmosphere for your bread to grow. Bake for 30 to 35 minutes, or until the loaves are dark golden brown on top and make a hollow sound when you thump them on the bottom.

➡ Transfer the loaves to wire racks and let cool for at least 1 hour before serving. Once the loaves have cooled completely, they can be stored in a paper bag (plastic seals out the air and keeps the bread from breathing, which turns it too soft) at room temperature for 2 to 3 days. You can also freeze this bread, well wrapped in plastic wrap, for up to 2 weeks.

ROSEMARY AND OLIVE OIL FOCACCIA

1¾ cups (420 grams) water, at body temperature (when you put your finger in it, it should feel neither cold nor hot)

1 teaspoon active dry yeast or 0.2 ounce (5 grams) fresh cake yeast

3½ cups (490 grams) unbleached all-purpose flour

1¼ cups (190 grams) bread flour

3 teaspoons kosher salt

2 tablespoons sugar

¾ cup (150 grams) olive oil

Big handful of medium-coarse yellow cornmeal for the baking sheet

2 tablespoons roughly chopped fresh rosemary

MAKES ONE 10-BY-15-INCH FOCACCIA (ENOUGH FOR 8 SANDWICHES OR 12 PIECES FOR THE DINNER TABLE)

At Flour, we bake all the bread for our popular sandwiches, and this is the coveted recipe. It produces thick slices of focaccia that are soft and hearty at the same time. A table of a dozen or so regular customers (we affectionately call them "The Table" because they have occupied the same communal table every weekday morning since almost the day we opened) routinely orders slices of it toasted. We bake off dozens and dozens of these sheets throughout the day to sate The Table and the rest of our customers. If you don't have time to bake it off, the dough keeps well in the fridge for 2 days or so. Just be sure to deflate it by punching it down if you don't use it the next day.

⇒ In the bowl of a stand mixer fitted with the dough hook attachment, combine the water and yeast and let sit for 20 to 30 seconds to allow the yeast to dissolve and activate. Dump the all-purpose flour, bread flour, 1 teaspoon of the salt, and the sugar onto the water and carefully turn the mixer on low speed. Let the dough mix for about 30 seconds. (To prevent the flour from flying out of the bowl, turn the mixer on and off several times until the flour is mixed into the liquid, and then keep it on low speed.) When the dough is still shaggy looking, drizzle in ½ cup (100 grams) of the oil, aiming it along the side of the bowl to keep it from splashing and making a mess.

⇒ With the mixer still on low speed, knead the dough for 4 to 5 minutes, or until it is smooth and supple. The dough should be somewhat sticky but still smooth and have an elastic, stretchy consistency. If it is much stiffer than this, mix in a few tablespoons water; if it is much looser than this, mix in a few tablespoons all-purpose flour.

(Alternatively, combine the water and yeast in a large bowl, and then add the other ingredients as directed and mix with a wooden spoon. Once the oil is incorporated, dump out the dough onto a floured work surface and knead for 6 to 8 minutes, or until smooth and supple.

➡ Lightly oil a large bowl. Transfer the dough to the oiled bowl, and turn the dough to coat it with oil. Cover the bowl with an oiled piece of plastic wrap or a lint-free damp cloth. Place the bowl in a draft-free, warm place (78 to 82 degrees F is ideal; an area near the stove or in the oven with only the pilot light on is good) for 2 to 3 hours. The dough should rise until it is about double in bulk.

➡ Once the dough has risen, flour your hands and your work surface and turn the dough out of the bowl. Gently stretch the dough into a rectangle about 10 by 15 inches. Sprinkle the cornmeal onto a baking sheet to keep the dough from sticking, and place the dough rectangle on the sheet. Generously flour the top of the dough, and then cover it loosely but completely with a piece of plastic wrap or a lint-free damp cloth. Place in a warm area for another hour or so, or until the dough rises a bit and gets puffy and pillowy.

➡ Position a rack in the center of the oven, and heat the oven to 425 degrees F.

➡ When the dough is ready, remove the plastic wrap and dimple the dough all over, using all ten fingers and firmly poking straight down into the dough all the way to the bottom. Sprinkle the rosemary evenly over the top, drizzle evenly with the remaining ¼ cup (50 grams) oil, and then sprinkle evenly with the remaining 2 teaspoons salt.

➡ Bake for 35 to 45 minutes, or until completely golden brown on the top and bottom. Lift the dough and make sure the underside is browned before pulling it out of the oven, or you will end up with soggy focaccia. Let cool on the pan on a wire rack for about 30 minutes, or until cool enough to handle, then cut into serving pieces.

➡ The focaccia will keep in a closed paper bag at room temperature for up to 3 days, or tightly wrapped in two layers of plastic wrap in the freezer for up to 2 weeks. If frozen, thaw at room temperature for 3 to 4 hours and refresh in a 300-degree-F oven for 5 minutes, or refresh, directly from the freezer, in a 300-degree-F oven for 12 to 15 minutes.

Same recipe, different flavors

OLIVE FOCACCIA: Add 1 cup (140 grams) chopped assorted pitted olives along with the rosemary. Proceed as directed.

PIZZA: We use this dough for our individual pizzas. The recipe makes about a dozen 6- to 7-inch round pizzas. Or, you can use about half the dough to make a 14-inch round pizza. Top with your favorite tomato sauce and toppings. At Flour, our most popular pizzas include our Three-Cheese Pizza, with tomato sauce, ricotta, mozzarella, and Parmesan; our Tarte Flambée, with caramelized onions (see Country Ham, Cheddar and Tomato Quiche variations, page 241), crème fraîche, fresh thyme, smoky bacon, and Gruyère; and our Aloha Pizza, with tomato sauce, Canadian bacon, pineapple, and mozzarella.

DRIED-FRUIT FOCACCIA

1 cup (160 grams) dried cranberries

1 cup (160 grams) golden raisins

1 cup (160 grams) dark raisins or dried cherries

About 3 cups (720 grams) hot tap water

1½ teaspoons active dry yeast, or 0.4 ounce (10 grams) fresh cake yeast

2½ cups (350 grams) unbleached all-purpose flour

1½ cups (225 grams) bread flour

1½ teaspoons kosher salt

6 tablespoons (128 grams) honey

2 tablespoons finely grated orange zest (about 1 orange)

1 cup (200 grams) olive oil

Big handful of medium-coarse yellow cornmeal for the baking sheet

2 tablespoons sanding or pearl sugar

MAKES ONE 12-BY-15-INCH FOCACCIA (ABOUT 12 PIECES)

I lived in New York City for one summer during college—this was way before I ever thought I would end up in the food business—and there was a bakery near my apartment that made a wonderful dried-fruit focaccia. It was bready and soft and filled with raisins and cherries and cranberries. I could have eaten it every day. (Actually, I think I did.) I searched in vain for a replacement when I returned to Boston in the fall. It never occurred to me that I might be able to replicate it myself, not until I switched gears years later and became a professional pastry chef. What seemed so daunting before was suddenly within reach. I had already developed a focaccia recipe for our sandwiches at Flour. Surely I could tweak the recipe to replicate the fruity focaccia I remembered from that summer in New York City. The adjustments were simple: add honey and orange zest to our original focaccia recipe, along with dried fruits. They worked like a charm. This focaccia makes fantastic toast for breakfast, or you can dress it up with a drizzle of honey and a scoop of vanilla ice cream for a quick dessert.

➡ In a large bowl, combine the cranberries, golden raisins, and dark raisins and pour the hot water over them. Let sit for about 30 minutes. Drain, reserving the water. Let the water cool to room temperature, then measure 1⅓ cups (320 grams) and reserve. Discard the remainder.

➡ In the bowl of a stand mixer fitted with the dough hook attachment, combine the 1⅓ cups soaking water and the yeast and let sit for 20 to 30 seconds to allow the yeast to dissolve and activate. Dump the all-purpose flour, bread flour, salt, honey, and orange zest onto the water and carefully turn the mixer on low speed. Let the dough mix for about 30 seconds. (To prevent the flour from flying out of the bowl, turn the mixer on and off several times until the flour is mixed into the liquid, and then keep it on low speed.) When the dough is still shaggy looking, drizzle in ¾ cup (150 grams) of the oil, aiming it along the side of the bowl to keep it from splashing and making a mess.

With the mixer still on low speed, knead the dough for 3 to 4 minutes, or until it is smooth and satiny. When you pinch the dough, it should have an elastic, stretchy consistency. If it is much stiffer than this, mix in a few tablespoons water; if it is much looser than this, mix in a few tablespoons all-purpose flour.

Add the plumped cranberries and golden and dark raisins and mix on low speed for 1 to 2 minutes, or until they mix into the dough somewhat. Stop the mixer and remove the dough from the bowl. Continue kneading the dough by hand on a floured work surface until the fruit is completely mixed in. The dough will be sticky and tacky and wet.

(Alternatively, combine the water and yeast in a large bowl, and then add the other ingredients as directed and mix with a wooden spoon. Once the oil is incorporated, dump out the dough onto a floured work surface and knead for 5 to 6 minutes, or until smooth and satiny. Then add the plumped dried fruits and continue kneading until the fruit is completely mixed in.)

Lightly oil a large bowl. Place the dough in the oiled bowl, and turn the dough to coat it with oil. Cover the bowl with an oiled piece of plastic wrap or a lint-free damp cloth. Place the bowl in a draft-free, warm place (78 to 82 degrees F is ideal; an area near the stove or in the oven with only the pilot light on is good) for 2 to 3 hours. The dough should rise until it is about double in bulk.

Once the dough has risen, flour your hands and your work surface and turn the dough out of the bowl. Gently stretch the dough into a rectangle about 12 by 15 inches. Sprinkle the cornmeal onto a baking sheet to keep the dough from sticking, and place the dough rectangle on the sheet. Lightly flour the top of the dough, and then cover it loosely but completely with a piece of plastic wrap or lint-free damp cloth. Place in a warm area for another hour or so, or until the dough rises a bit and gets puffy and pillowy.

Position a rack in the center of the oven, and heat the oven to 425 degrees F.

When the dough is ready, remove the plastic wrap and dimple the dough all over, using all ten fingers and firmly poking straight down into the dough all the way to the bottom. Drizzle the remaining ¼ cup (50 grams) oil evenly over the top, and sprinkle evenly with the sanding sugar.

Bake for 30 to 40 minutes, or until completely golden brown on the top and bottom. Lift the dough and make sure the underside is browned before pulling it out of the oven or you will end up with soggy focaccia. Let cool on the pan on a wire rack for about 30 minutes, or until cool enough to handle, then cut into serving pieces.

The focaccia will keep in a closed paper bag at room temperature for up to 3 days, or tightly wrapped in two layers of plastic wrap in the freezer for up to 2 weeks. If frozen, thaw at room temperature for 3 to 4 hours and refresh in a 300-degree-F oven for 5 minutes, or refresh, directly from the freezer, in a 300-degree-F oven for 12 to 15 minutes.

PARMESAN AND BLACK PEPPER WHOLE-WHEAT FOCACCIA

2 cups (450 grams) water, at body temperature (when you put your finger in it, it should feel neither cold nor hot)

1 teaspoon active dry yeast, or 0.2 ounce (5 grams) fresh cake yeast

2 cups (280 grams) unbleached all-purpose flour

3 cups (492 grams) whole-wheat flour

1 tablespoon kosher salt

2 tablespoons sugar

1 cup (200 grams) olive oil

Big handful of medium-coarse yellow cornmeal for the baking sheet

½ cup (50 grams) freshly grated Parmesan cheese

1 teaspoon freshly cracked black pepper

MAKES ONE 10-BY-15-INCH FOCACCIA (ENOUGH FOR 8 SANDWICHES OR 12 PIECES FOR THE DINNER TABLE)

Customers clamored for a whole-wheat version of our focaccia and it tooks months of testing before we were happy with the result. Whole-wheat flour adds a nutty flavor to breads, but it can also make the bread dense and heavy. We introduced some all-purpose flour into the mix to lighten it up and that was the magic ticket.

⇒ In the bowl of a stand mixer fitted with the dough hook attachment, combine the water and yeast and let sit for 20 to 30 seconds to allow the yeast to dissolve and activate. Dump the all-purpose flour, whole-wheat flour, 2 teaspoons of the salt, and the sugar onto the water and carefully turn the mixer on low speed. Let the dough mix for about 30 seconds. (To prevent the flour from flying out of the bowl, turn the mixer on and off several times until the flour is mixed into the liquid and then keep it on low speed.) When the dough is still shaggy looking, drizzle in ¾ cup (150 grams) of the olive oil, aiming it along the side of the bowl to keep it from splashing and making a mess.

⇒ With the mixer still on low speed, knead the dough for 4 to 5 minutes, or until it is smooth and supple. The dough should be somewhat sticky but still smooth and have an elastic, stretchy consistency. If it is much stiffer than this, mix in a few tablespoons water; if it is much looser than this, mix in a few tablespoons all-purpose flour.

(Alternatively, combine the water and yeast in a large bowl, and then add the other ingredients as directed and mix with a wooden spoon. Once the oil is incorporated, dump out the dough onto a floured work surface and knead for 6 to 8 minutes, or until smooth and supple.)

⇒ Lightly oil a large bowl. Transfer the dough to the oiled bowl, and turn the dough to coat it with the oil. Cover the bowl with an oiled piece of plastic wrap or a lint-free damp cloth. Place the bowl in a draft-free, warm place (78 to 82 degrees F is ideal; an area near the stove or in the oven with only the pilot light on is good) for 2 to 3 hours. The dough should rise until it is about double in bulk.

(continued)

➡ Once the dough has risen, flour your hands and your work surface and turn the dough out of the bowl. Gently stretch the dough into a rectangle about 10 by 15 inches. Sprinkle the cornmeal onto a baking sheet to keep the dough from sticking, and place the dough rectangle on the sheet. Generously flour the top of the dough, and then cover it loosely but completely with a piece of plastic wrap or lint-free damp cloth. Place in a warm area for another hour or so, or until the dough rises a bit and gets puffy and pillowy.

➡ Position a rack in the center of the oven, and heat the oven to 425 degrees F.

➡ When the dough is ready, remove the plastic wrap and dimple the dough all over, using all ten fingers and firmly poking straight down into the dough all the way to the bottom. Sprinkle the Parmesan evenly over the top, drizzle evenly with the remaining ¼ cup (50 grams) oil, and then sprinkle evenly with the remaining 1 teaspoon salt and the pepper.

➡ Bake for 35 to 45 minutes, or until completely golden brown on the top and bottom. Lift the dough and make sure the underside is browned before pulling it out of the oven, or you will end up with soggy focaccia. Let cool on the pan on a wire rack for about 30 minutes, or until cool enough to handle, then cut into serving pieces.

➡ The focaccia will keep in a closed paper bag at room temperature for up to 3 days, or tightly wrapped in two layers of plastic wrap in the freezer for up to 2 weeks. If frozen, thaw at room temperature for 3 to 4 hours and refresh in a 300-degree-F oven for 5 minutes, or refresh, directly from the freezer, in a 300-degree-F oven for 12 to 15 minutes.

DOUBLE-CORN CORN BREAD
WITH FRESH THYME

1 cup (200 grams) coarse yellow cornmeal

2½ cups (350 grams) unbleached all-purpose flour

2 teaspoons baking powder

1 teaspoon baking soda

1¼ teaspoons kosher salt

¼ cup (½ stick/56 grams) unsalted butter, melted and cooled

¼ cup (50 grams) canola oil

¼ cup (55 grams) packed light brown sugar

2 eggs

1 cup (240 grams) milk

¾ cup (180 grams) crème fraîche

1 cup (160 grams) fresh or frozen corn kernels

1 tablespoon chopped fresh thyme

MAKES ONE 9-BY-13-INCH LOAF (ABOUT 12 PIECES)

We offer this corn bread each holiday season. We make pans and pans of it and cut it into large squares, which get snatched up as quickly as we can wrap them up. Some corn breads are sweet and some are not. This version is somewhere in between. The batter includes a little sugar, along with a heap of corn kernels, which adds to the sweetness. A generous addition of fresh thyme gives it a satisfying background savory accent. As with most of the recipes in this book that call for crème fraîche, seek out the real thing. Sour cream is an okay substitute, but the bread won't be as rich or yummy.

➡ Position a rack in the center of the oven, and heat the oven to 350 degrees F. Butter a 9-by-13-inch baking dish.

➡ In a large bowl, stir together the cornmeal, flour, baking powder, baking soda, and salt until combined. In a medium bowl, whisk together the melted butter, oil, and brown sugar until a thick slurry forms. Whisk in the eggs, one at a time, and then whisk in the milk and crème fraîche.

➡ Pour the egg-sugar mixture into the cornmeal mixture, and then, using a rubber spatula, fold together until all of the cornmeal is completely incorporated. Fold in the corn kernels and the thyme until they are evenly distributed throughout the batter. The batter will be thick and pasty. Spread the batter evenly in the prepared pan.

➡ Bake for 40 to 50 minutes, or until the top is light golden brown and the center springs back when you poke it in the middle with a fingertip. Let cool completely in the pan on a wire rack, then cut into about 12 serving pieces.

➡ The corn bread can be stored, tightly wrapped in plastic wrap, at room temperature for up to 2 days or in the freezer for up to 2 weeks. If frozen, thaw at room temperature for 3 to 4 hours and refresh in a 300-degree-F oven for 8 minutes, or refresh, directly from the freezer, in a 300-degree-F oven for 15 to 18 minutes.

BUTTERMILK BISCUITS
WITH PARSLEY AND SAGE

2½ cups (350 grams) unbleached all-purpose flour

1½ teaspoons baking powder

½ teaspoon baking soda

1½ teaspoons kosher salt

½ cup (1 stick/114 grams) cold unsalted butter, cut into 8 to 10 pieces, plus 2 tablespoons (¼ stick/28 grams), melted

½ cup (120 grams) cold nonfat buttermilk

½ cup (120 grams) cold heavy cream

1 cold egg

1 tablespoon finely chopped fresh sage

1 tablespoon chopped fresh parsley

MAKES EIGHT 3-INCH BISCUITS

A few years ago, a customer ran into Flour and waited patiently in line to pick up a dozen of these biscuits. When he got back to his double-parked car, he found a bright orange ticket slapped on his windshield. He called us when he got home to say that the ticket was worth it. He had devoured two of the biscuits during his drive home and was swooning. We originally developed this recipe at the request of one of our chefs, who was making a chicken potpie for a special one day. We ate so many of them that we decided we should make them for our customers, too! We now offer them on our holiday menu and they sell out each time. Make sure your butter, buttermilk, cream, and the egg are cold, and work the dough as little as possible. You'll be rewarded with light, fluffy biscuits every time.

→ Position a rack in the center of the oven, and heat the oven to 350 degrees F.

→ Using a stand mixer fitted with the paddle attachment (or a handheld mixer), mix together the flour, baking powder, baking soda, and salt on low speed for 10 to 15 seconds, or until combined. Scatter the butter pieces over the top and beat on medium-low speed for about 1 minute, or until the butter is broken down and the mixture resembles coarse crumbs.

→ In a small bowl, whisk together the buttermilk, cream, egg, and sage until thoroughly mixed. On low speed, pour the buttermilk mixture into the flour mixture and beat for 10 to 15 seconds, or until the dough just comes together. There will still be a little loose flour mixture at the bottom of the bowl.

→ Remove the bowl from the mixer stand. Gather and lift the dough with your hands and turn it over in the bowl, so that it picks up the loose flour at the bottom. Turn over the dough several times until all of the loose flour is mixed in.

➡ Dump the dough onto a work surface and pat it into a layer about 1 inch thick. Using a 3-inch round biscuit or cookie cutter, cut out biscuits and place them on a baking sheet. Gently bring together the dough scraps, pat them into a layer about 1 inch thick, and cut out more biscuits until all of the dough is used up. You should have 8 biscuits total. (At this point, the biscuits can be tightly wrapped in plastic wrap and frozen for up to 1 week. Proceed as directed, baking the biscuits directly from the freezer and adding 5 to 10 minutes to the baking time.)

➡ Bake for 40 to 45 minutes, or until the biscuits are entirely golden brown. Let cool on the sheet on a wire rack. In a small bowl, mix together the melted butter and the parsley, and brush the tops of the biscuits while they are still warm.

➡ The biscuits taste best on the day they are baked, but they can be stored tightly wrapped in plastic wrap at room temperature for up to 1 day. Refresh them in a 300-degree-F oven for about 10 minutes before serving.

Acknowledgments

When I was in third grade we drew posters in school titled "All About Me." We listed our favorite color, we had pictures of our family, and we created lists such as "When I Grow Up I Want to . . . ." My Grown-Up Bucket List read "1. Write a book, 2. Become President of the United States, 3. Learn how to ice skate." In that order. I had my priorities straight, even at eight years old.

I assumed that writing a book would be a solo venture: just me and a computer. The reality is that writing this cookbook was one of the most collaborative and other-people-influenced projects I've embarked upon, not to mention one of the most enjoyable. This book would not have happened, period, without help from the following people.

My thanks to Lydia Shire for taking a chance on me and giving me that invaluable first opportunity to work in a professional kitchen, allowing me to discover my life passion. Rick Katz welcomed me with open arms into his bakery when I realized I belonged on the sweet side of the kitchen; I thank him for his careful strict teaching, his faultless recipes (many of which are included in this book), and his lifelong lesson that what matters most is making pastries that you love. I am grateful to my dear friend Jody Adams for taking me under her wing as her pastry chef and for teaching me so much about not just how to be a better chef but also a better leader. Thanks to Francois Payard for the whirlwind introduction to classic French pastry that influences my work still. Thank you to Jamie Mammano for letting me test recipes on him ad nauseum when I was his pastry chef and for being a truly terrific boss and friend.

To Bobby Flay for challenging me to a Throwdown, which put our sticky buns on the map. (Thank goodness we won!) Thank you to Doc Willoughby for giving me the confidence to put pen to paper and encouraging me in my early writing forays. Thanks to the chefs and pastry chefs who have influenced me and taught me so much over the years, some of whose recipes are adapted here: Rose Levy Beranbaum, Amy Scherber, the late Robert Steinberg, Amanda Hesser, Johnny Iuzzini.

If not for my rock star co-author Christie Matheson, this book would still be a pipe dream. Thanks to her for her gentle prodding and constant cheerleading and most of all her unwavering support and guidance. Thanks to Stacey Glick, my fabulous agent, for holding my hand while Christie held the other. To Bill LeBlond, my editor, for being such an ardent believer in me and this book and for his wonderful friendship. To Sarah Billingsley, my other editor, for her unabashed pleasure in reading and baking her way through these recipes and for her meticulous editing. I loved working with Joe Keller of Keller+Keller and thank him for the gorgeous photos and for making the process so fun. Denise Drower Swidey brought her trademark energy and determination to the photoshoots as our stylist and was a dream to work with. I had three awesome testers who helped test each recipe mulitple times—thanks to Mary Kate Paris, Meredith Lubking, and Melissa Suderman. Thank you as well to the students at Cambridge Culinary who also volunteered to test recipes. And thank you to Cathy Greve, whose delightful printing graces many of these pages as well as the walls of Flour, our T-shirts, our mugs, our signs.

At Flour I can't thank enough my two right-hand people. Nicole Rhode, our executive pastry chef, ran the kitchen seamlessly in my relative absence allowing me to focus on this book. Thank you, Nicole, for always being such an absolute delight to work with and for being so contagiously enthusiastic about anything and everything pastry and Flour. Aaron Constable, our general manager, is the face of Flour in so many ways. Thank you so much Aaron for your incredible good cheer, your unflagging dedication to Flour, your perpetual patience with me in all of my craziness, and your understanding of what makes me and Flour tick. I also have to thank Korinn Koslovsky ("crumb coat: friend or foe?!") who guided Flour in the early years; Sarah Powers for helping test recipes and for running the F2 pastry kitchen while I was constantly in the way working on the book; Rita Alipranda, whose official role as dishwasher does little to describe her true role as Flour's mascot and mom. Huge thanks to the whole Flour team at both F1 and F2 for making me so proud every day with your amazing work and the joy you bring to our customers.

I have the very best parents in the world. Mom and Dad, thank you for always believing in your *bao-bei*, for proclaiming everything I baked as a kid to be the best, even when my experiments weren't quite edible, for not thinking I was nuts when I dropped a lucrative career in management consulting to go sweat in a kitchen (well maybe you did but thanks for not telling me), and for loving me so relentlessly. Your unconditional support and belief in me have allowed me to take the chances I have with my career, Flour, and this book. Thank you to my brother Christopher for being a great brother and guinea pig back in the early days when I would make you eat whatever I was testing in the kitchen.

Most of all, thank you to my husband, Christopher—my best friend, my most reliable critic, my ultimate pie tester—for bringing endless laughter and love into my life. You make me believe anything is possible and with you everything is. I know you don't think it could possibly be true but I love you more than ice cream.

—Joanne Chang

Thanks to Joanne Chang for letting me tag along. (There's a reason everyone thinks you're spectacular: You are. And, yes, your recipes are, too.) Thanks to Christopher Myers, the only guy around cool enough for Jo. Thanks, as always, to my wonderful agent, Stacey Glick. Thanks to team Chronicle, especially the ridiculously talented Sarah Billingsley, Bill LeBlond, David Hawk, and Peter Perez. Thanks to Joe Keller for the drool-worthy photos. And endless thanks to the loves of my life, Will and Ellie (who supervised the photo shoot from a Baby Bjorn and greatly enjoyed the amenities at F2).

—Christie Matheson

table of equivalents

Liquid/Dry Measurements

U.S.	Metric
¼ teaspoon	1.25 milliliters
½ teaspoon	2.5 milliliters
1 teaspoon	5 milliliters
1 tablespoon (3 teaspoons)	15 milliliters
1 fluid ounce (2 tablespoons)	30 milliliters
¼ cup	60 milliliters
⅓ cup	80 milliliters
½ cup	120 milliliters
1 cup	240 milliliters
1 pint (2 cups)	480 milliliters
1 quart (4 cups, 32 ounces)	960 milliliters
1 gallon (4 quarts)	3.84 liters
1 ounce (by weight)	28 grams
1 pound	448 grams
2.2 pounds	1 kilogram

Oven Temperatures

Fahrenheit	Celsius	Gas
250	120	½
275	140	1
300	150	2
325	160	3
350	180	4
375	190	5
400	200	6
425	220	7
450	230	8
475	240	9
500	260	10

Lengths

U.S.	Metric
⅛ inch	3 millimeters
¼ inch	6 millimeters
½ inch	12 millimeters
1 inch	2.5 centimeters